Physics and the Modernist Avant-Garde

Explorations in Science and Literature

Series Editors:

John Holmes, Anton Kirchhofer and Janine Rogers

Explorations in Science and Literature considers the significance of literature from within a scientific world view and brings the insights of literary study to bear on current science. Ranging across scientific disciplines, literary concepts, and different times and cultures, volumes in this series will show how literature and science, including medicine and technology, are intricately connected, and how they are indispensable to one another in building up our understanding of ourselves and of the world around us.

Published titles

Biofictions, Josie Gill
Imagining Solar Energy, Gregory Lynall
The Diseased Brain and the Failing Mind, Martina Zimmermann
Narrative in the Age of the Genome, Lara Choksey
Writing Remains, Edited by Josie Gill, Catriona McKenzie, Emma Lightfoot
Rereading Darwin's Origin of Species, Richard G. Delisle, James Tierney
Twins and Recursion in Digital, Literary and Visual Cultures, Edward King

Forthcoming titles

The Social Dinosaur, Will Tattersdill

Physics and the Modernist Avant-Garde

Quantum Modernisms and Modernist Relativities

Rachel Fountain Eames

BLOOMSBURY ACADEMIC
LONDON • NEW YORK • OXFORD • NEW DELHI • SYDNEY

BLOOMSBURY ACADEMIC
Bloomsbury Publishing Plc
50 Bedford Square, London, WC1B 3DP, UK
1385 Broadway, New York, NY 10018, USA
29 Earlsfort Terrace, Dublin 2, Ireland

BLOOMSBURY, BLOOMSBURY ACADEMIC and the Diana logo are
trademarks of Bloomsbury Publishing Plc

First published in Great Britain 2023
Paperback edition published 2024

Copyright © Rachel Fountain Eames, 2023, 2024

Rachel Fountain Eames has asserted her right under the Copyright, Designs and
Patents Act, 1988, to be identified as Author of this work.

For legal purposes the Acknowledgements on pp. x–xi constitute an
extension of this copyright page.

Cover design by Rebecca Heselton
Cover image © MirageC/Getty Images

All rights reserved. No part of this publication may be reproduced or transmitted
in any form or by any means, electronic or mechanical, including photocopying,
recording, or any information storage or retrieval system, without prior
permission in writing from the publishers.

Bloomsbury Publishing Plc does not have any control over, or responsibility for,
any third-party websites referred to or in this book. All internet addresses given in this
book were correct at the time of going to press. The author and publisher regret any
inconvenience caused if addresses have changed or sites have ceased to exist,
but can accept no responsibility for any such changes.

A catalogue record for this book is available from the British Library.

A catalog record for this book is available from the Library of Congress.

ISBN: HB: 978-1-3502-9982-5
PB: 978-1-3502-9986-3
ePDF: 978-1-3502-9983-2
eBook: 978-1-3502-9984-9

Series: Explorations in Science and Literature

Typeset by Integra Software Services Pvt. Ltd.

To find out more about our authors and books visit www.bloomsbury.com
and sign up for our newsletters.

for
ELIZABETH FOUNTAIN EAMES
(1924–2020)

Contents

Illustrations ix
Acknowledgements x

Introduction 1
Poetry and physics 5
The age of revolutions: An overview of physics in the period 1905–45 9
   Relativity theory 10
   The emergence of quanta 14
   Visualizing the atom 15
   The quantum revolution 17
The New York avant-garde 23
Four New York poets 30

1 Relative measure: William Carlos Williams's Einsteinian poetics 39
   Cubist poetics in *Spring and All* (1923) 43
   Complex mathematics: Williams encounters Einstein 54
   Revising relativity: The second version of 'St Francis Einstein of the Daffodils' 63
   'The only reality that we can know is MEASURE': Einstein in *Paterson* 70

2 Mina Loy's energy physics 75
   Parody physics: Loy's futurist satires 80
   Physics without parody: 'Parturition' (1914) 94
   Loy's atomic spiritualism 107
   The man of electric vitality: *Insel* (1933–6) 118
   Back to the bomb: Rethinking atomic dissolution 126

3 The Baroness Elsa Von Freytag-Loringhoven's physical systems 131
   Dada's cult of indeterminacy 133
   Smashing Duchamp's glass: The Baroness against the Dada scientists 145
   Quantum dissolution in Weimar Berlin 152
   'Life is science': Finding order through science 162

4	**The quantum poetics of Wallace Stevens and Max Planck**	**179**
	The visualizability question and the poetic image	184
	The image in superposition: Stevens and Surrealism	196
	Stevens's phantom problem	205
	'Invisible or visible or both': An abstracted poetics	213
Conclusion		**225**
Appendix 1 – Parallel timeline		232
Bibliography		235
Index		249

Illustrations

1 Juan Gris, *Guitar and Clarinet* (1920), oil on canvas, 73 × 92 cm, Kunstmuseum Basel, 2297   49
2 Juan Gris, *Flowers* (1920), conté crayon, gouache, oil, wax crayon, wallpapers, printed white wove paper and newspaper on canvas, 54.9 × 46 cm, The Metropolitan Museum of Art, New York   51
3 Giacomo Balla, *Street Light* (*c.* 1910–11), oil on canvas, 174.7 × 114.7 cm, The Metropolitan Museum of Art, New York, 7. 1954   96
4 Marius de Zayas, 'Abstract Caricature of Alfred Stieglitz,' *Camera Work* 46 (1914), 41   138
5 Hannah Höch, *Cut with the Dada Kitchen Knife through the Last Weimar Beer-Belly Cultural Epoch in Germany, 1919–20*, collage, mixed media, 144 × 90 cm, Museen der Staatlichen Museen zu Berlin, NG 57/61   156
6 Elsa von Freytag-Loringhoven, *Perspective*, *c.* 1922–4. Red and green ink on paper. Elsa von Freytag-Loringhoven papers, Special Collections & University Archives, University of Maryland Libraries   167
7 Elsa von Freytag-Loringhoven, 'since space is immeasurable', *c.* 1924. Black ink on paper. Elsa von Freytag-Loringhoven papers, Special Collections & University Archives, University of Maryland Libraries   169
8 Salvador Dalí, *Invisible Sleeping Woman, Lion, Horse*, 1930, oil on canvas, 52 × 60 cm, Private Collection, Paris   203

Acknowledgements

This book was completed in the chaos of unprecedented times, bookended by illness, and as such I offer twice as many thanks to everyone who helped to make it possible. First, I must give my sincerest thanks to Professor John Holmes, and Dr Will Tattersdill and John Fagg, whose unerring enthusiasm and support, incisive critique and encouragement helped make this book what it is. Thanks also to Professor Michael Whitworth and Dr Nathan Waddell. This work was generously funded by Midlands3Cities and I am immensely grateful for the wealth of opportunities their support has given me.

To my parents, who helped me up the mountain and never doubted me for a minute, all my love and thanks. Thanks also to Bel Aguas, Hannah Comer, Rhiannon Cogbill, Sarah Alpert, Naya Chatzimichali, Niamh White and Ann Heatley, for their feedback and support; and, of course, to Bruce Murray, for his wise words and eternal patience.

Special thanks to the archivists and curators at the Beinecke Rare Books and Manuscripts Library, British Library and University of Maryland Special Collections for their assistance navigating their collections; to Roger Conover for his kind permission to reproduce Mina Loy's works here; and to Roderigo de Zayas for his assistance and permission to reproduce his father's caricature of Alfred Stieglitz. Extracts from William Carlos Williams's poetry are reprinted by kind permission of Carcanet Press and New Directions Publishing. Images by Hannah Höch, Salvador Dalí and Giacomo Balla are reprinted with the kind permission of DACS.

Finally, to Granny, who introduced me to the wonders of black holes and the strangeness of Freud in one sitting, and to whom this thesis is dedicated – thank you for inspiring me and reminding me that 'all shall be well, and all manner of thing shall be well'.

'St. Francis Einstein of the Daffodils,' by William Carlos Williams, from THE COLLECTED POEMS: VOLUME I, 1909–1939, copyright ©1938 by New Directions Publishing Corp. Reprinted by permission of New Directions Publishing Corp.

'The Red Wheelbarrow' by William Carlos Williams, from THE COLLECTED POEMS: Volume I, 1909–1939, copyright ©1938 by New Directions Publishing Corp. Reprinted by permission of New Directions Publishing Corp.

'To a Solitary Disciple,' by William Carlos Williams, from THE COLLECTED POEMS: VOLUME I, 1909–1939, copyright ©1938 by New Directions Publishing Corp. Reprinted by permission of New Directions Publishing Corp.

'The Rose (The rose is obsolete)' by William Carlos Williams, from THE COLLECTED POEMS: VOLUME I, 1909–1939, copyright ©1938 by New Directions Publishing Corp. Reprinted by permission of New Directions Publishing Corp.

Introduction

On 21 December 1930, *The New York Times* ran a curious headline. 'Science Needs the Poet', wrote the art critic, Edward Alden Jewell, calling for artists to embrace the potential of quantum mechanics and usher in a new cultural renaissance:

> What we need is a Lucretius who will imbibe at the spring of Einstein, Planck, Schroedinger and Heisenberg, compose a modern 'De Rerum Natura' and interpret the mystery and beauty that lie in and beyond the electron and space, curved and finite.[1]

Where the rigorous machine of Newtonian physics 'made no allowance for man's spiritual yearnings,' he wrote, 'science in the form of mathematical physics waxes more idealistic with every discovery':

> Miracles? The poet will discover them in Planck's quantum theory, which explains radiation as if it were composed of bullets instead of waves. Quanta of light and electrons fly about with no respect for the old remorseless laws of cause and effect, and behave as if they were endowed with free will. [...] Matter is a mere wraith. An atom is something ghostly from which radiations emanate. The cosmos is no longer a machine which moves in a predictable way.[2]

In centuries past, he says, poets had a firm grasp of the science that shaped their world and played a vital role in its interpretation. So why do they not do the same in the twentieth century, where the wild discoveries of Albert Einstein and Max Planck, Werner Heisenberg and Niels Bohr, had opened up a new and seemingly magical arena of physics – one which, through replacing a deterministic, mechanized world with a strange one, presented a new potential for science to appeal to the human spirit?

---

[1] 'Science Needs the Poet', *The New York Times*, 21 December 1930, 47.
[2] Ibid.

It is an interesting proposal, but perhaps one which, in 1930, came a little too late. Jewell might have been surprised to find that – to some extent – what he asked for already existed and had done for decades. Poets had been turning over the discoveries of modern physics, considering their value for art, and generating new forms of poetry to suit the transformed world they described. In fact, modernist writers were among the earliest adopters of Einsteinian ideas, finding value in them before they reached mass popularity.[3] Michael Whitworth has shown that debate about relativity appeared on the pages of modernist periodicals before the sensationally popular expositions of the 1920s and 1930s, Arthur Eddington's *The Nature of the Physical World* (1928) and James Jeans's *The Mysterious Universe* (1930).[4] The new physics was a common point of discussion among them from at least as early as 1910, and its value for poetry was widely recognized among the modernist writers.

William Carlos Williams believed that '[t]he work of Einstein merges into' the character of modern poetry, an idea he imagined could be articulated through a shift in poetic meter.[5] He argued that the findings of modern physics reflected directly upon the arts: '[i]t is the poetic conception (see Einstein's reported statement...) of the universe that is the correct one. Its forms are best seen in the poetic form of an age.'[6] Between 1918 and 1919, T. S. Eliot 'frequently invoke[d] science as a reference point for his ideal of poetry' and later suggested that science lay at the heart of the modernist project of 'trying to reconcile ancient feeling with modern thought and science'.[7] The modern age, he said, was represented by the figure of Einstein.[8] By 1930, in New York, Louis Zukofsky was hard at work translating a biography of Einstein, with a preface by the physicist himself. Einstein's words, Zukofsky thought, were the most satisfying part of the project: '[m]aybe I am learning something about language.'[9] Modernist writers,

---

[3] Katherine Ebury, *Modernism and Cosmology: Absurd Lights* (New York: Palgrave Macmillan, 2014), 5–6.
[4] Michael H. Whitworth, 'Natural Science', *T. S. Eliot in Context*, ed. Jason Harding (Cambridge: Cambridge University Press, 2011), 340–2.
[5] William Carlos Williams, 'The Poem as a Field of Action', *Selected Essays of William Carlos Williams* (New York: Random House, 1954), 283.
[6] William Carlos Williams, *The Embodiment of Knowledge* (New York: New Directions, 1974), 7.
[7] Whitworth, 'Natural Science', 340; T. S. Eliot, 'An Emotional Unity' (1927), The Beinecke Rare Books and Manuscripts Library, YCAL MSS 24/20, Folder 399.
[8] T. S. Eliot, 'London Letters' (1921), The Beinecke Rare Books and Manuscripts Library, YCAL MSS 34/20, Folder 401. This was apparently a highly contested accolade. As I discuss in Chapter 4, Wallace Stevens would later decide that it was the age of another physicist, Max Planck. See: Wallace Stevens, 'A Collect of Philosophy', *Opus Posthumous* (Faber & Faber, 1957), 201–2.
[9] Louis Zukofsky in Mark Scroggins, *The Poem of a Life: A biography of Louis Zukofsky* (New York: Shoemaker and Hoard, 2007), 39.

then, were not only attentive to the new physics, but actively engaged in shaping its transmission and formulating ideas about its influence and legacy.

Science had become a valuable commodity for a poet. Tim Newcomb has characterized the early twentieth century as a period in which national values were so strongly in favour of science, technology and commodification that the continuance of poetry, both in publication and as a respected profession, came under threat.[10] In part, this threat came from the shifting interests of the common readership. As Whitworth notes, '[t]o the conservative Henry Newbold, concluding a survey of modern poetry in 1931, it seemed that the common reader was more interested in "the wonders of science and its transitory universe" than in poetry, taking more delight in physics than metaphysics.'[11] Yet this may not simply have been a case of lacking interest, but of shared market. Jeans and Eddington's books often weaved in metaphysical undercurrents and wider epistemological questions, inspiring awe and interest in the challenging concepts they discussed.[12] The appetite was still there but had seemingly been diverted in favour of forms more accessible than poetry. If, as Jewell describes, physics had begun to provide some of the wondrous matter expected of poetry, there is a sense in which the poet had to contend not only with the cultural authority of science, but also with science's offering of new ways to imagine the world and one's place in it.

Public interest in physics had been galvanized since the turn of the century as the fruits of applied physics became more accessible to the average person. Electricity entered the home, telephones and radios soon followed, and great feats of engineering had changed the landscape of urban life, from the advanced structural developments of the modern city to the vehicles which were soon to pass through them in their thousands. These technical innovations prompted lively debates about the changing conditions of modern life, bolstered by the booming mass-circulation of transatlantic print publications. Generalist periodicals, where science articles abutted literary reviews, presented a complex matrix of information about new discoveries and their suggested impacts upon the readers' everyday lives. Physics was further applied to new fields: communication, psychology and medicine. The development of X-ray imaging

---

[10] John Timberman Newcomb, *How Did Poetry Survive?* (Urbana: University of Illinois Press, 2012).
[11] Michael Whitworth, 'The Clothbound Universe: Popular Physics Books, 1919–39', *Publishing History*, 40 (1996), 56.
[12] Eddington's book had itself emerged from a smaller essay titled 'The Domain of Physical Science' in Joseph Needham's *Science, Religion and Reality* (1925), while Jeans ended his description of the new theories with a chapter on their metaphysical implications.

and radiotherapy around the turn of the century evoked as many anxieties as solutions (see Chapter 2). This modern world was a world understood through an increasingly scientific imagination.[13]

This book examines the way four poets working in America – William Carlos Williams, Mina Loy, the Baroness Elsa von Freytag-Loringhoven and Wallace Stevens – engaged with this scientific imagination. Taking these writers as case studies, I propose a way of reading modernism which attends to writers' interdisciplinary interests, exploring the intersection of literature, physics and the discourses of modern art. This work challenges the view that these subjects do not readily overlap by exploring the way in which these poets utilized concepts from physics, often mediated through cultural interplay with the visual arts. These poets engage with physics to achieve new effects in poetry, developing scientifically inflected metaphors, novel approaches to poetic form, and revitalized ideas about what a poem might be. This book examines the world systems and strategies each writer developed through which to interpret the often-turbulent world around them, uncovering a shared desire to frame modern experience in scientific terms. More broadly, I explore how each writer forged aesthetic meaning through the integration of scientific ideas, methodologies and vocabularies, into new forms of art. What emerges is a sense not only of the currency of physics for the modern poet, but of the shared challenges faced in the early twentieth century by writers, artists and scientists alike, and the corresponding ways in which, across each of these fields, people sought to overcome them.

These poets' interest in physics has a shared point of origin in New York during the 1910s and 1920s, mediated through their engagements with the international avant-garde arts scene that coalesced there. Visual art and the concepts of physics became entangled in their poetry in striking ways, offering insight into the complex cross-disciplinary character of modernist creative networks. Williams experienced the manipulation of perspective and measure in Cubism before proposing the radical introduction of Einsteinian measure into poetry; Mina Loy came of age as a poet satirizing the Italian Futurists' rhetoric of electric vitality; the Baroness embraced Dada's chaos of chance, uncertainty and electro-machinic bodies before developing her own cosmology devoted to 'abstract science'; and Wallace Stevens articulated his concerns about the limitations of imagery and role of the imagination in

---

[13] Alfred North Whitehead, *Science and the Modern World* (Cambridge: Cambridge University Press, 1927), 12.

poetry, first through allusion to Surrealism, before advancing a poetics of abstraction that paralleled contemporary perceptions about the limitations of the scientific imagination.

Poetry and physics

These writers' fusion of poetry and science developed during a period of shifting cultural values in the West and was shaped by the cosmopolitan networks of New York. They were exposed to an increasing amount of information from an ever more eclectic set of sources as artists moved in greater numbers across the Atlantic, bringing with them ideas from Europe, and returning overseas with fresh insights from America. This was a period of intense artistic collaboration, experimentation, innovation and discovery. Expatriate Europeans, fleeing the war, sought artistic asylum among the skyscrapers, joining the vibrant salons of the city's arts scene, such as Alfred Stieglitz's coterie at 291 Fifth Avenue (1905–17) and Alfred Kreymborg's *Others* (1915–19) group. In this deeply collaborative environment, writers rubbed shoulders with painters, actors, dancers, performance artists, photographers and well-monied patrons of the arts. It was also a space in which science and technology became synonymous with modernity; to live in the city was to live among the fruits of modern science, from hyper-modern skyscrapers and bridges to automobiles and electric lighting. Globally renowned scientists like Albert Einstein crossed both geographical and field boundaries as heralds of new scientific ideas and humanitarian messages from Europe, giving public talks and taking over the headlines.[14] This culture of 'rampant boundary crossing' fostered experimentation across field lines, which were for these cosmopolitan artists much more flexible and porous than America's lionization of expertise and the trend towards specialization shaping American colleges might have encouraged.[15] These artists were cultural magpies picking up the 'broken fragments of systems' in the fracturing world

---

[14] Milena Wazeck, *Einstein's Opponents: The Public Controversy about the Theory of Relativity in the 1920s*, trans. Geoffrey S. Koby (Cambridge: Cambridge University Press, 2014), 6.

[15] Mark S. Morrisson, *Modernism, Science, and Technology* (London: Bloomsbury Academic, 2017), 44. John Higham writes that, in contrast to Europe's relative ambivalence, 'by 1920… America had embraced the specialist and sanctified the expert with an enthusiasm unmatched anywhere else. [Generating the popular image of] a scientist whose narrow ruthlessly focussed intelligence was as distinctively American as Emerson's scholar had once seemed'. John Higham, 'The Matrix of Specialization', *Bulletin of the American Academy of the Arts and Sciences* 33, no. 5 (February 1980), 13.

around them.¹⁶ This magpie tendency often led to deeper consideration of new systems that might come in the place of those modernity had thrown out: new scientifically inflected forms for poetry, mind-bending new content to fill it with, and an opportunity to develop new systems of aesthetic and epistemic order in a world which often seemed on the brink of crisis.

These poets often framed themselves and their work in scientific terms, raising the profile of their beleaguered art form by enabling them to take advantage of an association with science and technology which were centres of financial and intellectual capital.¹⁷ By adopting the vocabulary and forms of science, poets were able to argue the value of poetry, relating it to 'public reality' and to 'convince Americans that they needed a new kind of poetry'.¹⁸ The project of associating poetry with the rigors of science appears in the rhetoric of Ezra Pound, forming a vision of the modernist agenda which sought to resolve the epistemological gap between the material (industrial, economic) and non-material (intellectual, spiritual) worlds. Ian Bell describes how Pound embraced the masculinized language of science as a means of imposing a new order and purpose upon poetry, a discipline which had come to be seen as effeminate.¹⁹ Pound desired to reframe poetry as a disciplined technical craft, and claimed openly that '[t]he arts, literature, poesy, are a science just as chemistry is a science'.²⁰ Appealing to science, adopting its technical vocabulary and reputation for rigor, precision and (importantly) difficulty, challenged the loss of value ascribed to poetry within modern culture. He argued for the interrelation of literature and science, stating in 1915: 'The arts and the sciences together. Any conception which does not see them in their interrelation belittles both.'²¹

Peter Middleton identifies two ways in which modernist writers forged this alignment. First, he says, they claimed authority for poetry as a form of technology.²² We see this in the way Williams describes a poem as a 'machine made of words', or the Baroness describes Joyce as the 'engineer' of *Ulysses*.²³ The second approach was to liken poetic vision to the vision of the new physics

---

[16] T. S. Eliot, *Selected Essays*, 3rd ed. (London: Faber & Faber, 1991), 138–9.
[17] Peter Middleton, *Physics Envy: American Poetry and Science in the Cold War and after* (Chicago & London: University of Chicago Press, 2015), 35; see also: Newcomb, *How Did Poetry Survive?*.
[18] Lisa Steinman, *Made in America* (New Haven & London: Yale University Press, 1987), 21.
[19] I. F. A. Bell, *The Critic as Scientist: The Modernist Poetics of Ezra Pound* (London: Methuen, 1981).
[20] Ibid., 46.
[21] Ibid., 83.
[22] Middleton, *Physics Envy*, 35.
[23] William Carlos Williams, 'Introduction to The Wedge', *Selected Essays of William Carlos Williams* (New York: New Directions, 1969), 256; Elsa von Freytag-loringhoven, 'The Modest Woman', *The Little Review* 7, no. 2 (Summer 1920), 37.

provided by Einstein and quantum mechanics.[24] This is apparent in the effusive demands of the Futurist F. T. Marinetti, working to break his subjects down into particles and wave-forms, inviting a 'wireless' poetry stripped of connecting syntax; or when Loy likens her protagonist's hyper-artistic perception to radio communication, electromagnetism and radioactivity in her novel *Insel* (1930).[25] In this book, I show that these practices are just the surface of a much deeper conceptual relationship between modernist writing, avant-garde art and physics, but, by 1930, these areas of culture were much more intertwined than is often recognized.

An awareness of this connection between modernism and physics has gained ground in the scholarship of the last two decades, with a number of dedicated studies teasing out the mechanics of their interrelation. Most of this work has attended to canonical British writers, especially Virginia Woolf, D. H. Lawrence and W. B. Yeats. Whitworth and Rachel Crossland, for example, have both offered in-depth examinations of the relationship between Einstein's ideas and the attitudes of Woolf and Lawrence to science in their writing.[26] In her study of modernist cosmologies, Katherine Ebury has turned a similar lens on modernist Irish writers Yeats, Joyce and Beckett.[27] Yet few studies have taken a similar approach to work done in America, despite evidence that the American modernists were as interested in science as their European counterparts. This may be in part due to the fact that the term 'science' in North American literary scholarship 'has been used far more commonly to refer to "technology", and the discipline has been more open to considerations of applied science'.[28] The most influential studies in this context, Lisa Steinman's *Made in America* (1987) and Cecilia Tichi's *Shifting Gears* (1987), centre on modernist writers' responses to technological innovations. To my mind, however, grouping technology with the highly conceptual areas of modern physics can be detrimental if – as seems to be the case – it distracts us from paying due attention to American writers' interests in more theoretical scientific concepts. As I will show, attending to these writers' interactions with physics can be tremendously productive, drawing out a remarkable array of creative interactions and interpretations,

---

[24] Middleton, *Physics Envy*, 35.
[25] F. T. Marinetti, 'Electrical War', *Futurism: An Anthology*, ed. Lawrence Rainey, Christine Poggi, et al. (New Haven & London: Yale University Press, 2009), 103; Mina Loy, 'Insel Draft 2', The Beinecke Rare Books and Manuscripts Library, MSS 6/3, Folder 41, 89.
[26] Michael Whitworth, *Einstein's Wake* (Oxford: Oxford University Press, 2000); Rachel Crossland, *Modernist Physics* (Oxford: Oxford University Press, 2018).
[27] Ebury, *Modernism and Cosmology*.
[28] Whitworth, *Einstein's Wake*, 7.

from the manipulation of (see Chapter 1) poetic measure to the depiction of a scientifically inflected understanding of human spirituality (see Chapters 2 and 3). An exception to this prioritization of technology is Peter Middleton's *Physics Envy* (2015), which attends to the discourses of modern physics in the late modernist period, during the Cold War. Middleton's starting point – the end of the Second World War – is broadly speaking my end point, as the public perception of physics was profoundly altered by the advent of atomic weapons (see Chapter 2), and part of the work of this thesis is to address the gap in the field left by those earlier studies.

This study does not take physics as a conceptual framework through which to interpret modernist poetics, as Daniel Albright does in *Quantum Poetics* (1997), but rather follows the precedents set by the handful of critics mentioned above, who have examined the complex relationship between modernist texts and physics through a historicist lens.[29] I read the transmission of scientific ideas through culture as a series of cross-disciplinary conversations. This is grounded in the idea that 'literary texts do more than thematize scientific theories'.[30] Instead, '[t]hey actively shape what the scientific theories signify in cultural contexts'.[31] Furthermore, just as 'changes in physical theories inspire changes in a culture's general attitudes ... art both responds to and shapes' the meaning of scientific theories outside of the laboratory.[32] For each of the writers I discuss, their employment of scientific concepts is shaped by their relationship with and understanding of the purpose of poetry itself. For instance, Williams and Stevens are invested in elevating poetics and the role of the poet through their association with scientific ways of seeing and representation, asking questions about what happens when artistic endeavours are approached through a scientific lens; Loy and the Baroness, in contrast, provide examples of a highly networked remediation of scientific concepts, which offers readers insight into the values and meanings ascribed to physics in the early twentieth century. Together, reading these poets enables us to see how ideas from science ripple through different countries and intellectual spheres; from the elites of 'high Modernism' to the outer reaches of the avant-garde, they offer up new ways for us to think about the meaning of physics and its cultural significance.

[29] Daniel Albright, *Quantum Poetics: Yeats, Pound, Eliot, and the Science of Modernism* (Cambridge: Cambridge University Press, 1997).
[30] Serpil Opperman, 'Quantum Physics and Literature: How They Meet the Universe Halfway', *Anglia* 133, no. 1 (2015), 97.
[31] N. Katherine Hayles, *How We Became Posthuman: Virtual Bodies in Cybernetics, Literature, and Informatics* (Chicago & London: The University of Chicago Press, 1999), 21.
[32] Susan Strehle, *Fiction in the Quantum Universe* (Chapel Hill: The University of North Carolina Press, 1992), 8.

In earlier studies of physics and literature, the experimental proof of Einstein's general theory of relativity in November 1919 has been, perhaps unduly, prioritized as a turning point, after which Einstein shot out of obscurity to worldwide fame.[33] Crossland rightly notes that although the experiment transformed public awareness of Einstein's theory, it should not necessarily be seen as a watershed moment in regard to public awareness of modern physics, and the oft-quoted 'Revolution in Science' headline from *The Times* on 7 November should be seen as the culmination of a growing public interest fostered by the press and popular science writers.[34] I join Crossland in beginning not in 1919 but 1905, in order to show that many of the ideas and concerns of the new physics in circulation among the poets I discuss relied less upon a single moment of change than a gradual culmination of ideas, often facilitated by the appearance of new technologies which brought their implications into a tangible realm.

The age of revolutions: An overview of physics in the period 1905–45

Most overviews of the modernist period touch upon physics as a cultural influence, most often citing the importance of Einstein, and occasionally also gesturing to quantum mechanics.[35] In the span of a few decades, advances in physics and applied physics technologies transformed modern life, from the introduction of electricity, telephones and radios into the home, to the devastating end to the Second World War through America's use of atomic bombs in Hiroshima and Nagasaki. This accompanied a dramatic shift in the way scientists visualized the physical world, both at the macroscopic scale (uncovering the structure of space-time) and at the microscopic scale (with a series of advances in ideas about the fundamental particles of matter). Bestselling expositions of the new physics 'encouraged the literary culture of the 1920s to understand the revolution in physics as a dramatic rupture, what we would now term a "paradigm shift".[36] However,

---

[33] Crossland, *Modernist Physics*, 2–3.
[34] Ibid.
[35] Julian Hanna, *Key Concepts in Modernist Literature* (New York: Palgrave Macmillan, 2009), 40–1; Jane Goldman, *Modernism, 1910–1945: Image to Apocalypse* (New York: Palgrave Macmillan, 2004), 59–63; Philip Yew and Alex Murray (eds.), *The Modernism Handbook* (London, New York: Continuum Books, 2009), 60–1; John Smart, *Modernism and after: English Literature 1910–1939* (Cambridge: Cambridge University Press, 2008), 22; David Bradshaw and Kevin J. H. Dettmar, *A Companion to Modernist Literature and Culture* (New Jersey: Blackwell Publishing, 2006), 39–43; Tim Armstrong, *Modernism: A Cultural History* (Malden, MA: Polity Press, 2005), 115–22.
[36] Whitworth, *Einstein's Wake*, 111.

it is worth bearing in mind as we go forward that, as Gavin Parkinson notes, the most striking and influential theories of the new physics 'are best viewed as supplementing and inflecting classical, Newtonian mechanics rather than simply replacing it'.[37] Although this project is primarily concerned with physics through the lens of modernist artistic experimentation, a grounding in the history, conceptual detail and reception of relativity, quantum theory and new models of the atom, as well as practical applications of physics, is vital for understanding the nature of these ideas within the wider modernist culture. We begin with arguably the most famous of these, Einstein's theories of relativity.

Relativity theory

First published in 1905, Einstein's theory of Special Relativity explained how to interpret motion between objects in inertia. The theory's major proposal was to reject the idea of absolute space and absolute time, suggesting instead that time and space are related and relative to the frame of reference from which they were measured. For Einstein, the world looks very different depending on whether you are moving or stationary; measurements taken from a (very) high-speed train will differ from those made by someone standing on a railway embankment. Einstein suggested that this difference is not simply a matter of personal perception mediated by a 'real' measurement, but that both measurements are valid and true. Rather than prioritizing, for instance, the measurement made on the moving train over that of the person on the embankment (or vice versa), he suggested that what matters is the speed the two are moving in relation to one another. This theory worked only in 'special' instances where the frames of reference were moving in a straight line at a uniform speed, hence the name Special Relativity. As we will see in Chapter 1, the notion that space and time expand and contract dependent on velocity encouraged a reconsideration of measurement in other areas, including art and poetics.

In his own popular exposition in 1916, Einstein drew the example above from the relatively new phenomenon of train travel, and its implications for standard time.[38] During the latter half of the nineteenth century, the railway system had initiated a widespread restructuring and standardization of public time, with practical implications that quickly spread around the world.

---

[37] Gavin Parkinson, *Surrealism, Art and Modern Science: Relativity, Quantum Mechanics, Epistemology* (New Haven and London: Yale University Press, 2008), 11.
[38] Albert Einstein, *Relativity: The Special and General Theory* (New York: Pi Press, 2005), 18.

Einstein grew up during this period of transition, before the notion of unified time could be taken for granted, as discussions about the standardization of time had begun to alter the way people lived their lives. Prior to cross-country rail networks, each town and city ran according to its own localized time, with little need to synchronize, but the demands of uniform train timetables led to the introduction of standardized 'railway time' in Britain in the 1840s, an idea which spread across Europe and to the United States alongside the development of railway networks over the following decades. In 1891, Einstein's native Germany still had five different time-zones, but coordinated their railroad services in 1893, amid international confusion which continued for almost two decades, with standard time introduced internationally in 1912.[39] Yet by 1905, when Einstein published his theories, this shift was well underway: standard time-zones had been introduced and, for anyone outside of a laboratory or philosophy department, time was becoming more stable and unified than ever before.

Yet, through his railway carriage thought experiments, Einstein threatened to undo the idea of standardized time, at least so far as physical processes are concerned. His theories suggested that time and space were tightly interlinked in a four-dimensional space called the *space-time continuum*, formed of the three spatial dimensions (height, length, depth) and a fourth dimension, time.[40] He described the 'relativity of simultaneity', demonstrating how flashes of lightning at two points on a railway track which appear simultaneous from the embankment do not appear (and are, in fact, not) simultaneous when observed from a moving train carriage.[41] Things which appear to happen simultaneously only do so when seen from a shared inertial reference frame; the moment you or the thing you are observing moves, time dilates. Time itself was shown to expand and contract based on an object's speed, tied up with a number of other mind-bending effects: scientific rulers (to use Einstein's example) expand or contract, gaining or losing mass based on the speed at which they are moving relative to the observer. The one vital exception is the propagation of light, which maintains a constant speed (of 300,000 km/second) regardless of frame of reference.[42] Einstein brought time and space together into the new hybrid *space-time*, introducing a non-Euclidean universe in which mass and energy were equivalent ($E = MC^2$) – that is, the faster

---

[39] Stephen Kern, *The Culture of Time and Space, 1880–1918* (Cambridge, MA: Harvard University Press, 1983), 12–14, 23.
[40] Einstein, *Relativity*, 23.
[41] Ibid., 34–7.
[42] Ibid., 25–8.

an object moves, the greater its mass – and the gravity of massive objects could cause not only light (hitherto considered to travel only in straight lines) but time itself to bend.

The advent of these theories, sending ripples through an already turbulent world in the wake of the First World War, elicited a loaded set of existential questions about the nature of reality that captured the imaginations of scientists and laypeople alike, bringing unprecedented public attention to the field of physics itself.[43] Einstein's theories were not immediately appreciated, however. He was able to develop the General Theory of Relativity in relative obscurity, building upon the ideas of his teacher, Hermann Minkowski, to 'combine time with space, and to describe physical processes as inhabitants of the four-dimensional space, now referred to as *space-time*'.[44] On 29 May 1919, when the British physicist Arthur Eddington and his team recorded the first experimental proof of the theory during an expedition to photograph the solar eclipse on the West African island of Principe, the theory was thrust to the forefront of the media and public attention. Their photographs proved Einstein's prediction that the immense gravity of the sun should cause light to bend around it, distorting the image of the stars as they move relative to Earth. These results led the *New York Times* to run the dramatic headlines: 'Stars All Askew in the Heavens', 'Men of Science More or Less Agog over Results of Eclipse Observations', adding, for the sake of their alarmed readership, 'Stars Not Where They Seemed or Were Calculated to Be, but Nobody Need Worry'.[45]

This coverage catapulted Einstein to fame hitherto unknown for a physicist. 'Before 1919 almost no one outside of physics knew of Albert Einstein. After 1919 almost no one did not know of him.'[46] Although physics was already of interest to some artists and writers, Einstein's fame drew increased curiosity from those seeking modern forms of expression and understanding – and inspired responses from modernist writers, one of which, William Carlos Williams's poem 'St Francis Einstein of the Daffodils', is a focal point of the first chapter of this book. Yet Einstein's theories were not universally welcomed. Many scientists on both sides of the Atlantic were reluctant to accept this new structure for

---

[43] Elizabeth Cornell, 'Louis Untermeyer's Poetic Engagement of the Popularization of Einstein's Relativity Theory', *South Central Review* 32, no. 2 (Summer 2015), 63.
[44] Roger Penrose, 'Introduction', *Albert Einstein, Relativity: The Special and General Theory*, trans. Robert W. Lawson (New York: Pi Press, 2005), xi.
[45] 'Stars All Askew in the Heavens', *The New York Times* (10 November 1919), https://timesmachine.nytimes.com/timesmachine/1919/11/10/118180487.pdf [Accessed 9 January 2020].
[46] Stanley Goldberg cited in Crossland, *Modernist Physics*, 2.

the universe.⁴⁷ Writers had difficulty translating Einstein's theories to non-specialist readers; Bertrand Russell attributed much of relativity's difficulty to just how drastically the common reader needed to rethink their common-sense understanding of space and time.⁴⁸ In some areas, the very complexity of the theory itself was a sign of Einstein's genius, but elsewhere its impenetrability elicited confusion. Alongside the many serious attempts to get to grips with relativity, a minor industry of satirical cartoons and articles grew up, presenting the exaggerated strangeness and absurdity of the theories' consequences.⁴⁹ One commentator described it as a science that 'would surely have satisfied [Lewis Carroll's] Alice': 'For no one can be sure of his shape now; because size depends upon speed. All motion is relative. If Alice had moved fast enough she could have diminished her weight. All students of physics to-day know mass and energy are essentially the same thing.'⁵⁰ Yet the difficulty of the theory was also one of the reasons for its popularity, providing intrigue and puzzlement for a readership who enjoyed a challenge. Demand for popular explanations of the theory was high. In 1920, the *Scientific American* ran an essay contest, offering $5,000 to the person able to give the best explanation of the Special and General Theories of Relativity.⁵¹

Numerous expositions, including Einstein's own, were printed in English and often ran into multiple editions.⁵² Katy Price has traced a shifting attitude to the theory, offering a picture of 'public frustration about the difficulty of Einstein's theory in the early 1920s, yielding by the 1930s to the sense that cosmic speculation had become a popular pastime'.⁵³ General Relativity offered, for the first time, a reliable picture of the structure of the universe as a whole, weaving space, time and gravity into one elegant theory.⁵⁴ Elizabeth Cornell says that, in America, '[p]ublic attention on Einstein and his theory subsided somewhat by

---

⁴⁷ Robert P. Crease and Alfred Sharff Goldhaber, *The Quantum Moment* (New York: W. W. Norton & Co., 2014), 40.
⁴⁸ Bertrand Russell, *A B C of Relativity* (London: Routledge, 1997), 11.
⁴⁹ For an overview of press interpretations of Einstein's theory on both sides of the serious and satirical divide, see: Katy Price, *Loving Faster Than Light: Romance and Readers in Einstein's Universe* (Chicago & London: The University of Chicago Press, 2012), 42–73.
⁵⁰ Alexander McAdie, 'Relativity and the Absurdities of Alice', *The Atlantic Monthly* (June 1921), https://www.theatlantic.com/magazine/archive/1921/06/relativity-and-the-absurdities-of-alice/303933/ [Accessed 7 January 2020].
⁵¹ Alan J. Friedman and Carol C. Donley, *Einstein: As Myth and Muse* (Cambridge: Cambridge University Press, 1985), 16.
⁵² Albert Einstein, *Relativity: The Special and General Theories* (London: Methuen, 1920); C. P. Steinmetz, *Four Lectures on Relativity* (New York: McGraw-Hill, 1923); Bertrand Russell, *A B C of Relativity* (New York: Harper & Brothers, 1925), to name a few.
⁵³ Price, *Loving Faster Than Light*, 3.
⁵⁴ Penrose, *Albert Einstein, Relativity*, xvii.

the end of 1920, but the German scientist returned to the spotlight even more strongly when he visited the United States in the spring of 1921'.[55] As we will see in Chapter 1, Williams took inspiration from this visit.

The emergence of quanta

As some physicists looked to the stars for proof of the shape of the universe, others were looking in the opposite direction, hunting for answers about the shape of its smallest constituents. Exploration of the behaviour of matter and energy at very small scales led to the second and perhaps more controversial revolution in early-twentieth-century physicists' world-picture: the rise of quantum physics. Quantum theory emerged from work on the relation between frequency, intensity and temperature conducted by the German physicist Max Planck at the turn of the century.[56] Planck examined a phenomenon called blackbody radiation. A blackbody is a 'perfect absorber of energy',[57] a surface which appears black because it absorbs all forms of radiation (e.g. light and heat) which fall on it. He discovered that at low frequencies, such as the low-level radiation of blackbodies, Wein's law about the smooth distribution of radiation broke down.[58] To create a successful model for blackbody radiation, he was forced to treat energy in quantized chunks or particles – 'pieces of energy' – rather than as a continuous wave.[59] To describe the relationship between these quanta of energy and their wave frequency, he introduced a mathematical constant (now known as Planck's constant) into his equations. Energy, it seemed, worked as a wave at large scales, but at the smallest scales broke down and behaved more like particles. By being forced to accept the quantum nature of energy transmission, Planck had discovered a limitation of Classical Physics, the first sign that the laws physicists had abided by for centuries did not apply on the smallest scales

---

[55] Cornell, Louis Untermeyer's Poetic Engagement of the Popularization of Einstein's Relativity Theory, 51.
[56] For a fuller account of Planck's work, see Helge Kragh, *Quantum Generations* (Princeton, NJ: Princeton University Press, 1999), 58–63.
[57] 'Blackbody', *Encyclopaedia Britannica* (Encyclopaedia Britannica inc., 2016), https://www.britannica.com/science/blackbody [Accessed 9 January 2020].
[58] This law, developed by the German physicist, Wilhelm Wein, described the relationship between temperature and peak wave-length emission. This relationship was described by a smoothly distributed radiation curve, which peaks at the dominant wavelength, corresponding to the colour of light emitted by the body. As the heat of a body increases, Wein said, the dominating wavelength is displaced towards the shorter (blue) end of the spectrum. At low temperatures, however, Planck discovered that the blackbody radiation curve behaved in a way that was not explained by this law.
[59] John Gribbin, *In Search of Schrödinger's Cat* (London: The Folio Society, 2012), 36.

of measurement.⁶⁰ Planck announced his discovery in December 1900, but the idea of energy quanta was at that time considered by most to be little more than a 'mathematical trick' designed to fix his equations.⁶¹

As quantum theory developed, the concept of quanta was integrated into more areas of physics, offering solutions to long-standing puzzles in thermodynamics and gravitation. It was not until Einstein insisted that the quantum behaviour Planck had observed was the true nature of light that the implications of energy quanta began to be realized. In 1905, Einstein wrote that light 'is not continuously distributed over an increasing space but consists of a finite number of energy quanta which are localized at points in space, which move without dividing, and which can only be produced or absorbed as complete units'.⁶² Light was emitted not in continuous waves but in quantized packets, now known as photons; more intense light was simply a higher density of photons of the same energy, while different coloured lights (or lights of different frequencies) were the result of photons containing higher or lower amounts of energy.⁶³ By 1923, this theory had ushered in new discussions about the nature of waves and particles which led to a second wave of quantum theories and the development of the quantum model of the atom.

Visualizing the atom

The twentieth century saw the transformation of atomic physics, with the birth of new technologies – the cloud chamber and electrostatic machines, the early forerunners of today's Large Hadron Collider – used to discover and detect the behaviour of subatomic particles. A flurry of experiments by Ernest Rutherford and others led to new theories about the shape and structure of the atom and, as we will see in Chapter 2, influenced Mina Loy's representation of the *human* body and its interactions. The model accepted at the turn of the century, Thomson's plum pudding model (1897), so-called because it envisaged the atom as an enclosed lump of positive charge dotted with electrons like bits of fruit in a plum pudding, was challenged by Rutherford in 1909. This model had been popular for its simplicity and monistic nature but, as Kragh points out, its value for

---

[60] Ibid., 39.
[61] Ibid., 37; for a more technical account of earlier atomic models, including the 'vortex atom' which led to Thomson's model and of the scientific details behind these developments, see Kragh, *Quantum Generations*, 44–53.
[62] A. B. Arons and M. B. Peppard, 'Einstein's Proposal of the Photon Concept – a Translation of the *Annalen der Physik* paper of 1905', *American Journal of Physics* 33, no. 5 (May 1965), 368.
[63] Gribbin, *In Search of Schrödinger's Cat*, 43.

illuminating other aspects of physics and chemistry were 'suggestive analogies rather than deductions based on the details of the model'.[64] Under Rutherford's scrutiny, it fell short. He realized that, far from being a solid whole, atoms must be made up mostly of empty space, with a charged nucleus at its centre, which exerted a field of force to contain its electrons. This shift from a pudding-like mass to a vast empty space with miniscule particles constituted a monumental epistemological shift in our understanding of matter: the matter that makes up everything we know is nowhere near as solid as our intuitions would suggest. There was a problem with this model, too, however: it did not explain what kept the electrons from being sucked in by the electrostatic attraction of the nucleus. Rutherford's atom would inevitably collapse in on itself. Bohr's elegant solution to this problem in 1913 integrated the principles of quantum theory into the model of the atom, proposing fixed concentric circular orbits (known as 'shells' or 'quantum levels') around the nucleus. These shells corresponded to the quanta of energy held by electrons in their fixed paths of orbit, much like how the planets orbit the sun, but with no possible orbits in between the quantum levels. This model became known as the Planetary Model and explained many chemical questions about the behaviour of electrons and their availability for chemical reactions.

Despite its elegance, Bohr's model failed. The idea of orbits relied heavily on classical mechanics, while the idea of energy quanta came from quantum theory, two systems that followed distinctly different rules.[65] Because of its elegant simplicity, however, it gained widespread popularity, and has remained a popular way of visualizing the atom. This is because the energy contained in each shell corresponded to a certain quantum of energy, which cannot be further broken down. Electrons can move between shells by either emitting or absorbing a quantum of energy. When they do, they don't glide up or down from shell to shell, but 'leap' instantly from one to the other. This is the origin of the term 'quantum leap'.

For the writers I consider in this book, the Planetary Model would have been the most accessible, both due to its clarity and simplicity, and because of the richness of imagery its comparison to the solar system provided. For some writers it offered a neat image of a consistently structured physical world, where the largest and smallest phenomena work according to mirroring systems. Despite being precisely the intuition later developments in quantum

---

[64] Kragh, *Quantum Generations*, 46.
[65] Ibid., 45–6.

theory came to overthrow, the notion of macro-/micro-similarity evoked by the Planetary Model offered a well of inspiration, some results of which I examine in Chapters 2 and 3. Appealing though it might have been to see Bohr's model as the bridge between the Classical and Quantum world, this understanding of the atom has since been disproven in almost every aspect, and was soon replaced by another quantum model which remains widely accepted by experts today.

The Quantum Mechanical Model, developed by Erwin Schrödinger in 1925, firmly integrated quantum principles into the structure of the atom, shifting away from describing the exact path of electrons to predicting the *probability* of finding an electron at a given point. This model depicts the nucleus not as a speckled mass or concentric shells, but as a compact body surrounded by an electron cloud of variable density. From pudding to solar system to cloud in less than two decades: the rapid development of atomic models offers a sense of wider epistemological shifts taking place across physics, with radical changes taking place over only a few years.

The quantum revolution

With the advent of quantum mechanics, the world-picture of physics grew less solid, more complicated and harder to visualize. The two major revelations of quantum mechanics are that the world is formed of things which are both particles and waves at the same time, and that, at a subatomic level, nothing can be predicted with absolute certainty. Einstein's proposal that light *is* both wave and particle was extended to apply to electrons and other subatomic particles, too. This sparked a major debate among scientists about the validity of the terms 'wave' and 'particle' themselves (which I discuss in Chapters 3 and 4) and it also raised deep questions about the nature of scientific observation. Developments in physics broadly follow the same pattern: theories are put forward based on theoretical or practical problems faced by the physicist, then tested through empirical experimentation and observation to provide a proof. Occasionally this works in the opposite direction, with observed effects leading scientists to theorize about them. In both cases, the act of *observation* is vital to the eventual proof or dismissal of the theory, and without observational evidence no theory can be considered true. Since the Enlightenment, this has been how science had proceeded, and it had long seemed inviolable as a method of exploring the natural world. With more and more refined equipment to aid their observations, twentieth-century experimentalists were able to detect the detail of their theories with greater and greater accuracy, and it seemed it would go on that way indefinitely. Then came the quantum revolution.

Born out of the disruption caused by the First World War, the 'quantum generation' of physicists, including Werner Heisenberg, Paul Dirac, Wolfgang Pauli and Pascual Jordan, came of age in the early 1920s. Compared to those of Planck and Einstein's generations, '[t]hey had no ingrained training in classical physics to overcome, and less need than even so brilliant a scientist as Bohr of half-measures to retain a flavour of classical ideas in their theories of the atom.'[66] With Planck's notion of constants and Bohr's incomplete atom model, as well as Einstein's use of statistics to account for details of atomic spectra, they were equipped for a second wave of developments.

One of the central features of quantum mechanics is Heisenberg's Uncertainty Principle. Heisenberg understood that particles on a quantum scale behave very differently from those large enough to be seen through a microscope. At this level the terms physicists are usually concerned with – such as the velocity and position of a particle – do not simply apply. Normally the direction and velocity of an object would allow you to predict its position at a given time, the same way you might predict that a train leaving New York at a certain time and speed will arrive at its destination on time. For quantum particles, this is not the case. Here, '[t]he more accurately we know the position of a particle, the less accurately we know its momentum, and vice versa.'[67] One measurement precludes the other. Importantly, Heisenberg showed this was not an issue with the devices used to take the measurements, or with the scientists' capacity or competency, but rather an insight into the nature of the quantum phenomena themselves. That is, '[t]here is no such thing as an electron that possesses both a precise momentum and a precise position.'[68] Uncertainty had to be accepted as a fundamental structural aspect of the universe. Because of this, Heisenberg argued, '[m]echanical quantities, such as position and velocity, should be represented not by ordinary numbers but by abstract mathematical structures called "matrices".'[69]

This discovery had widespread implications, both within science and for the perception of the new physics in the public realm. First, quantum phenomena can be represented only as abstractions; second, their very nature precludes complete knowability; and, finally, what we know about a particle is determined

---

[66] Ibid., 52.
[67] Ibid., 139.
[68] Gribbin, *In Search of Schrödinger's Cat*, 140.
[69] M. A. Eastwood, 'Heisenberg's Uncertainty Principle', *QJM: An International Journal of Medicine* 110, no. 5 (May 2017), 335.

by what we choose to measure and how we set up our experiment. Quantum physics at this point broke off not only from the laws of Classical physics, but also from describing behaviour that is easy to visualize. As we saw with the quantum model of the atom, electrons could no longer be determined by single points in orbit but by clusters of probabilities. Quantum mechanics, as Heisenberg put it, is 'a matter of processes that, though still experimentally observable in their effects and rationally analysable by mathematical means [...] no longer allow us to form any image of them'.[70] If the relativity theories posed a challenge for writers to illuminate without resorting to complex mathematics, quantum mechanics posed an even greater one, as the terminology used began to break down and lose its applicability.

The evolution of quantum mechanics was characterized by a series of instances in which scientists had to confront linguistic challenges; their discoveries demanded new forms of articulation to express work which resisted the easy understanding both of those funding their research and their scientific colleagues. Heisenberg and Bohr scrabbled to find a way of describing these new wave-particles. In the autumn of 1926, they met in Copenhagen for evenings of rigorous and heated discussion about how best to proceed. They came to differing conclusions. Bohr accepted the imagery of waves and particles as restricted metaphors. In the atomic domain, he suggested, descriptions should adhere to the complementarity principle, whereby the 'complete knowledge of phenomena on atomic dimensions requires a description of both wave and particle properties.'[71] While in a practical sense, the wave-particle nature of subatomic phenomena collapses when measured, displaying either wave- or particle-like properties, Bohr argued that taken together these properties 'present a fuller description than either of the two taken alone'.[72] Through the concept of complementarity, Bohr maintained the ability to talk in a meaningful way about phenomena which were otherwise resistant to traditional imagery. In contrast, Heisenberg stepped away from language and insisted that the only meaningful way to discuss quantum phenomena was through mathematics. In his 1927 paper, he strove to resist 'any customary images of atoms and permitted his theory to determine the meanings of symbols'.[73] In other words, he came to

---

[70] Werner Heisenberg, *Across the Frontiers*, ed. Ruth Nanda Ashen, trans. Peter Heath (New York: Harper & Row, 1974), 12.
[71] 'Uncertainty Principle', *Encyclopaedia Britannica* (Encyclopaedia Britannica inc., 1998), https://www.britannica.com/science/complementarity-principle [Accessed 10 January 2020].
[72] Ibid.
[73] Arthur J. Miller, *Imagery in Scientific Thought* (Cambridge, MA: The MIT Press, 1986), 253.

terms with and embraced the abstraction demanded by quantum mechanics, a move which, while valuable to mathematically minded scientists, only reinforced the feeling that physics was becoming increasingly arcane and inaccessible. The road to these conclusions was long and fraught; I will return to the outcomes and implications of this crisis of language and imagery in more depth in Chapter 4.

In short, quantum mechanics exposed a number of frailties in the old Classical mechanics: our potential for accurate knowledge of subatomic phenomena had limitations; Newtonian physics were not universal; and at the level of the electron, it becomes difficult to describe physical behaviour in traditional terms. There is one more important revelation from quantum mechanics that it is worth glossing here, for it had considerable implications for modern understandings of perception and reality: the observer effect. Every quantum experiment raises a serious problem. The very act of observing interferes with the subatomic phenomenon being observed. This effect is the result of the fact that 'we have to interfere with the atomic processes in order to observe them at all'.[74] Quantum phenomena are fundamentally altered through the act of observation, a realization which aroused serious epistemological questions. As we will see in Chapters 3 and 4, the implications of this renewed attention to the relationship between the object and the observer extended beyond the laboratory, provoking a reconsideration of the viewer's relationship with art and the role of the imagination in creative production.

In the wake of a war which had caused massive material and epistemic uncertainty in its own right, it is easy to see how a statement from scientists foregrounding uncertainty as a fundamental aspect of the universe might be misinterpreted. By the late 1920s, quantum leaps and uncertainty principles had become polymorphous metaphors, applied in the popular footnote press to everything from the Wall Street Crash to football results. In 1929, for instance, the *New York Times* ran a tongue-in-cheek article attributing to Heisenberg the sudden change of cause-and-effect links between stock prices and earnings.[75] Gavin Parkinson notes that the French philosopher Gaston Bachelard argued that 'an "epistemological break" had taken place due to the entirely new forms of rationality demanded by the seemingly nonsensical results achieved by physicists observing behavior on the subatomic scale'.[76] In 1931, the *New York Times* ran a

---

[74] Gribbin, *In Search of Schrödinger's Cat*, 107.
[75] 'By-Products', *The New York Times*, 3 November 1929, 4.
[76] Gavin Parkinson, 'Surrealism and Quantum Mechanics: Dispersal and Fragmentation in Art, Life, and Physics', *Science in Context* 17, no. 4 (2004), 558.

full-page article by science writer Waldemar Kaempffert, who emphasized the importance of digesting the barrage of new theories that had emerged since the turn of the century, and their implications for future knowledge. The headline ran:

> HOW TO EXPLAIN THE UNIVERSE? SCIENCE IN A QUANDARY; One After Another the Theories Put Out by the Scientists Have Been Exploded and Now Science in Its Uncertainty Has Been Forced to Become Idealistic and to Drop the Idea of a Mechanical Universe A Universe of Spirit.[77]

Kaempffert captured the disturbing nature of quantum theory:

> We are trying to explain reality, the universe, the objects we see and feel. We must of necessity explain them in terms of electrons, the elements of which they are composed. We find ourselves baffled [...] Hence we can never know anything definite about an atom and therefore about a world composed of atoms. Pure chance reigns. The concept of cause has no meaning in the atom.[78]

In popular discourse, quantum physicists' claims were extrapolated, exaggerated and applied to other areas of knowledge. Just as it had become common to invoke relativity as a means of dismissing an argument, references to quantum leaps, complementarity, wave-particle duality and observer interference gradually found their way into common parlance. The theory aroused as many misinterpretations as it did expositions and, as Julie M. Johnson notes, '[c]onfronted with a mathematical construct which has been transmuted into a metaphysical theory and blended with parallel philosophical and psychological ideas, it is often difficult to separate one thread from another and trace it directly back to its origins'.[79]

While for some the strangeness of quantum behaviour initiated an epistemological crisis, others were more inclined to think it presented an opportunity for creative emancipation. In a review of Eddington's *New Pathways in Science* (1935), the science writer and literary journalist J. W. N. Sullivan proposed that the new theories opened a door for artists and writers to embrace science and integrate it into new forms of knowledge:

> Everybody but a few die-hards is pleased with the new modesty that science has developed. It is no longer necessary for mystics and artists, in mere self-defence,

---

[77] Waldemar Kaempffert, 'How to explain the Universe? Science in a Quandary', *The New York Times* (11 January 1931), 120.
[78] Ibid.
[79] Julie M. Johnson, 'The Theory of Relativity in Modern Literature: An Overview and "The Sound and the Fury"', *Journal of Modern Literature* 10, no. 2 (June 1983), 220.

to ignore the scientific outlook. Science has become aware that its knowledge is a particularly restricted kind of knowledge. Also, it has no exclusive claim to truth. It is admitted that there may be kinds of knowledge which are valid, even though they have not been, and cannot be, reached by scientific methods.[80]

Quantum theory underwent as many misinterpretations as relativity, not least because it provoked as much (if not more) confusion and approbation within the field of physics as it did in the world outside it. Quantum theory, with its dissolution of the subatomic world that had once been assumed to be solid into a system of strange wave/particle simultaneities, probabilities, statistics and uncertainties, seemed to feed the same anxieties relativity had engendered among its detractors: namely, it challenged the intuitive world view of Classical Physics upon which the foundations of physics had rested. Heisenberg sums up the key revelations of the new physics thus:

> Relativity and the quantum theory have revealed basic structures in nature that were previously unknown. In relativity theory we are concerned with the structure of space and time; in quantum theory with the consequences of the fact that every measurement in the atomic field requires an act of intervention.[81]

As Parkinson notes, '[a]lthough the implications for knowledge of Relativity and quantum mechanics were first recognised by the handful of physicists mainly responsible for the formulation of those theories, the epistemology that emerged from them was developed and made known to a larger public by philosophers of science, historians of science and philosophers.'[82] This process, through which complex mathematical ideas filtered out into public understanding, took place gradually over the course of the first half of the century.

The New Physics, then, introduced a varied and often surreal epistemology which encompassed concepts that challenged earlier perceptions of science and demanded a reconsideration of ideas which had shared implications both for the scientist and the artist. The challenges of visualization, the relationship between observer and observed, complementarity, spacio-temporal measurement, abstraction and the need to develop a meaningful language through which to express the new discoveries form an important point of intersection between science and the arts.

---

[80] J. W. N. Sullivan, 'Science and Philosophy: Sir Arthur Eddington's New Book', *The Observer* (3 March 1935), 4.
[81] Heisenberg, *Across the Frontiers,* 19.
[82] Parkinson, 'Surrealism and Quantum Mechanics', 4.

The New York avant-garde

Quantum mechanics disturbed those who discovered it because of its apparent discontinuity with all that had gone before. Einstein rejected its randomness and non-linearity, partly for aesthetic reasons: 'God does not play dice with the universe.'[83] Similar misgivings were spread through the scientific community on both sides of the Atlantic. Crease and Goldhaber describe how 'American physicists who had been attracted to their calling by its elegance, beauty, predictability, and universality were struggling with an upstart theory that was – by contrast – ugly, weird, unpredictable, and apparently quite specialized.'[84]

By the 1910s, a classically trained artist might have begun to feel the same way about their own field. Art faced its own series of revolutions in this period.[85] Charismatic movements touting bombastic manifestos and employing shocking techniques designed to signal their newness – Fauvism, Cubism, Futurism, Surrealism, Dada – all vied to cast off the fustiness of nineteenth-century modes of representation and present the world in striking and modern ways. The work they produced is often challenging and esoteric, pushing outwards from the boundaries of realism towards abstraction, humour, polemic and satire. New techniques were developed by artists experimenting with photography, film, collage and non-mimetic sculpture; new subjects were found in the bustle of urban life, the machinery of war and modern industry, and scientific forms; and artists proposed radically new ideas about the purpose and audience of art.[86] In the arena of avant-garde art, ideas entered a playground of experimentation, in which their aesthetic and philosophical potential was stretched and manipulated, often in ways that invited scorn from their audiences, sometimes in ways that questioned or openly threatened their validity, but occasionally, too, in ways which would go on to transform the wider cultural understanding of those ideas. For all the writers I discuss, physics is entangled with the innovations of modern art; their individualized employment of scientific ideas, at the level of form, content or overarching ontology, draws upon and feeds back into the broader

---

[83] Vasant Natarajan, 'What Einstein Meant when He Said "God does not play dice…"', *Resonance* (July 2008), 659–60.
[84] Crease and Goldhaber, *The Quantum Moment*, 40.
[85] For an in-depth overview of the history of modern art, see: Elizabeth C. Mansfield and H. Harvard Arnason, *A History of Modern Art: Painting, Sculpture, Architecture, Photography* (New Jersey: Prentice Hall PTR, 1998); Wendy Steiner, *Venus in Exile: The Rejection of Beauty in Twentieth-century Art* (New York: Simon & Schuster, 2001).
[86] Robert L. Herbert, 'The Arrival of the Machine: Modernist Art in Europe, 1910–25', *Social Research* 64, no. 3 (Fall 1997), 1273.

networked understanding of physics and its relationship with the arts during this period. Just as the field of physics was not homogenous, with scientists' ideas shifting and evolving as the century progressed, we can expect to find similar contradictions and variations among the artists' remediation of scientific ideas. With this in mind, it is important to have an overview of some of the key movements active in New York in the 1910s and 1920s – Cubism, Futurism, Dada and Surrealism – as they form a vital intermediary throughout each of my case studies.

European art erupted onto the American stage as part of the celebrated Armory Show of February 1913. This vast exhibition, which took over the 26,000 square feet of New York's 69th Regiment Armory's drill hall with 1,300 international artworks, brought new forms of experimental European art to a mainstream American audience for the first time.[87] Conservative audiences were in for a shock: they were faced with dramatic experiments in composition, fragmentation, colour and movement, with whole galleries dedicated to forms of art that were not only controversial but, to some, entirely unintelligible. A cartoon by Alek Sass in the *New York World* on 17 February 1913 illustrated the shock of American art critics who visited the show: a strait-laced art critic visits the show, growing more and more alarmed with each gallery he enters.[88] By the third gallery he is on his knees; by the fifth he is being rushed away in an ambulance. In addition to traditional values, many of these critics feared the changed 'interpretative machinery that accompanied the new art, which seemed to shake the very foundations of the American art world': it challenged American taste-makers by enabling the public to form their own opinions, not only of the quality of a painting or sculpture but also of what Art itself was or could be.[89] The American art historian and critic Royal Cortissoz decried the modernist artists' work as 'not only incompetent, but grotesque', stating he was 'absolutely sceptical as to their having any claim whatever to being works of art'.[90] But what were these scandalous new artworks, and what was the thinking behind the artists creating them?

Cubism was developed in Paris between 1907 and 1914 by Pablo Picasso and George Braque, whose influences included the artistic styles of Paul Cezanne

---

[87] Darcy Tell, 'The Armory Show at 100: Primary Documents', *Archives of American Art Journal* 51, no. 3–4 (Fall 2012), 11, 15.
[88] Alek Sass, 'Nobody Who Has Been Drinking Is Let in to See This Show'. *New York World*, 17 February 1913.
[89] JoAnne M. Mancini, '"One Term Is as Fatuous as Another": Responses to the Armory Show Reconsidered', *American Quarterly* 51, no. 4 (December 1999), 838, 839–40.
[90] Royal Cortissoz cited in ibid., 850.

and African art. The first phase of the movement, known as Analytical Cubism (1907–12), involved the broken-down representation of still life and portrait subjects from multiple perspectives, adopting a technique of sharp geometric fragmentation and overlapping perspectival layers. Figures and objects were distorted and flattened, with a tendency for monochromatic palettes of blue, green or tan. After 1912, Cubism developed a more mature style, with a greater use of colour and form, fracture and overlapping, which drew together elements within a composition through contrasting lines and textures. This style became known as Synthetic Cubism because of its greater concern with unity to synthesize different forms into flat representations which challenged common perceptions of three-dimensional space. Synthetic Cubism adopted new techniques, such as collage, to create depth and verisimilitude, with artists integrating found items such as newspaper clippings or wallpaper into their compositions. This intellectualized style of painting broke the shackles of earlier mimetic art, proposing new approaches to form and perspective that pushed against traditional ideas of beauty. Cubism presented 'a view or perspective on "reality" and life which is also manifested in literature' primarily through an 'attitude of originality, of making new through techniques of defamiliarization'.[91] Cubism's rejection of traditional modes of representation opened the door to more and more experimental forms of expression in art in following decades. As I show in Chapter 1, these techniques inspired Williams to experiment with new ways of presenting compact, fragmented perspectives in his poetry, utilizing the line-breaks and empty space around words in a poem to expand the significance of his stripped-back language.

Italian Futurism burst onto the scene in February 1909, when Marinetti's *Manifesto of Futurism* found its way onto the pages of first the Italian magazine *La gazetta dell'Emilia* and then the French newspaper *Le Figaro*.[92] Marinetti 'proclaimed the birth of a new literary and social movement' with a radical new approach to art.[93] The futurists rejected inherited artistic traditions and promoted a cutting-edge, youthful aesthetic grounded in modern technology,

---

[91] Jan-Louis Kruger, 'William Carlos Williams' Cubism: The Sensory Dimension', *Literator* 16, no. 2 (August 1995), 197.

[92] Although Futurism also flourished as a distinct movement in Russia, the influence of Futurism on the poets discussed in this thesis comes primarily from Italian Futurism. F. T. Marinetti, 'Manifesto del Futurismo', *Gazzetta dell'Emilia* (5 February 1909); F. T. Marinetti, 'Manifeste du futurisme', *LE FIGARO*, LV 3, no. 51 (Saturday 20 February 1909), 1; further information on the publication history of this first manifesto can be found in Paulo Tonini, *I Manifesti del Futurismo Italiano 1909-1945* (Gussago: Edizioni dell'Arengario, 2011), 6–7.

[93] Richard Kostelanetz, 'Futurism (Italian)', *A Dictionary of the Avant-Gardes*, 2nd ed. (New York and London: Routledge, 2001), 231.

scientific advancements and kinetic dynamism rendered on canvas through bold, graphic geometry, vibrant colours and lines of force. Futurism's hymn to modernity expanded into experiments with new forms of music and sound poetry, as well as bombastic, often politically inflected manifestos, and unsyntactical 'telegraphic' forms of literature.[94] As we will see in Chapter 2, Loy's engagement with Futurism pushed her towards a poetry bursting with the language of electromagnetism.

Dada emerged in 1916 Zurich, growing out of the ruins of war as artists began to reject systems of order and meaning that had come before. The movement was shaped by its negations: anti-establishment, anti-rationalist, anti-capitalist, even anti-art. One of its founders, Hugo Ball, said that the Dadaist 'knows that this world of systems has gone to pieces, and that the age which demanded cash has organized a bargain sale of godless philosophies'.[95] Dada greeted the political and epistemological crises of the decade with a destructive push for greater disruption and artistic chaos. Its proponents revelled in the detritus of modernity, integrating found objects, repurposed materials, new technologies and innovative techniques to demand a reassessment of art's cultural value. In New York, Dada was rooted in experiments from 1915, drawing upon Marcel Duchamp's ideas of anti-art, which exploded accepted definitions of art held by galleries and artistic institutions. The term came to New York later than Europe, despite the similarities of the projects taking place on either side of the Atlantic, and so New York Dada is often considered a retrospective category for similar anti-establishment aims and practices to those enacted in Zurich and Paris.[96] However, by the time of her publication in *The Little Review* in 1919, the Baroness was hailed by its editor, Jane Heap, as 'the only one living anywhere who dresses Dada, loves Dada, lives Dada'.[97] In Chapter 3, I explore how Dada's chance-based aesthetics inflected the Baroness's receptiveness to the systems and methodologies of the new physics.

Surrealism took up Dada's interest in irrationality, turning it towards constructive rather than destructive ends. Influenced by advances in psychoanalysis – and the

---

[94] See Kostelanetz, 'Futurist Music', *A Dictionary of the Avant-Gardes*, 2nd ed. (New York and London: Routledge, 2001), 233–4.
[95] Hugo Ball, 'Dada Fragments (1916–1917)', *The Dada Painters and Poets: An Anthology*, ed. Robert Motherwell (Belknap: Harvard University Press, 1989), 51.
[96] As Amelia Jones notes, 'New York Dada' is a term which 'was only retroactively, from the early 1920s, labeled as such by the popular press and, self-servingly, by the European Dada movement'. During this period, it was taken up and celebrated by *The Little Review*, especially in relation to the Baroness when she appeared on their pages. Amelia Jones, *Irrational Modernism* (Cambridge, MA: The MIT Press), 11.
[97] Jane Heap, 'Dada – ', *The Little Review* (Spring 1922), 46.

mystical implications of the new physics – Andre Breton expounded the movement's desire to resolve the division between conscious and unconscious experience through an art which questioned the value of realism and rationalism as a holistic method of interpreting modern experience: 'I believe in the future resolution of these two states, dream and reality, which are seemingly so contradictory, into a kind of absolute reality, a *surreality*.'[98] Parkinson argues that Surrealism exists 'at the crossroads of physics, philosophy, psychoanalysis and politics'.[99] He identifies a continuous engagement with relativity and quantum mechanics, which evolved into a rejection of nuclear physics in the cold war era, a pattern I see mirrored in Loy's changing ideas about atomic dissolution in Chapter 2.[100] Furthermore, Surrealism's interrogation of the irrational through optical illusion and superposition techniques generated debate around the ideal multivalence of images in modern poetry, influencing Stevens's techniques of representation in Chapter 4.

Each of these art movements was engaged to a greater or lesser extent with a trend towards abstraction. It is fascinating to see how certain of Heisenberg's comments on science hold true if the word 'science' is replaced with 'art': 'When contemporary [art] is compared with that of earlier periods, it is often asserted that in the course of its development this [art] has become ever more abstract.'[101] In both fields, abstraction was met with scepticism from traditionalists. How could Science, a field based on empiricist observation, rely on unobserved abstractions? How could Art, a field concerned with representation, step away from representing the observed world? For Heisenberg, science's increased abstraction was 'positively repellent' and 'only partially compensated by the great practical success which science can point to in its application to technology'.[102] For Einstein, it enabled a revolution in physics long before the means to experimentally verify his findings existed. For Royal Cortissoz, it led to art he believed was the 'grotesque' result of 'invertebrate and confusing thinking';[103] for other art critics, such as D. S. MacColl, abstraction brought the promise of a 'quickened consciousness of the value and meaning of life itself'.[104]

---

[98] Andre Breton, 'Manifesto of Surrealism', *Manifestos of Surrealism*, trans. Richard Seever and Helen R. Lane (Ann Arbor: The University of Michigan Press, 1969), 14.
[99] Parkinson, 'Surrealism and Quantum Mechanics', 4.
[100] Ibid., 8.
[101] Werner Heisenberg, 'Abstraction in Modern Science', *Across the Frontiers*, ed. Ruth Nanda Anshen, trans. Peter Heath (New York: Harper & Row, 1974), 70.
[102] Ibid.
[103] Royal Cortissoz, 'The Post-Impressionist Illusion', *Century* 85 (April 1913), 805.
[104] D. S. MacColl, 'The International Exhibition', 25, in JoAnne M. Mancini, '"One Term is as Fatuous as Another": Responses to the Armory Show Reconsidered', *American Quarterly* 51, no. 4 (December 1999), 833–70, 859.

Whether seen as repellent or rich in potential, abstraction gained traction across both science and art; its discourses, problems and opportunities were widely discussed and led to a cultural shift. The need for a 'balance between abstraction and representation' preoccupied many of the artists and scientists discussed in this book.[105] Abstraction is, primarily, a perspectival shift – 'the act or process of leaving out of consideration one or more qualities of a complex object so as to attend to others'[106] – which 'represents the possibility of considering an object or group of objects under one viewpoint while disregarding all other properties of the object'.[107] Impressionism, for instance, isolated its interest in an analytical, scientifically inflected interrogation of light effects; likewise, Cezanne's concern with 'the geometrical forms underlying the confusion of nature' were highly influential in both visual and literary art.[108] Creative interpretation of the possibilities of abstraction led the cubists to render the concept of simultaneity, Duchamp to render movement through time and poets to delve deeper and deeper into what makes a poem a poem. In these instances, art broke free of the assumption that it should strive to be an obvious and realistic rendering of its subject and took on new, often 'dispassionate and intellectual' forms.[109]

Heisenberg neatly summarizes the mindset with which these artists approached their work, describing how the 'interplay, or struggle, if you will, between the contents to be expressed and the restricted means of expressing it seems… – much as it is for science – the unavoidable precondition for the emergence of genuine art'.[110] Physics became more abstract, art became more abstract and poetry became more abstract in part because of this self-interrogation of their own methods and modalities, and reaction against the restrictions of the past. Indeed, as we shall see, each of the poets I discuss in this book had a stake in this struggle between abstract and concrete reality: Williams wrangled with 'ideas' and 'things'; Loy with the nature of abstraction itself; the Baroness wrestled with abstract intellectualism and sensual organicism; and Stevens's oeuvre is a hymn to the great battle between what he termed 'reality' and the 'imagination'.

---

[105] Daniel R. Schwarz, "'The Serenade of a Man Who Plays a Blue Guitar': The Presence of Modern Painting in Steven's Poetry", *The Journal of Narrative Technique* 22, no. 2 (Spring 1992), 71.
[106] Michael J. Hoffman, *The Development of Abstractionism in the Writings of Gertrude Stein* (Philadelphia: University of Pennsylvania Press, 1965), 28.
[107] Heisenberg, 'Abstraction in Modern Science', 71.
[108] Alfred H. Barr Jr, *Cubism and Abstract Art* (New York: The Museum of Modern Art, 1936), 20, 26.
[109] John Golding, *Cubism: A History and an Analysis 1907–1914*, 3rd ed. (Cambridge, MA: Harvard University Press, 1988), 100.
[110] Heisenberg, 'Abstraction in Modern Science', 147.

This highly experimental period in the art world coincided with a new, scientifically inflected understanding of the artists' work: as 'Art' was seen to designate objects for private pleasure, radical artists instead chose to describe their works as 'laboratory experiments', and their creativity as a process of discovery and innovation.[111] Writers, too, discussed their work in terms of scientific investigation. Increasingly the language of the laboratory crept into poetic discourse: Williams described the experimental writing of Joyce and Stein as 'great laboratory work', for example, while Loy pursued new interpretations of the body-mind relationship in her 'ego laboratory'.[112]

The years preceding the eruption of the First World War saw a brief 'prophetic and utopian phase' in the arts, which seemed to set out 'the arena of agitation and preparation for the announced revolution, if not the revolution itself'.[113] The idea of revolution, so familiar in modernism as a process of rupture and transformation tightly encapsulated in Pound's maxim 'make it new', held wide currency in this period of political and social upheaval, but it did not mean the same thing for everyone. Heisenberg complicates the idea of comparing 'revolutions' in the arts and sciences by asserting a fundamental difference in how they come about in each sphere. He concludes that revolutions in science are motivated not by a drive for newness for its own sake (as seen in avant-garde art), but rather by a drive for conservatism: 'By changing as little as possible; by concentrating all efforts on the solution of a special and obviously still unsolved problem, and by proceeding as conservatively as possible in doing so.'[114] Novelty, for scientists, held none of the intrinsic value granted to it by the avant-gardes, despite – as in the case of Quantum Physic – leading to some of science's most rapid periods of development.

If Heisenberg felt that 'nothing is more unfruitful than the maxim that at all costs one must produce something new', the same does not apply to the early-twentieth-century arts scene.[115] Maurice Raynal, art critic and friend of Picasso, describes the artistic activities of this period as a veritable spree of interdisciplinary looting among artists: 'Poetry, prose literature, philosophy

---

[111] Herbert, 'The Arrival of the Machine', 1283.
[112] William Carlos Williams, 'Embodiment of Knowledge [1/2]' (c. 1928–1930), YCAL MSS 116/40, The Beinecke Rare Books and Manuscripts Library, Folder 1018; Mina Loy, 'History of Religion and Eros', *Stories and Essays of Mina Loy* (Illinois and London: Dalkey Archive Press, 2011), 237.
[113] Renato Poggioli, *Theory of the Avant Garde* (Oxford: Oxford University Press, 1968) cited in Marjorie Perloff, *The Futurist Moment: Avant-Garde, Avant Guerre, and the Language of Rupture* (Chicago: University of Chicago Press, 2003), xvii.
[114] Heisenberg, Abstraction in Modern Science, 151.
[115] Ibid.

and science – all were eagerly ransacked [...] all the procedures of the sciences and metaphysics – played their part.'[116] Yet it is important here to consider the difference in aim and purpose between science and art, and the uses to which they put their resources. Sam Halliday has rightly noted that although in many cases science and technology provide 'a vocabulary and set of concepts', they do not 'circumscribe the imaginative uses to which these were put.'[117] Writers and artists have the freedom to play fast and loose with fact, turning their sources towards aesthetic goals. Whether their new world-pictures are loosely or intricately attached to scientific discoveries, the early-twentieth-century artists I discuss rarely intended them for a scientific audience; their art is personal, emotional, political, provocative, but they are rarely 'scientific' in a technical sense. There were, nevertheless, scientists among their audience – and they were also magpies, at times responding creatively to the form and content of modern art and literature. Niels Bohr appreciated the work of the Cubist Jean Metzinger, whose work may have influenced Bohr's ideas about Complementarity;[118] Erwin Schrödinger wrote his own poetry, fusing scientific and poetic imagery and bringing his literary imagination to bear on his expression of scientific ideas;[119] and Werner Heisenberg responded to modern art in a series of lectures and essays, commenting on its affinity with modern science.[120] The free-flowing nature of these concepts means that we should not go looking in the literature and art of the modernists for direct or scientifically accurate transpositions of hard science, but rather approach each instance on its own terms, attentive to the intricate threads interaction they represent.

Four New York poets

In each of the cases I discuss here, the relationship between the poet and the physics their work engages with is complicated and multidimensional, often shifting over time. For some, the relationship was functional and instructive; for

---

[116] Maurice Raynal cited in Donley and Friedman, *Einstein*, 21–2.
[117] Sam Halliday, *Science and Technology in the Age of Hawthorne, Melville, Twain, and James* (London: Palgrave, 2007), 3.
[118] Christophe Schinckus, 'From Cubist Simultaneity to Quantum Complementarity', *Foundations of Science* 22 (2017), 709–16. https://doi.org/10.1007/s10699-016-9494-7
[119] Tzveta Sofronieva 'Erwin Schrödinger's Poetry', *Science & Education* 23 (2014), 655–72. https://doi.org/10.1007/s11191-013-9579-4
[120] Werner Heisenberg, *Across the Frontiers*, ed. Ruth Nanda, trans. Peter Heath (New York: Harper &Row, 1974).

others, it became a cross to bear. For Williams, this meant a growing conviction that Einstein's relativity had profound implications for the form of poetry; for Loy, the atomic bomb led to a jarring reconsideration of long-held philosophies of atomic dispersal. For the Baroness, physics evolved from artistic plaything and epistemological joke in the 1910s towards a life-affirming set of 'sense laws' during the 1920s, while Stevens found a representative for the modern mind in the abstract theories of Planck.[121]

All four of them came of age as writers in mid-1910s, where they took part in the avant-garde arts scene that flourished in New York's Greenwich Village, and this book takes New York as a vital point of intersection between them. Williams and Stevens were born nearby, in New Jersey and Pennsylvania, respectively, while Loy from Britain and the Baroness from Germany both found their way to New York in complex personal circumstances amid the tide of European expatriates that washed into the city during the war. Avant-garde New York broadly prioritized modernist values: newness, innovation, experimentation, *vers libre* and the quest to find a fitting idiom for modern experience. American-born poets like Williams were engaged in the hunt for a new, distinctly American poetic identity, seeking a style and idiom that could encompass and represent their particular time and place. Expatriates like Loy brought with them their experience of the European avant-gardes of France and Italy, offering their American readers poems that were at once formally innovative and scandalously sexy. The bohemian arts scene thrived on controversy, playfulness and an enthusiastic embrace of new technologies and techniques like photography, collage and kinetic sculpture. Fostered by wealthy patrons and collectors such as Walter and Louise Arensberg, and the busy work of new galleries and spaces for performance established by Julien Levy and Alfred Stieglitz, the cosmopolitan melting pot of New York became a centre for artistic experimentation. While the works discussed in this book are not limited to those produced during these writers' time in New York, the frenetic conditions of this time and place serve as an ontological anchor for us as we consider their approaches to the fusion of art, poetics and science; that is to say that the city's distilled culture of international, intermedial and interdisciplinary fusion is representative of a wider, distinctly Modernist, approach to writing.

Despite their separate interests and poetic styles, the paths of these writers intersected during this vibrant period in New York's artistic history. Williams

---

[121] Elsa von Freytag-Loringhoven, 'Selections from the Letters of Elsa Baroness von Freytag-Loringhoven', *Transition* (February 1928), 26.

lived just over the water in Rutherford, practicing medicine during the week and 'sneak[ing] away mostly on Sundays to join the gang' in the coteries of the Manhattan high-rises.[122] Stevens, likewise, flitted in and out, mingling with the Arensberg circle, and attending exhibitions at the New York galleries as he balanced his life of letters with his growing reputation in the conservative world of the insurance business. Loy brought her futurist credentials across the Atlantic in 1916 as she arrived to join the group that formed around the new magazine, *Contact*, gaining a reputation as the *New York Evening Sun*'s exemplary 'Modern Woman' by the following year.[123] According to Roger Conover, it was 'common to couple the names of Mina Loy and William Carlos Williams' in the 1910s and 1920s, and not only for their poetic talents; Williams was very enamoured with Loy, but playing husband and wife in the Provincetown Playhouse's production of Kreymborg's *Lima Beans* in October 1916 was as close as they got to romantic entanglement.[124]

Another misplaced flirtation brought Williams into contact with the Baroness, who hounded him with her affections and unexpected nudity until he was forced to take up boxing to fend her off.[125] Although Stevens once admired the Baroness's innovative costume choices, he too unwittingly caught her attention. The 'relentlessly-clothed' poet is said to have 'avoided going south of 14th street for fear of meeting her.'[126] When mounting their 'defense of art' against the censorship threat of the *Ulysses* trial in 1921, the editors of *The Little Review* arranged for the Baroness and Loy to be photographed together by Man Ray for a special issue, although there is little evidence to suggest the women knew one another well.[127] It is unclear whether Stevens and Loy knew one another personally, but when conceiving the avant-garde image of his new project, *Others*, Kreymborg picked them out especially as essential contributors to ensure the magazine's success. They were both published alongside Williams in successive issues of *Others* in 1915.[128]

---

[122] William Carlos Williams, *The Autobiography of William Carlos Williams* (New York: New Directions, 1967), 136.
[123] Linda Arbaugh Taylor, 'Lines of Contact: Mina Loy and William Carlos Williams', *William Carlos Williams Review* 16, no. 2 (Fall 1990), 26.
[124] Roger Conover cited in ibid., 27.
[125] Williams, *The Autobiography of William Carlos Williams*, 163–9.
[126] Tony Sharpe, *Wallace Stevens: A Literary Life* (London: Macmillan Press, 2000), 84–5; John J. Trause, 'William Carlos Williams and the Baroness', *The Rutherford Red Wheelbarrow*, ed. Jim Kline (Patterson, NJ: White Chickens Press, 2011), 173.
[127] Carolyn Burke, *Becoming Modern: The Life of Mina Loy* (New York: Farrar, Straus and Giroux, Kindle ed., 2012), 298.
[128] Mina Loy, 'Love Songs. I–IV', *Others* 1, no. 1 (1915), 6–8; Wallace Stevens, 'Peter Quince at the Clavier', *Others* 1, no. 2 (August 1915), 31–4; William Carlos Williams, 'Pastoral', 'Pastoral. II', 'The Ogre', 'Appeal', *Others* 1, no. 2 (August 1915), 23–5; Sharpe, *Wallace Stevens*, 83.

Each chapter of this book examines one of these four poets' relationships to physics through their connections with one or more modern art movement/s. Chapter 1 explores William Carlos Williams's development of new approaches to poetic measure, and his eventual development of the 'variable foot' through an analysis of his cubist technique. I examine the way in which Williams's approach to poetry was inflected by his interest in pictorial Cubism, and in particular the way in which cubist ideas of measurement were fused with developments in popular understandings of Einsteinian space-time in Williams's depiction of Einstein's arrival in New York in his occasional poem 'St. Francis Einstein of the Daffodils' (1921).

In Chapter 2, I read Mina Loy's work through the lens of modern energy physics and particle theory, tracing the complex ebb and flow of ideas about particle interaction and atomic dissolution in her work. I show how much of Loy's writing employs Futurist ideas of atomic dissolution, an idea which she utilized to produce striking interrogations of human sexuality and spiritual transcendence. This chapter shows the fluidity with which Loy's ideas evolved, following her through her engagement with Christian Science and, later, with the surrealist painter Richard Oelze in the 1930s, to show how her early interest in physics developed into a complicated and idiosyncratic metaphysics of radioactivity, electromagnetism and inter-atomic energy.

Chapter 3 examines the role of the Baroness Elsa von Freytag-Loringhoven in New York's vibrant and chaotic Dada scene, beginning with an examination of the poet-artist's relationship with the 'playful physics' of Marcel Duchamp. I read the Baroness's Dada as a response to the international crisis of the war, following her shifting understanding of physics from the machinic to the cosmological as she was forced into exile in Weimar Berlin. By contrasting prevailing attitudes with Dada's intentional systemic rupture during the interwar period, I show that the kind of physics which had been a matter of play in New York became a lifeline for the displaced Baroness as she sought in vain to rejoin to her colleagues and friends.

My final chapter interrogates Wallace Stevens's claim that Planck was the most characteristic thinker of the first half of the twentieth century by investigating the intersections of the two men's epistemologies. Examining the idiosyncratic world of poetic abstraction developed by Stevens alongside the quantum physicists' search for a viable syntax for quantum behaviour, I show how Stevens's and the physicists' lines of enquiry into the seemingly irrational, unvisualizable and deeply abstract nature of reality led them to consider similar problems of language, representation, process, meaning and value.

Williams, Loy, Stevens and the Baroness each engage with physics in a different way, variously adapting scientific ideas for experimentations with poetic form, using metaphors and images from physics to imbue their work with a cutting-edge, scientifically inflected, and distinctly modern flavour, and adopting and adapting the methodological trappings of science – of experiment and abstraction – to underpin their work with the written word. Modernist poetry played a part in shaping the cultural reception of figures like Einstein (for instance with Williams arguing the importance of integrating Einstein's new measurement into modern cultural aesthetics), and of articulating the impact of new scientific theories upon the non-scientific reader (by linking them to human experience as Loy and the Baroness do or, as Stevens does, publicly drawing links between science and politics, philosophy, history, and the modern cultural and intellectual life). Writers like Williams, who openly stated his interest in integrating Einsteinian measure into poetry, necessitate different handling from those like Stevens, whose interest in physics is a matter of shared concerns, rather than explicitly stated intention. Indeed, the variety of ways in which writers' concerns intersected with those of the physicists during this period is of vital importance, both for how we trace fields of influence and in shaping our intentions in doing so. As we begin to tease out these connections, we should take George Levine's advice and recognize 'the variousness and incompleteness of writers' and scientists' interrelations'.[129] The fluidity with which ideas move through culture means that no one means of characterizing the relationship will be adequate for any subject. As Whitworth puts it, 'literary fugitives flee the bank vaults of science in all directions, and a single searchlight cannot track them down.'[130] Thus, the work of this book necessarily shifts in relation to each poet's own sensibility and interests as I seek for each an appropriate and individual solution to what Crossland has called the 'balancing act' between tracing paths of direct influence and *zeitgeist*.[131] There are some cases in which cause-and-effect models are appropriate, for instance when Williams names Einstein's relativity theory as the starting point for his new approach to poetic metrics, but in other cases the source of a poet's language or ideas is much less explicit. Sometimes the evidence available requires a model which acknowledges that ideas move through culture not in simple streams but rather through what Hayles has called a flow of 'turbulent

---

[129] George Levine cited in Middleton, *Physics Envy*, 39.
[130] Whitworth, *Einstein's Wake*, 2.
[131] Crossland, *Modernist Physics*, 7.

complexity', in which no single field or source is privileged and the relationship between literature and science is 'not a one-way street'.[132]

In the case of Loy, for example, whose archives tantalizingly include what appear to be references from books gesturing to her reading on wave mechanics ('Theory of Vibrations', 'vib. mechanics', 'resistance effect'), topical reading is by no means her only source of physics ideas.[133] As I show in Chapter 2, Loy's understanding of physics is particularly complex as it passes through, merges with, and is amplified by a vast array of wider discourses including technology and machines, Futurism, Surrealism, Spiritualism, nationalism and fascism, and sexuality and feminism, before it finds its way into her writing. Moreover, Loy's writing works in dialogue with these ideas and movements, shaping her readers' perceptions of physics as a means for articulating modern concerns by bringing its language and principles to bear on other cultural discourses.

Some writers leave less of a paper trail: the Baroness's references to 'abstract science', for instance, do not come with an easy point of reference. In cases like this, it is necessary to reconstruct 'the moment's discourse' according to a broader 'fields of force' model, described by Whitworth as a means to 'ascribe scientific knowledge to an author in the absence of particular reports of reading or of conversations'.[134] Viewing the passage of ideas through culture as 'being propagated through a heterogenous, discontinuous medium' and attenuated at particular points enables discussion of the work of writers who did not write about the books they read or leave an easy-to-catalogue library behind them. However, we cannot simply assume a uniform understanding of a scientific concept, for instance, across the whole of society.[135] Some line of transmission still needs to be identified. In my study, this role is played by the visual arts.

Well-known poets such as Williams and Stevens pose different challenges to scholars than those whose work has been little discussed, and so while each chapter of this book is underpinned by archival research, my chapters on Loy and the Baroness have benefited most from extensive work in their archives at the Beinecke Rare Books and Manuscripts Library and the University of Maryland Special Collections. Unpublished works, such as Loy's poem 'Impossible Opus', gesture to a deeper interest in physics than has previously been acknowledged.

---

[132] N. Katherine Hayles, 'Turbulence in Literature and Science: Questions of Influence', in *American Literature and Science*, ed. Robert J. Scholnick (Lexington, KY: The University Press of Kentucky, 1992), 242.
[133] Mina Loy, 'History of Religion and Eros' notes and drafts [1/2], Mina Loy Papers, The Beinecke Rare Books and Manuscripts Library, Yale University, YCAL MSS 778/5, Folder 158.
[134] Whitworth, *Einstein's Wake*, 18.
[135] Ibid.

Here, Loy brings cutting-edge technical terms, like 'super-matter' and 'cyclotrone' [sic], into a poem about the juggernaut machinery of the modern age and its primeval roots in *Homo sapiens*' evolutionary imperative towards using basic tools.[136] Coupled with other fragmented notes in her papers – one tantalizingly reads 'Atom smashing? What? Dynamo' – we get a sense of Loy grappling with the more experimentalist side of atomic physics, where physicists were developing specialized accelerators designed to smash subatomic particles into one another and see what flew out.[137] In Chapters 2 and 3 especially, I deal with material that has been much less discussed than that of the other two chapters, and as such I have provided greater background detail for my arguments to redress the balance, in the knowledge that less prior scholarship exists to offer grounding for my reader.

My work is concerned with ideas in process; as such, I approach each of the poets I discuss on their own terms. In particular, I take the terminology they use – whether from physics or art or philosophy – in context. Working with unsettled ideas, whose meanings and language continually shifted throughout their lifetimes, we find many moments of slippage, in which theories and movements overlap, sometimes blurring at the edges. In part, this is because the writers I discuss were actively involved in the formation of these movements; in part also it is because, at a time when experimentation had become central to poetic practice, these poets refused to be constrained by a single world view. We see this in Chapter 2, for example, in the gamut of idealisms Mina Loy passed through and fused together; or in Chapter 3 in the way Stevens skirts the edges of the surrealist movement without ever quite classing himself as a surrealist. Unconstrained by tradition, these writers were free to take up and creatively reinterpret ideas from the public domain, and in doing so they sometimes step away from 'pure' understandings of the concepts they discuss. After all, whatever exposure they had to the science itself, these poets are not scientists (even when they claim to be) and their work ought not to be judged on its 'correctness' or scientific merit. Each of these poets engaged with science that had already been mediated, found in news articles and popular science books, heard at public lectures, discussed across the dinner table, and thus their work offers a magnified vision of wider cultural perceptions of physics. With each chapter, then, I have chosen to be guided by the poet's own journey through these ideas,

---

[136] Mina Loy, 'Impossible Opus', Mina Loy Papers YCAL MSS6 / 5, The Beinecke Rare Books and Manuscripts Library, Folder 96.
[137] Mina Loy, 'History of Religion & Eros' notes and drafts (1/2), The Beinecke Rare Books and Manuscripts Library, Folder 157.

embracing the slipperiness of connections where they arise as a natural part of the artistic process, which can tell us a great deal about the changing culture in which they worked.

The following study reveals a heterogeneous community of writers working with physics using profoundly different techniques to create innovative approaches to writing. As we shall see, however, they share a common interest in boundary crossing, their work standing in opposition to the increasing field specialization of the academy, and in particular they find in physics a set of concepts and imagery well fitted to descriptions of modern experience. Their engagement with physics is often turbulent, developing in surprising and provocative ways over the course of their careers, and revealing the many ways in which literature, visual art, and science speak to one another during this period, as people sought new ways of imagining and understanding the nature not only of the universe but of humanity's place within it.

1

Relative measure: William Carlos Williams's Einsteinian poetics

> *How can we accept Einstein's theory of relativity, affecting our very conception of the heavens about us of which poets write so much, without incorporating its essential fact – the relativity of measurements – into our own category of activity: the poem.*[1]

Speaking at the University of Washington in 1948, William Carlos Williams proposed an understanding of poetry as a form of expression that must be responsive to the perceptions and experiences of the modern world. In this talk, entitled 'Poetry as a Field of Action', he suggested integrating the new physics of Einstein into poetic practice as part of a wider argument that the very nature of poetry had shifted along with the technological advances of the twentieth century. This shift had affected the accepted subjects for poetry, such that it had become natural that 'the modern poet has admitted new subject matter into his dreams… the whole armamentarium of the industrial age to his poems', but, Williams suggests, while most modern poets had conceded to include the everyday and the industrial as subjects in poetry, they had largely resisted the integration of new forms of experience into the structural bases of poetry, line and meter.[2] 'Here we are unmoveable,' he said, '[b]ut here is precisely where we come into contact with reality.'[3] This sets the foundation for his conception of a poetry whose structure – its materiality on the page and existence as an object in its own right – shapes its own reality; a poetry whose metrics and form are its essential aspects; and a poetry whose modern content is mirrored in its measures. Williams saw relative measurement as an 'opportunity to expand the structure, the basis, the actual making of the poem', as he worked on his Modernist epic,

---

[1] William Carlos Williams, 'The Poem as a Field of Action', *Selected Essays of William Carlos Williams* (New York: Random House, 1954), 283.
[2] Ibid., 282.
[3] Ibid., 283.

Paterson (1946–8).⁴ The lecture set an agenda for Williams's experimentation with inter-line form, and his development of the 'variable foot', which was to influence many later poets, including Charles Olson, Charles Tomlinson and Thom Gunn.⁵

Williams's use of Einsteinian physics to propose 'sweeping changes top to bottom of poetic structure' has strong links with his earlier programme for an interdisciplinary approach to poetry through the visual arts.⁶ By examining the milieu in which he first came to apply ideas from science and mathematics to the practice of poetry, I suggest that the integration of relativity into poetic measure was, to Williams, a logical extension of ideas that, through his exposure to the avant-garde movements in art during the first two decades of the century, manifested in his poetry even before he came to articulate them through the language of science. Williams's poetic development was rooted in his experiences of the avant-gardes of visual art in New York and Paris, particularly in the theories of the cubists, who presented new forms of representation that incorporated advances in geometry and mathematics. I argue that the language and concepts provided by the widespread interdisciplinary interest in Einsteinian relativity in the 1940s, wherein Cubism became entangled with modern physics, gave Williams a means of expressing and contextualizing a vision for poetry which he had been working towards since as early as the mid-1910s.

To assess the interlinking of these three aspects of poetry, art and physics, it is important to consider the contemporaneity of Williams's poetic career with the theories he was later to adopt as the basis for his 'revolution' in poetic structure, and with the evolution of Cubism.⁷ Williams published his first collection of poetry in 1909, engaged in a wide variety of literary experiments throughout the 1910s – including the surrealist *Kora In Hell* (1918) improvizations – and reached the height of his 'cubist phase' by 1923 with *Spring and All*.⁸ Einstein's theory was put forward first as 'special relativity' in a paper in 1905, refined into 'general relativity' by 1915, and then experimentally proven by the British scientist Arthur Eddington and his team in 1919. As such, relativity theory grew alongside Williams, reaching public attention in the years immediately

---

⁴ Ibid., 291.
⁵ Williams's late metrical conception of the poetic 'foot' as aligned more closely to breath and intonation than to syllabic length. Exact definition of the 'variable foot' remains a matter of debate – see Eleanor Berry, 'William Carlos Williams' Triadic-Line Verse: An Analysis of Its Prosody', *Twentieth Century Literature* 35, no. 3 (1989) 364–88.
⁶ Ibid., 281.
⁷ Ibid.
⁸ Jan-Louis Kruger, 'William Carlos Williams's Cubism: The Sensory Dimension', *Literator*, 16, no. 2 (August 1995), 196.

preceding Williams's first consistent attempts at seeking a revolutionary voice for poetry. By the mid-1920s, Williams was reading and writing to his friends about Einstein's physics, enjoying and recommending Steinmetz's lectures on relativity in 1926 and Whitehead's *Science and the Modern World* (1925).[9] As discussed in my introduction, the cubist school is generally seen to have been developed principally by Picasso and Braque between 1907 and 1925, and is commonly divided into two stages – Analytical Cubism (1907–12) and Synthetic Cubism (1912 onwards) – making it contemporaneous to the developments both of Einstein's theory and Williams's early poetics.

By the time of 'Poetry as a Field of Action' (1948), interpretations of the cubist movement which viewed its innovations in relation to Einsteinian relativity and non-Euclidean geometry were common, if erroneous. Linda Dalrymple-Henderson has shown the widespread misinterpretation of the movement, which was formed ahead of Eddington's expedition, in a pre-war France more influenced by late-nineteenth-century dimensional geometries than twentieth-century physics.[10] Williams's lecture took place amid a flurry of influential works by art critics between 1945 and 1948, particularly from Paul Laporte, László Moholy-Nagy, Clement Greenberg and Alexander Dorner, which sought to cement the link between Cubism and modern physics, and guided the public understanding of Cubism for much of the century.[11] Williams was heavily influenced by his interest in Cubism, which went beyond simple appreciation into wider considerations of its concepts and their applicability to his own art. In his early years, he aspired to be a painter himself, though he eventually gave it up for medicine and poetry, maintaining his interest through his involvement with the artists of New York. In his autobiography he describes how he would 'have arguments over cubism which would fill an afternoon [alongside] a comparable whipping up of interest in the structure of the poem'.[12]

From 1910 onwards, the New York avant-garde scene exposed Williams to an artistic circle that celebrated not only artistic experimentation and

---

[9] Mike Weaver, *William Carlos Williams: The American Background* (Cambridge: Cambridge University Press, 1971), 40.
[10] Linda Henderson, 'Four Dimensional Space or Space-Time? The Emergence of the Cubism-Relativity Myth in New York in the 1940s', *The Visual Mind*, 2nd ed. (Cambridge, MA: MIT Press, 2005).
[11] Ibid.; see also Paul Laporte, 'The Space-Time Concept in the Art of Picasso', *Magazine of Art* 41, no. 1 (1948), 26–32; 'Cubism and Science', *Journal of Aesthetics and Art Criticism* 7 (1949), 243–56; László Moholy-Nagy, *The New Vision* (New York: Wittenborn, 1946); László Moholy-Nagy, *Vision in Motion* (Chicago: Paul Theobold, 1947); Alexander Dorner, *The Way Beyond 'Art'* (New York: Wittenborn, 1947).
[12] William Carlos Williams, *The Autobiography of William Carlos Williams* (New York: New Directions, 1967), 136.

boundary-pushing but also a willingness to adopt and integrate theory from other disciplines into art.[13] Throughout this period, Williams saw himself as part of the wide and diffuse art scene which incorporated poets as well as artists: 'We were restless and constrained, closely allied with the painters. Impressionism, Dadaism, Surrealism applied both to painting and the poem.'[14] Critics who have commented on Williams's relationship with visual art agree that Cubism had the most influence upon his approach to poetry.[15] He describes the watershed moment of the 1913 Armory Show ('I went to it and gaped along with the rest'), where he was delighted by strikingly modern cubist works such as Duchamp's controversial *Nude Descending a Staircase*, recalling how he 'laughed out loud when [he] first saw it, happily, with relief'.[16] Bram Dijkstra has argued that this involvement with the New York arts scene was the turning point which led Williams to generate his own style of poetry, encouraging him to reject the traditions and derivative styles that characterized his earlier works.[17] As we shall see, the revolutionary transformation of art taking place there shaped Williams's early understanding of the Poet, casting the artist as an involved observer with a dynamic and relative frame of reference, and foregrounding the importance of measure to innovations in modern art. It also encouraged him to see the potential of non-artistic theories about reality to offer innovative approaches to artistic representation.

Williams's understanding of physics was informed in the first instance by his exposure to late-nineteenth-century developments in the field of geometry represented in cubist art. The first section of this chapter will explore this grounding to show how these ideas became fused with Einsteinian measurement in Williams's work. Once we understand the visual language Cubism offered Williams as a way of exploring ideas of measurement and interconnection in his early poetry, the linkage between the poet's cubist interests and the prospect of a new form of measurement presented by Einstein's theories becomes more intuitive. I will then discuss Williams's representation of Einstein in detail

---

[13] Bram Dijkstra, *The Hieroglyphics of a New Speech: Cubism, Stieglitz, and the Early Poetry of William Carlos Williams* (Princeton, New Jersey: Princeton University Press, 1969); Christopher J. MacGowan, *William Carlos Williams's Early Poetry: The Visual Arts Background* (Ann Arbor, Michigan: UMI Research Press, 1984); Kruger, 'William Carlos Williams's Cubism', 195–213, among others.

[14] Williams, *Autobiography*, 148.

[15] Rob Fure, 'The Design of Experience: William Carlos Williams and Juan Gris', *William Carlos Williams Newsletter*, 4, no. 2 (Fall 1978), 10–19; Dijkstra, *The Hieroglyphics of a New Speech*; MacGowan, *William Carlos Williams's Early Poetry*.

[16] Williams, *Autobiography*, 134.

[17] Dijkstra, *The Hieroglyphics of a New Speech*, 48–9.

through a close analysis of two different versions of his poem 'St Francis Einstein of the Daffodils' to analyse how the development of this poem reflects Williams's own deepening understanding of the physicist's ideas and their implications for art and poetry. We will then return to the claims in 'Poetry as a Field of Action' in order to assess the impact of the fusion of ideas from physics and visual art for Williams's poetic practice.

Cubist poetics in *Spring and All* (1923)

The idea of measure as central to Cubism was expounded by Guillaume Apollinaire, the French poet and foremost critical exponent of the movement. Williams encountered Apollinaire's *Les Peinteurs Cubistes* (1913) in translation as part of the spring 1922 number of *The Little Review* devoted to Francis Picabia which, he told the editor, he 'enjoyed thoroughly, absorbedly'.[18] Here, Apollinaire describes the Cubism with which Williams was familiar, but he reframes it in terms which revolve around the development and necessity of a new measure in art:

> The painters have been led quite naturally and, so to speak, by intuition, to preoccupy themselves with possible new measures of space, which, in the language of modern studios has been designated briefly and altogether by the term the *fourth* dimension.[19]

This was art transformed by a new approach to its subjects, moving away from the 'purely human conception of beauty' of classical art, towards a style that foregrounded the plasticity of objects in space, their existence and aesthetic value not simply on the canvas but on the universal stage:

> The art of the new painters takes the infinite universe as the ideal, and it is this ideal that necessitates a new measure of perfection, which permits the artist to give to the object proportions which conform to the degree of plasticity to which he desired to bring it.[20]

Apollinaire gives the sense of an art in which the material object is entirely plastic, flexible to the touch of the artist, with measures relative only to the

---

[18] William Carlos Williams, 'The Reader Critic', *The Little Review* 9, no. 1 (Autumn 1922), 60.
[19] Guillaume Apollinaire, 'Aesthetic Meditations on Painting: The Cubist Painters—First Series: I–VII', *The Little Review*, 8, no. 2 (Spring 1922), 13; original: 'themselves'.
[20] Ibid.

artist's aesthetic desires. Throughout the three articles, Apollinaire explicitly attributes the innovative style of Cubism to a scientific methodology applied to art, claiming that 'Geometry, the science which has for its scope space, its measurement and its relations, has been from time immemorial the rule even of painting', something which the 'scientific cubists' brought to the forefront of their styles.[21] Although they did not perceive it in these terms themselves, the cubists introduced a new approach to proportions that acquired a flexibility analogous to the relative measures of post-Einsteinian perception, in which frame of reference and speed are the main determinants of spatial dimensions. Apollinaire's young artists 'who think in plastic' manifested in their painting the aspirations Williams had for his own art: an 'attempt to render plastic the inner constitution of objects', and the manipulation of measure and spatial relations was their key tool for doing so.[22]

Through its reconsideration of visual geometries, Cubism appealed to Williams in its rebellion against traditional modes of seeing and representation and presented vital new ways of rendering the object-reality of modern experience. Like Williams later, the cubists explored 'possible new measurements of space', embracing a new geometrical landscape which rejected the universality of Euclidean geometry.[23] They realized that dimensional geometry in mathematics had become incompatible with earlier conceptions of dimensionality in art. Where the rendering of three-dimensional objects on a two-dimensional canvas was well established through traditional rules of perspective, the cubists sought to introduce further dimensions to the two-dimensional space.

Analytical Cubism dissected the 'inherent geometrical forms of the object' through fragmentation, while Synthetic Cubism combined fragmentation and composition to bring 'identifiable elements into one plane of relations where the object is preserved with a greater concern with design and unity'.[24] Both sought to shake off the expectations of *mimesis* in art in favour of foregrounding the fact of the painting as an object in its own right, examining the interrelation and intersection of geometries within objects. Importantly, Apollinaire compared the geometrical interests of the cubists with the structures of written

---

[21] Ibid., 13, 18.
[22] Pamela A. Genova, 'The Poetics of Visual Cubism: Guillaume Apollinaire on Pablo Picasso', *Studies in 20th Century Literature* 28, no. 1 (2003), 55; Williams cited in Peter Halter, *The Revolution in Visual Art and the Poetry of William Carlos Williams* (Cambridge: Cambridge University Press, 1994), 60.
[23] Apollinaire, 'Aesthetic Meditations on Painting', 13.
[24] 'Cubism', *The Princeton Encyclopedia of Poetry and Poetics*, 4th ed. (Princeton, NJ: Brogan Tate, 2012), 321 –2; Kruger, 'William Carlos Williams's Cubism', 200.

language: 'geometry is to the plastic arts what grammar is to the art of the writer'.[25] This comparison is particularly generative if considered alongside Williams's early experiments. If the cubists could manipulate geometry, opening new perspectives on their subjects, the poet might do the same through the fracturing and manipulation of grammar structures and lexical units.

A simple form of cubist fragmentation can be found in one of Williams's most famous poems, 'The Red Wheelbarrow', which first appeared in *Spring and All* in 1923:

So much depends
upon

a red wheel
barrow

glazed with rain
water

beside the white
chickens[26]

The rigid, compressed stanzas, each shaped like a barrow on the page, fracture objects into their constituent parts. The wheelbarrow is broken down and defamiliarized: the wheel and the barrow are separated by sharp enjambment, while other aspects of the scene, the colour of the chickens, the type ('rain') of the water, are cut away from the objects they describe. In *Spring and All*, this poem is followed by the statement that: 'The fixed categories into which life is divided must always hold. [...] But they exist – not as dead dissections'.[27] I suggest that these dissections mirror Apollinaire's observation that an artist like 'Picasso studies an object as a surgeon dissects a body', and that for Williams the act of dissecting both the object and the line that represents it introduces a similar vitality to that of Picasso's art, and sets a basis for his later experiments with measure.[28] The subject is fragmented and reconstituted in the process of reading, the links between words and their referents is shattered and rebuilt by making

---

[25] Apollinaire, 'Aesthetic Meditations on Painting', 13.
[26] William Carlos Williams, *Spring and All* (New York: New Directions, 2011), 74.
[27] Ibid., 75.
[28] Apollinaire, 'Aesthetic Meditations on Painting', 12; the comparison between Picasso and the surgeon is also made in the second instalment, 'Aesthetic Meditations on Painting: The Cubist Painters—Second Series', *The Little Review*, 9, no. 1 (Autumn 1922), 45.

the reader aware of the gap between perception and formalization: between the moment when an object is seen as an impression (of colour, of light) and the moment it is rationalized as a familiar object (rainwater causing the glaze, chickens). The poem's ambiguities appear in the spaces between words and lines as much as in the words themselves, demonstrating the vitality and importance of the fragmented line as a structural unit in Williams's poetics. Williams took from Apollinaire's Cubism the 'rejection of an art that is purely representational', realizing, as he writes in *Spring and All*, 'the falseness of attempting to "copy" nature' and, like the cubists, he sought instead a reconsideration of values: a new mode of seeing the relations between objects and their parts.[29]

Although challenges to the 'Cubist-Relativity myth' now shape our understanding of how Cubism itself developed, the erroneous connection still retains an important historical influence.[30] Tony Robbin has convincingly argued for analytical Cubism's foundation in a four-dimensional geometry, emerging from nineteenth-century projective geometry and the hyper-cube mathematics of Jouffret.[31] He demonstrates the influence of this geometry – in which the fourth dimension was not considered to be Time but an additional plane – on Picasso's early cubist works of 1910.[32] Here, modes of seeing space were central to Cubism's innovation: 'Cubism was no vacuous formal improvisation; it rocked Western painting because it offered a new way of seeing space that was considered to be truer to life.'[33] Picasso sought to render the fourth dimension through geometries of line which pressed beyond the surface appearance of the subject to reveal an image that was closer to reality. Henderson also shows that Picasso and Braque were concerned with this geometrical fourth dimension rather than Einsteinian physics. She points, however, to a widespread perception in the 1940s of a strong link between Cubism, relativity, and non-Euclidean geometries, which emerged as earlier geometrical conceptions of *n*-dimensionality faded from public attention.[34] Thus, while there is some evidence that Williams's favourite cubist, Juan Gris, was a student of Einstein's

---

[29] Marjorie Perloff, *The Futurist Moment: Avant-Garde, Avant Guerre, and the Language of Rupture* (Chicago, IL: University of Chicago Press, 2003), 111; Williams, *Spring and All*, 28.
[30] Linda Dalrymple Henderson, 'The Image and Imagination of the Fourth Dimension in Twentieth-Century Art and Culture', *Configuration* 17, nos. 1–2 (Winter 2009), 131–60.
[31] Tony Robbin, *Shadows of Reality: The Fourth Dimension in Relativity, Cubism, and Modern Thought* (New Haven, CT: Yale University Press, 2006).
[32] Specifically, *Portrait of Daniel-Henry Kahnweiler* (1910) and *Portrait d'Ambroise Vollard* (1910); Robbin, *Shadows of Reality*, 29–33.
[33] Robbin, *Shadows of Reality*, 40.
[34] Henderson, 'The Image and Imagination of the Fourth Dimension in Twentieth-Century Art and Culture', 131–60.

work alongside Poincaré and geometry under the mathematician Maurice Princet during the war, this myth of influence may have informed Williams's understanding of Cubism more than the artist himself.[35] For the purposes of this study, I am not concerned with the truth of whether Picasso and Braque, or even Gris, shaped their movement around relativity physics (as evidence suggests they did not), but rather with the widespread *perception* of the link as Williams would have experienced it in the period when he was formulating his ideas of relative measure in poetry. By the mid-1920s, Williams had a clear appreciation of the value of mathematics for the poet. I suggest that Gris's Cubism offered Williams an entry-point for his explorations of the potential for mathematical and physical ideas in his poetic structure, and that in the period in which Cubism had come to be widely associated with relativity, it provided a springboard for Williams's poetic innovations.

Juan Gris was, for a time, not only Williams's favourite cubist, but his 'favourite painter'.[36] He saw in Gris a style 'that points forward to what will prove the greatest painting yet produced'.[37] Gris's Synthetic Cubism advanced an intellectualized style which foregrounded mathematical concerns, leading to work in which the subject appeared 'superimposed onto a schematic of geometrical pictorial substructure'.[38] Apollinaire described Gris's style as painting that 'aims first of all at a scientific reality', with 'clearness, scientifically conceived'.[39] Williams admired this approach, seeing in it an attempt 'to separate things of the imagination from life', both through eschewing mimetic realism and reinvigorating the subject through the deconstruction and reconstruction of its relations.[40] What differentiated Gris from Picasso and Braque, as the art historian John Golding asserts, is a sense of process and dissection, deconstruction of the solid subject and its multifaceted reconstruction on the canvas, though, as we have seen, Apollinaire associated the work of several major cubists with an approach to a scientific reality. Gris, however, works with the eye of the scientist, contained and careful. In his paintings the geometrical and relational foundations of the subject are made explicit.[41]

---

[35] John Golding, *Cubism: A History and an Analysis 1907–1914*, 3rd ed. (Cambridge, MA: Harvard University Press, 1988), 102.
[36] Williams, *Autobiography*, 318.
[37] Williams, *Spring and All*, 45.
[38] Golding, *Cubism*, 100.
[39] Apollinaire, 'Aesthetic Meditations on Painting: The Cubist Painters—Second Series—Continued', *The Little Review*, 9, no. 2 (Winter 1922), 49–51.
[40] Williams, *Spring and All*, 28.
[41] Golding, *Cubism*, 102.

This kind of Cubism excited Williams with the possibilities of approaching poetry with the manner of the visual artist, interested in the formal constituents of space and dynamics: lines, shapes, planes and colour. 'To a Solitary Disciple' (1920) demonstrates Williams's approach to deconstructing a scene and reconstructing it geometrically. It asks the reader to consider first the impression of linear geometries and interrelations in the scene, before filling in the gaps:

> Rather notice, mon cher,
> that the moon is
> tilted above
> the point of the steeple
> than that its color
> is shell-pink.[42]

Williams is deeply concerned with acts of seeing and perception, how they are mediated by our experience and the ways the untrained mind continually seeks to attribute terms and turn experience into cliché. This poem instructs us to reconfigure our perception, to visualize a traditionally romantic scene in new, geometrically inflected terms. Through fractured lines, Williams asks us to 'notice' the object in a way that is opposite to the standard way a viewer might experience an image. The moon appears to the reader first, with a focus on its relative position, its angle, the point of the steeple, solid and more important than its colour which is clarified only in the final line. By contrast, in a gallery, a visitor might catch a flash of colour before interpreting the shapes and their referents to come to perceive the full image of moon and spire. In giving the details in this order, Williams foregrounds the importance of the interrelations of forms within the scene, which we must 'grasp', before we can make statements about the objects they make up. The mode of seeing the poem encourages is rather that of the painter composing: the shapes and relations on the page are set down before they are overlaid with colour. Williams draws attention to the fundamental structures and forms, 'the dark / converging lines / of the steeple' in their purest form. This is set in tension with the non-functional ornamentation on the spire which ultimately fails (to Williams's delight) to ruin the integrity of its underlying geometry:

> perceive how
> its little ornament
> tries to stop them—
> see how it fails!

---

[42] William Carlos Williams, 'To A Solitary Disciple', *Collected Poems I 1909–1939* (Manchester: Carcanet Press, 2000), 104.

Here the subject is held in a state of ambiguity until its details have first been observed. Williams asks us to see the trees before the wood, to look through and beyond things, to their structural dynamism.

As Apollinaire noted, '[t]hat which differentiates cubism from the old schools is that it is not an art of painting, but an art of conception ... representing the concept of reality, or the created reality.'[43] It is characterized by a process of seeing which is less physiological than imaginative; the object is transmuted in the mind of the artist away from 'reality as seen' towards a rendering of its deeper relations.[44] The process of seeing from the inside out in this poem is reminiscent of the distortions explored by the cubist painters, whose images eschewed realism in order to seek a deeper understanding of the subject. Take, for example, Gris's still life *Guitar and Clarinet* (Figure 1) from the same year. Gris uses colour to blur the boundaries between his geometric objects, creating

Figure 1 Juan Gris, *Guitar and Clarinet* (1920), oil on canvas, 73 × 92 cm, Kunstmuseum Basel, 2297.

---

[43] Apollinaire, Aesthetic Meditations on Painting (Spring 1922), 17.
[44] Ibid.

an effect which is simultaneously crisp in its use of solid colours and lines, and fluid. Seen first through colour, the table pierces through the clarinet, is visible through the bottle, the wine glass and even the music score, while the texture of the clarinet is broken into patches of solid shade and wood-flecked light. The movement of the different spatial planes, where the objects and their backdrop move backward and forward through each other, creates dynamism within the painting. Similarly, the motion of geometries penetrating the obvious impressions of external colour in 'To a Solitary Disciple', generates a dynamic movement within the solid geometric object of the spire:

> See how the converging lines
> of the hexagonal spire
> escape upward—
> receding, dividing!

In *Spring and All*, Williams admires Gris's technique in manipulating the 'inevitable flux of the seeing eye toward measuring itself by the world it inhabits'.[45] Cubist paintings like this deny the viewer a comfortable frame of reference by which to measure themselves in relation to the subject, rejecting traditional ideas of perspective and realistic colour, and manipulating planar relations. Unlike traditional still lives, *Guitar and Clarinet* is a painting concerned not so much with its obvious subjects as with the interrelation and interpenetration of its subjects and the spaces they inhabit. This, Williams believed, offered insight into the deeper value of the object-subject within poetry, and opened new avenues for the depiction of the modern world.

For Williams, Gris provided an opportunity to see the world anew, throwing off connotation and cliché.[46] Williams's rejection of overused metaphor, 'The Rose', which first appeared in *Spring and All*, takes Gris's 1914 collage, *Flowers* (Figure 2) as inspiration for a poetry which reconsiders common imagery through a lens of geometry and form, revitalizing the worn-out cliché of the rose into a deeply penetrating object existing as a construct in a spatial frame:

> The rose is obsolete
> but each petal ends in
> an edge, the double facet

---

[45] Williams, *Spring and All*, 26.
[46] For further discussion of Gris's influence on Williams, see: James E. Breslin, 'William Carlos Williams and Charles Demuth: Cross-Fertilization in the Arts', *Journal of Modern Literature* 6, no. 2 (1977), 248–63.

cementing the grooved
columns of air – The edge
cuts without cutting
meets – nothing – renews
itself in metal or porcelain[47]

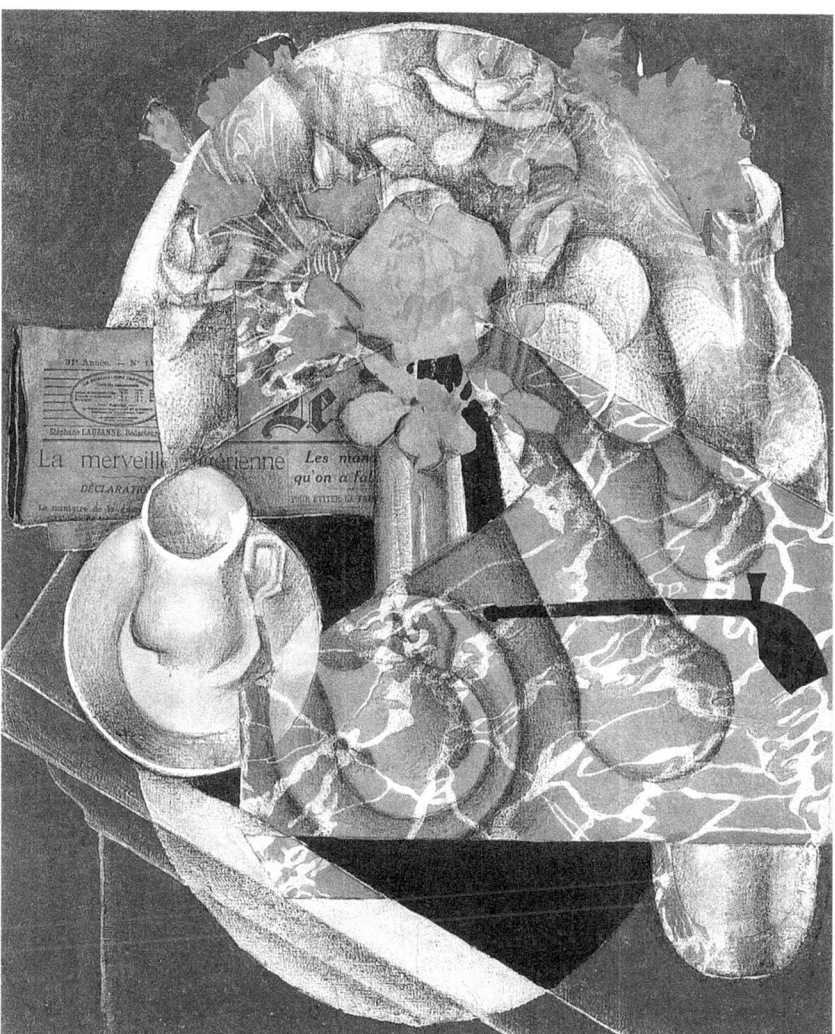

Figure 2 Juan Gris, *Flowers* (1920), conté crayon, gouache, oil, wax crayon, wallpapers, printed white wove paper and newspaper on canvas, 54.9 × 46 cm, The Metropolitan Museum of Art, New York.

[47] Williams, *Spring and All*, 30–1.

Here, Williams dissects the three-dimensional object of the rose with the eye of a cubist painter, breaking it down into its constituent planes and edges. As in 'The Red Wheelbarrow', the intersection of lines, mirrored by Williams's enjambment, draws attention to the fractured inter-relation of the rose's parts: 'each petal ends in / an edge', but these edges are constantly intersected by other lines and forms both within the poem's structure and visually. These intersections are not restrictive, but an act of renewal. 'The edge / cuts without cutting', the edges of the petals themselves still a part of the whole that makes up the flower and the flow which passes over and between edges, like the overlapping layers of colour which ignore the form of the subject in Gris's collage, 'renews / itself' in new materials, creating a sense of complementarity between the rigid geometrical forms of the dissected rose.

In *Flowers*, Gris builds onto a base of canvas, newspaper, woven paper and wallpaper, whose edges offer different planes of perspective over which the tableware, flowers and mirror spill and relate. In some places the edges are firm boundaries but, in others, objects are manipulated by the lens of the wallpaper, creating cuts across objects which serve to reshape and recolour rather than restrict their forms. Williams introduces caesura, cutting even finer intersections within his lines: 'meets – nothing – renews'. Here the space between words, inflected with a geometrical line which is as much a cut as a line of connection, is the point of regeneration. The distance between the words becomes a flexible plane of interrelation. 'Renews', being cut off from its object, 'itself', hangs in conceptual space, indicating a generalized renewal that results entirely from the fragmentations of line and stanza. Only when a word, an idea, a line ends 'the start is begun'.[48]

Spring and All is a book whose jagged prose frequently reaches hard but open edges. It is a sequence that embraces contradiction and renewal under the aegis of Spring – the symbolic point of beginning and ending. Williams describes composition as a visual act, but one fused with imagination and personality allowing the poet to free himself from the restrictions of *mimesis* and even from completion:

> In every composition, the artist does exactly what every eye must do with life, fix the particular with the universality of his own personality – Taught by the largeness of his imagination to feel every form which he sees moving within himself, he must prove the truth of this by expression.

---

[48] Ibid., 108.

> The contradiction which is felt.
> … Such a realization shows us the falseness of attempting to 'copy' nature.[49]

The reader feels these contradictions most keenly in the moments when sentences are left hanging, unfinished as, just before 'The Rose', Williams ends a paragraph 'Such work elucidates – ', rather than elucidating, or when ideas are introduced only to be curtailed mid-thought: 'I don't know what the Spanish see in their Velasquez and Goya but.'[50] *Spring and All* is full of these hanging phrases, which give the text the feeling of incompleteness, of being a work in progress, but there are moments when these breaks open up possibilities for the reader to complete the thought, such as 'When we name it, life exists. To repeat physical experiences has no –' or the single-line non-question 'What would have happened in a world similarly lit by the imagination'.[51] That Williams retains these half-thoughts suggests their value. In another, he hints that this value lies in the reader's natural human desire to fill in the gaps between thoughts, to find meaning between the lines: 'No man could suffer the fragmentary nature of his understanding of his own life –'[52]

The cubists introduced Williams to the plasticity of measure in art. Their geometries manipulated measure and favoured the dissection and reconstruction of the object and formed a basis for Williams's understanding of mathematics and science as sources of new conceptions of the poetic line. The potential of cubist techniques for opening up meaning in the spaces between objects, allowing for profound examination of the interrelation of objects in space, extended in poetry to the exploration of the deep relations between the constituent parts of the poem as objects in their own right. Poetic lines were subject to new forms of measurement, could be compressed, broken up, stripped of their old forms and connotations, and revitalized. For Williams, the realization of this freedom was the realization of a new form for poetry, one in which structure and measurement were to take precedent. Having embraced so strongly the new measures made available by cubist geometry, and in light of the gradual association of Cubism with Einsteinian measure in the following decades, the integration of further new forms of measurement into poetry was a logical progression in the development of Williams's poetics.

---

[49] Ibid., 27–8.
[50] Ibid., 30, 35.
[51] Ibid., 41, 43.
[52] Ibid., 38.

Complex mathematics: Williams encounters Einstein

> When Einstein promulgated the theory of relativity he could not have foreseen its moral and intellectual implication. He could not have foreseen for a certainty its influence on the writing of poetry.[53]

The cubist context allows us to position Williams's relationship with Einstein as an extension of his early experiments with form. Above, in a letter from the 1950s, Williams expresses a firm sense that Einstein's ideas impacted upon the writing of poetry. But how does Williams's use of cubist fracture and expansion relate to Einstein's relativity, and how do these, together, lead to the variable foot? As we have seen, Williams's embrace of the fragmented line is a means of liberating the potential of the empty (and flexible) space between words, and this provides the essential base for his concept of the poem as a field of action. A cubist shift away from seeing the poem as *mimesis,* towards a conception of the poem as a constructed object in its own right, enables a free treatment of the object on its own terms. If we approach Williams's first direct engagement with Einstein in the context of his cubist experiments, we can unpack the ways in which, as early as 1921, Williams was employing cubist techniques to approach the subject of relativity. Furthermore, even at this early stage, William's fusion of Cubism and relativity gestures towards the understanding of these concepts proposed by the art critics of the 1940s discussed by Henderson, particularly that of his contemporary, Lázslo Moholy-Nagy.

Williams's first direct engagement with Einstein appears in 'St Francis Einstein of the Daffodils' (1921). Written at the height of Williams's interest in developing a cubist approach to poetry, it employs many of the techniques of *Spring and All* but goes further in its exploration of shifting viewpoints by tethering them to Einstein's concepts of reference frames and simultaneity. First published in *Contact* shortly after Einstein's visit to New York in April–May the same year, 'St Francis Einstein of the Daffodils' has two versions, the second considerably shorter than the first. As we shall see, the first version of the poem draws out several fruitful aspects of Einstein's theory, and by comparing this with the later version, which appeared in *Adam and Eve in the City* (1936), we can see evidence of Williams's increasingly nuanced understanding of not only the cultural significance of Einstein's theories but also of the physics behind them leading up to his formulation of the 'Poem as a Field of Action'. A close reading of both versions of the poem alongside each other illustrates the congruence

---

[53] Williams, *Selected Letters*, 335–6.

of Williams's interpretation of relativity and his use of cubist approaches to rendering the scene. It also offers clues as to how these two aspects of theory came together in his poetry to generate new formal possibilities for Williams's later work.

In order to understand how a new and relativity-inflected measure emerges from the cubist broken line, it is important to recall the fundamental changes to our understanding of measure introduced by Einstein's theory in more detail, as well as its ongoing use by artists as a point of reference for new artistic experimentation. Einstein proposed that measure is relative to the observer's frame of reference and speed. As everything in the universe is in a state of constant motion, and the difference in the speed at which we are moving relative to objects around us is very small, the effect is unnoticeable to the naked eye; but an analogue of it was seen by artists and photographers (and by Einstein himself) in the development of high-speed vehicles such as trains and cars following the Industrial Revolution. In Cubism, difference of experience was linked to the visual plane, as Lászlo Moholy-Nagy demonstrates:

> There is clearly recognizable difference between the visual experience of a pedestrian and a driver in viewing objects. The motor car driver and the airplane pilot can bring distant and unrelated landmarks into spatial relationships unknown to the pedestrian. The difference is caused by the various speeds, vision in motion.[54]

While the cubists themselves did not link this with Einstein as such, later commentators and inheritors of the cubist legacy rapidly fused the ideas to suit their changing understanding of the physical world. For Williams, this conceptual advance was vital and significant.[55] The concept of capturing movement on the canvas, which Moholy-Nagy terms 'speed in motion', synonymous with 'simultaneous grasp', 'simultaneity and space-time' in Cubism, is the revelation by the artists that the experience of speed 'can be arrested, rendered, stretched, and compressed, in short, articulated [to] approach a vocabulary of space time'.[56] Furthermore, the rejection of the fixed perspective of the renaissance towards 'vision in motion' is a reframing of the process of seeing towards what Moholy-Nagy calls '*vision in relationships*'.[57] Relational considerations emerged at this

---

[54] Moholy-Nagy, *Vision in Motion* (Chicago, IL: Paul Theobold and Company, 1961), 245.
[55] James Paul Gee, 'The Structure of Perception in the Poetry of William Carlos Williams: A Stylistic Analysis', *Poetics Today* 6, no. 3 (1985), 375.
[56] Moholy-Nagy, *Vision in Motion*, 155, 247.
[57] Ibid., 114. Moholy-Nagy's emphasis.

time not only in visual art and poetry, but also in philosophy, with Heidegger's first steps towards Phenomenology, partly in response to the changed perceptions emerging from Einstein's theory. In *The Concept of Time* (1924), Heidegger offers a useful explanation of the outcome of Moholy-Nagy's observations, framing the new space-time as a product of its relations:

> The current state of this research [the measuring of nature within a system of space-time relations] is established in Einstein's relativity theory. Some of its prepositions are as follows: Space is nothing in itself; there is no absolute space. It exists merely by way of the bodies and energies contained in it. [...] Time too is nothing. It persists merely as a consequence of the events taking place in it. There is no absolute time, and no absolute simultaneity either.[58]

Thus, space and time exist only by virtue of relational activity, by the relationships between things (massive particles, objects, people) and their resultant forces acting within them. In physics, this understanding emerges from the same conceptual source as Cubism – projective geometry. Geometry, the study of the properties of space, interrelations, intersections and relative positions, shows that any alteration of a geometrical construct is relational; whether it is a Euclidian shape, or a product of non-Euclidian projective geometry, visual or mathematical, distortions produce a new set of relationships. As I will demonstrate, the 'complex mathematics' Williams gestures to in the earlier version of 'St. Francis Einstein of the Daffodils' is fundamentally a map of interrelation, and the poem itself becomes a field in which these relationships form and are moulded by the poet.[59]

The first version of this poem gives a reiterative portrayal of Einstein's first moments in New York and considers the scientist's influence and the potential of his work to reinvigorate what Williams saw as a stultified American social and creative consciousness.[60] Despite offering our most direct insight into Williams's early interest in the concepts of physics, the poem has rarely been considered in this light by critics.[61] Although it includes frequent references to and formal employment of Einsteinian concepts, Vainis Aleksa has argued that the poem demonstrates Williams's interest in Einstein's humanitarian mission (as an

---

[58] Martin Heidegger, *The Concept of Time*, trans. William McNeill (Hoboken, NJ: Blackwell Publishers, 1992), 3.
[59] William Carlos Williams, 'St. Francis Einstein of the Daffodils', *Contact* (Summer 1921), 3.
[60] Ibid., 2–4.
[61] The main exception is a very short paper by Carol Donley, 'A little touch of / Einstein in the night– Williams's Early Exposure to the Theories of Relativity', *William Carlos Williams* Newsletter, 4, no. 1 (Spring 1978), 10–13.

advocate of the Zionist movement) rather than any concern with physics. He suggests that 'for Williams... the visit announced a "Yiddishe springtime" rather than a rebirth of science'.[62] I would argue, however, that while this wording makes clear Williams's awareness of the humanitarian aspect of Einstein's visit, which was widely publicized, the nature of the poem gives evidence of a greater engagement with the concepts of special and general relativity than Aleksa acknowledges. Rather, Williams brings together aspects of the conceptual, artistic and the social, demonstrating Moholy-Nagy's idea that 'space-time is not only a matter of natural science or of esthetic and emotional interest. It deeply modifies the character of social ends'.[63]

Einstein visited New York City in April 1921, riding the wave of fame and media fanfare that had accompanied the experimental proof of his Theory of General Relativity by Arthur Eddington and his team in 1919. The discovery was heralded by the newspapers Williams would have read as 'Epochmaking'; it was widely reported on and became highly topical in factual articles, which attempted to explain or interpret the theory, as well as satirical spoofs in publications such as *The Atlanta*.[64] As Donley and Friedman, and Price, have aptly illustrated, the theories were widely discussed, if not widely understood; relativity rapidly became a commodity, increasingly adapted and reconstituted by the press, popularizers and cartoonists, to embody a shifting and ephemeral sense of incomprehensibility and awe.[65] The public and the press were similarly confused by Einstein's theories; they came to be known as the most significant scientific discovery no one could understand. Price shows examples of 'excerpts from newspapers, magazines, and books that display a deliberate misapplication of the new cosmology to familiar experience'.[66] This suggests that misunderstanding was not only a symptom but almost an aim for some of the journalists and writers of the period, particularly satirists.

As Aleksa notes, Williams's initial understanding of Einstein in 1921 was drawn from the accessible forms in which his theories appeared in these media. The first version of 'St Francis Einstein of the Daffodils' offers an amalgam of these

---

[62] Vainis Aleksa, 'Mythic Resonance in the *Contact* Version of "St. Francis Einstein of the Daffodils"', *William Carlos Williams Review* 24, no. 1 (Spring 1998), 40.

[63] Moholy-Nagy, *Vision in Motion*, 266.

[64] 'Eclipse Showed Gravity Variation: Hailed as Epochmaking', *The New York Times* (9 November 1919), 6; Donley, 'A little touch of / Einstein in the night – Williams's Early Exposure to the Theories of Relativity', 10.

[65] Katy Price, *Loving Faster Than Light: Romance and Readers in Einstein's Universe* (Chicago & London: The University of Chicago Press, 2012), 6.

[66] Ibid., 3.

confused interpretations, one that revels in its own chaos of representation.[67] Williams addresses the popular questions raised by Einstein's ideas as they crashed onto the American scene: if all things are relative, what is real? What happens to objective truth when all viewpoints offer different but equally valid measures? And how can this fragmented reality, in which all experiences are relative, be represented responsibly?

The cubist approach would be to render the subject from multiple viewpoints simultaneously and, as Moholy-Nagy put it, 'by seeing matters in a constantly changing moving field of mutual relationships'.[68] This is precisely the approach Williams takes in the first version of 'St. Francis Einstein'. The poem opens with a description of the scene as Einstein arrives in New York before going on to perform a distinctly cubist process of fracture and reconstruction of the same imagery to present the scene from multiple viewpoints. By repeatedly shifting the definition of Einstein's arrival in America – what begins as a singular event is fragmented into many reiterations and reinterpretations – Williams takes a field of language through recurrent shifts, demonstrating both the way that perspective inflects meaning and the value of syntactic arrangement in conveying meaning:

> In March's black boat
> Einstein and April
> have come at the time in fashion
> up out of the sea
> through the rippling daffodils
> in the foreyard of
> the dead Statue of Liberty
> whose stonearms
> are powerless against them
> the Venusremembering wavelets
> breaking into laughter –[69]

As the first description of the scene presented to us, we may be tempted to take the first stanza as the *ur*-definition; it contains the constituent parts which make up Williams's later reframings of the scene in a way that is perhaps the most acccpting of the pre-Einsteinian, Newtonian order of things. Einstein arrives

---

[67] Aleksa, 'Mythic Resonance in the *Contact* Version of "St. Francis Einstein of the Daffodils"', 40.
[68] Moholy-Nagy, *Vision in Motion*, 114.
[69] Williams, 'St Francis Einstein of the Daffodils', *Collected Poems*, 130; all quotations taken from this edition, 130–3.

conventionally (one implication of 'in fashion'), by boat into New York Harbour, bringing the life of spring to New York's dead culture. It is the arrival of the timely celebrity. Here, natural life sits distinct from a man-made death, the 'rippling daffodils' juxtaposed with the 'dead' and 'powerless' stone of the Statue of Liberty. The image is a fairly straightforward juxtaposition of living and dead; the stanza, a single sentence with two distinct parts. By its end, Williams's use of portmanteau ('stonearms', 'Venusremembering') hints punningly towards the implications of Einstein's theory, in which hitherto distinct concepts, such as space and time, blur to become part of the same complex of 'spacetime'.

In the following stanza, however, the event is defamiliarized. The same images shift in the poetic field, transforming the scene into a portent of a liberated future. The images and conflicts which existed, in the first stanza, in a more passive juxtaposition are forced into turmoil:

> Sweet Land of Liberty,
> at last, in the end of time,
> Einstein has come by force of
> complicated mathematics
> among the tormented fruit trees
> to buy freedom
> for the daffodils
> till the unchained orchards
> shake their tufted flowers –

Rather than Einstein being 'timely', the time marker becomes another pun: 'at last, in the end of time', so that Einstein's arrival becomes something long awaited, something monumental. As in *Spring and All*, the image of epistemological apocalypse implied by 'the end of time', an aspect favoured by the more overzealous misinterpretations of Einstein's theory, that suggested 'every measurement is subjective; that all "truth" is only relative; that science has abandoned cause and effect; that everything is relative', gives rise to chaos and torment, for which only Einstein can be an ordering force.[70] The necessity of Einstein's involvement, the sense that he must come 'by force of / complicated mathematics', conflates physics (the study of forces) with an impossible complexity which can only be described, almost dismissively here, as 'complicated mathematics'.[71] This mirrors

---

[70] Alan J. Friedman and Carol C. Donley, *Einstein: as Myth and Muse* (Cambridge: Cambridge University Press, 1985), 65.
[71] Richard Feynman cited in ibid.

contemporary reception of the theory, which was frequently couched in a vague language of bemusement, and which for years afterwards even brilliant physicists and science educators like Richard Feynman had to admit was elusive for non-mathematicians: 'There are circumstances in which mathematics will produce results which no one has really been able to understand in any direct fashion.'[72] Aleksa suggests that, for Williams, 'Einstein was not seen in our own terms as the archetype of cryptic and revolutionary science, but in the most widely accessible terms established by the "wise newspapers"'.[73] However, I would argue that the inclusion of this 'complicated mathematics' suggests a concern beyond the social sphere of Einstein's celebrity which, coupled with the experimental imagery of the poem, gestures explicitly towards the exact terms Aleksa dismisses.

What is clear here is that Williams understands that the essentially mathematical nature of relativity has wider implications for perception, and he demonstrates these later in the poem, in what are the fifth and sixth versions of the scene:

April Einstein	Einstein, tall as a violet
through the blossomy waters	in the lattice arbour corner
rebellious, laughing	is tall as a blossomy
under liberty's dead arm	peartree! The shell
has come among the daffodils	of the world is split
shouting	and from under the sea
that flowers and men	Einstein has emerged
were created	triumphant, St. Francis
relatively equal.	of the daffodils!
Oldfashioned knowledge is	
dead under the blossoming	
peachtrees.	

These renditions begin to embody aspects of the theory itself, from the conflation of 'Einstein and April' into the metaphorical embodiment of spring and new knowledge, 'April Einstein', to Williams's play on the American constitution ('relatively equal'). The fifth stanza (starting 'April Einstein') again transfigures the scene into one of riotous spring, the waters blossom, Einstein is 'rebellious, laughing' and 'shouting' his theories through shorter, higher-energy, emphatic lines.

---

[72] Ibid., 64.
[73] Aleksa, 'Mythic Resonance in the *Contact* Version of "St. Francis Einstein of the Daffodils"', 40.

Although it would be more than two decades before he articulated a theory for the potential of relative measure for poetry which engages these concepts, Williams's understanding of Einstein's relativity of measure as perceived from different frames of reference can be seen in the apparent contradiction that Einstein is simultaneously as 'tall as a violet' and as 'tall as a blossomy peartree'. This image, combined with the exclamatory triumph of these stanzas, moves away from an apocalyptic 'end of time' to celebrate the fact that 'The shell / of the world is split', and that 'Oldfashioned knowledge is dead', making way for a tide of epistemological freedom and renewed possibility. In conjunction with these breakages, we see new formations; the portmanteaus become more frequent, blending quality and object in an inversion of the fragmentation in 'The Red Wheelbarrow' (noticeably in the fourth stanza the 'rainwater' is left undivided). Earlier images break down and bleed into one another; the water takes on the aspect of the flowers, blossoming, while the previous stanza showed 'Venusremembering daffodils', as they are seen in the reflection of 'a great pool of rainwater'. As in the cubist fragments of *Spring and All*, breakage in 'St. Francis Einstein' ultimately leads to renewal.

As Williams shifts, repeats and resituates words in the field of the poem, they take on different inflections and present different impressions of the scene, as though setting down one after the other different media reports of Einstein's visit, with an ironic awareness of the relativity of those portrayals.

> Sing of wise newspapers
> that quote the great mathematician:
> A little touch of
> Einstein in the night –

Like the fragments of a cubist painting, and the differing accounts of the newspapers, Williams conveys the scene in a kaleidoscope of reiterations, taking for each a different frame of reference. As Williams has previously implied, the wisdom of the papers stretches only so far as to quote the scientist himself, the one man deemed to have grasped enough of the 'complicated mathematics' to speak with any authority. But these reiterations go further than the 'inevitable flux of the seeing eye' Williams sees in Gris's paintings. The changing inflections of each retelling impose a relativity of perception on the scene; in analogue to the repetitious attempts of the press to articulate the consequences of Einstein's discovery, the poem becomes a collage of impressions which grow into an increasingly frenzied attempt to pin down an authoritative description of an event which, by wider paradox of popular interpretations of relativity, necessarily has no single, verifiable measure. In doing so, Williams hits upon the wider epistemic trauma caused by the discovery; as Whitworth has shown, 'From its inception, relativity had caused dispute over whose authority counted.'[74]

The idea that 'everything is relative' led to widespread responses of delight, despair and confusion among those seeking applications for relativity in fields outside physics. If all is relative, how can any single account of an event be true? The relativity of 'truth' was an erroneous conclusion that arose from Einstein's revelation that 'measurements of time, space, and mass are relative to the individual observer's space-time reference frame'.[75] In the reality of the theory, however, nothing is uncertain or subjective about those measurements; they are true and agree for anyone sharing the reference frame. As such, while a multiplicity of simultaneous relative measures *exist*, only one is true for any particular frame; the poem is cubist in how it reframes the scene as it were from different angles within the same art object. In this poem, as in a cubist painting, an object can take on two or more aspects, as shown where 'there are both pinkflowered / and coralflowered peachtrees', and in the latter parts of the poem the wind simultaneously blows 'four ways, hot and cold'.

If, as I have argued, the first version of 'St. Francis Einstein' was an attempt to grapple with its subject through a cubist dissection, reconstruction, and side-by-side representation of the same scene, the 1936 version from *Adam and Eve and the City* may be seen as an admission of its failure. The first version does not offer the 'universal experience' that Williams sought for his poetry. If, as Dijkstra suggests, Williams believed 'universal experience [is] communicable only on the basis of an authentic perception of the object of the material world, which, he reasoned, [can] only stem from an accurate representation of the things we know', the poem rapidly becomes subject to the very terms the new physics was redefining: perception and knowledge.[76] In this, it falls down: the kaleidoscope approach does little to render the lived reality of relative experience, which is always seen by the individual through a single lens. The line poem, which asks by convention to be read in a linear fashion, stanza by stanza, does not have the same sense of simultaneity as a painting, which may be taken entire in an instant. The challenges of literary Cubism are different from those of cubist painting in exactly this respect: simultaneity, even as a result of fragmentation, is impossible to achieve in a traditional line poem, though it may, perhaps, be

---

[74] Whitworth, *Einstein's Wake*, 37.
[75] Friedman and Donley, *Einstein*, 65.
[76] Dijkstra, *The Hieroglyphics of a New Speech*, 8.

achieved in certain forms, such as the visual poems of Juliette Roche.[77] Williams's experiments never extended so far beyond tradition, but it is clear that by 1936 he had reached some resolution on his ideas about perception and relative experience. Compressed from 122 lines to 55, the second version of 'St. Francis Einstein' excises the repetitions of the original, presenting instead a poem that can be read as a single representation of the scene of Einstein's arrival spread across four stanzas. So we must ask why Williams would return to the poem in such detail, and perhaps more importantly, what shaped the changes he made for the later version.

Revising relativity: The second version of 'St Francis Einstein of the Daffodils'

It is clear that Williams's interest in physics extended beyond his early cubist experiments. In a 1925 essay on Marianne Moore he argued that a 'course in mathematics would not be wasted on a poet, or a reader of poetry, if he remember no more from it than the geometric principle of the intersection of loci: from all angles lines converging and crossing established points'.[78] If this recalls the intersecting lines of 'The Rose', whose existence is defined by its relations and implicit geometry as it 'penetrates space', it is because these ideas continued to deeply permeate Williams's poetic ideals.[79] Geometry is linked, for Williams, with clarity of artistic perception:

> [The poet] might carry it further and say in his imagination that apprehension perforates at places, through to understanding – as white is at the intersection of blue and green and yellow and red. It is this white light that is the background of all good work.[80]

Williams's geometries are active and interactive – they are the rapid vector-motion descriptions of shapes, curves that distort perception, moving lines of penetrating light, which shoot off from his objects and cut through the universe. They are mathematics in its active form, as physics, and they are an embodiment of 'vision in motion'. In describing Moore's poetry, he might as well have been

---

[77] Sacha Bru, 'Are We Modernists Yet? Avant-Garde, Temporality, History', BAMS, New Work In Modernist Studies Conference, 10 December 2015, Queen Mary University of London, Keynote Address.
[78] William Carlos Williams, *Selected Essays*, 122.
[79] Williams, *Spring and All*, 31.
[80] Williams, *Selected Essays*, 122.

describing his own. The mathematically determined vision of 'The Eyeglasses' (1923) from *Spring and All* equally reveals and clarifies the 'universality of things':

>   the favourable
>   distortion of eyeglasses
>   that see everything and remain
>   related to mathematics –[81]

Allying poetry with optics, Williams brings a sense of scientific clarity to the poet's mission; but this clarity was often to be challenged by his growing understanding of the uncertainties inherent in many of the predicates of relativity.

Williams's interest was fostered by his friend, the mathematician John Riordan, who recommended to him popular works that engaged with the social and philosophical implications of the new physics. In December 1926, Riordan gave him a copy of A. N. Whitehead's *Science and the Modern World*, which Williams read on the boat to Europe in September of the following year.[82] Their letters indicate that by this point Williams had also studied C. P. Steinmetz's *Four Lectures on Relativity and Space* (1923) at Riordan's recommendation, and the trajectory of his poetry thereafter demonstrates not only an attentive linking of relative perception, poetic form and aesthetics, but also a need to reconcile the ideas these books expounded with the lived experience of modern life. In particular, a clearer and more sophisticated understanding of the new physics presented the basis for the dramatic overhaul of 'Saint Francis Einstein of the Daffodils', leading to a version of the poem that dispenses with many of his earlier techniques in favour of concision and greater obscurity.

Whitehead's exposition of the history of science is coupled with an argument against the materialism and mechanism of previous centuries in favour of a system of events, fields of influence and complex processes. Here, Williams would have found an argument for a world view reconsidered in light of the new physics and focussed on a similar view of relationships and interaction as those we have seen from Moholy-Nagy and Heidegger. Relativity alters our understanding of reality by making us more aware of our own position within it; we constantly frame the world around us from our own reference point (determined, as we have seen, by our speed relative to the objects we are seeing). This much Williams grasped in 1921 with his recasting of Einstein's arrival from different reference frames, but Whitehead offered a complex argument which links this fundamental change

---

[81] Williams, *Spring and All*, 46.
[82] Weaver, *William Carlos Williams,* 47–8.

of perception with social, religious and philosophical implications. It is not simply that one can change one's frame of reference and justify any rendering of a scene or argument (as dinner table relativists might have it); frame of reference has a profound effect on the physical *reality* of a situation. 'So far as physics is concerned', writes Whitehead, separate bodies 'are wholly occupied in moving each other about, and they have no reality outside this function. In particular for physics, there is no intrinsic reality'.[83] He explains that 'primarily the spacio-temporal continuum is a locus of relational possibility'.[84] The space-time continuum is a construct in which fields exist and interact, and it is these interactions which define the field and which, in turn, define reality.

In trying to capture the message of Whitehead's dense argument, contemporary reviewers arrived at a description very similar to a formula for line poetry: 'The discontinuity which recent physics apparently requires in some of its primary objects is also provided, [Whitehead] suggests, in the repetition of simple pattern units, giving a series of wholes which are discrete even though the process within each unit is continuous.'[85] The appeal to Williams of a perception of reality based on relational possibility is mirrored in his reflection upon design in Cezanne's paintings:

> He put it down on the canvas so there would be meaning without saying anything at all. Just the relation of the parts to themselves. In considering a poem, I don't care whether it's finished or not; if it is put down with a good relation to the parts, it becomes a poem. And the meaning of the poem can be grasped by attention to the design.[86]

To understand relationships between aspects of an artwork, whether poem or painting, then, is to find its meaning. The pattern of things in the world is unified by perception, much as the relationships between words in a poem are solidified to understanding by the reader. To see – to perceive – is, in effect, to make real.

If the guiding idea behind Whitehead's foregrounding of events is drawn from visual perception, Steinmetz goes further in linking relativity's new geometries with optics; he states the Einsteinian proposition that 'length is not a fixed and invariable property of the body but depends upon the condition under which it

---

[83] Alfred North Whitehead, *Science and the Modern World* (Cambridge: Cambridge University Press, 1927), 193.
[84] Ibid.
[85] Charles H. Toll, 'Review: [Untitled]', *The American Journal of Psychology*, 38, no. 1 (1927), 140.
[86] Walter Sutton, 'A Visit with William Carlos Williams', *Minnesota Review*, 1, no. 3 (April 1961), 309–24 cited in Gee, 'The Structure of Perception in the Poetry of William Carlos', 376.

is observed'.⁸⁷ Mike Weaver has proposed that this description suggested relative line length to Williams, but this is not all. Steinmetz distinctly links the idea to visual perception, adding that relative measure applies even to light waves, the underlying source of our perception of colour. As Peter Halter says in his study of Williams and visual arts, 'to see, Williams is trying to demonstrate, is to perceive and feel the visual dynamics inherent in all forms and colors, and to assess the dynamic patterns that result from their interactions.'⁸⁸ Relativity removes any certainty about the relational aspects of an object. Colour is simply a result of the eye and brain's collective interpretation of light-waves which are by no means absolute, but in the same thrall to physical forces as any other object. Length is simply a property of physical perception. In these conditions, it is impossible to ask 'which is the "true colour"' or length of an object; the only available answer is a paradox: all and none, dependent on your frame of reference.⁸⁹ That Einstein might be tall as a tree or small as a flower, that a wheelbarrow might be red or grey in different weather, has a profound effect on the artist or poet seeking to portray 'ideas ... in things'.⁹⁰ For how do we define a 'thing' in a poem except by its physical attributes and their impression upon an observer?

In the second version of 'St Francis Einstein', we can see some of these considerations in action. The most obvious shift is one of measure, with the new opening formed of noticeably more erratic line lengths:

'Sweet land'
at last!
Out of the sea –
the Venusremembering wavelets
rippling with laughter –
freedom
for the daffodils!
– in a tearing wind
that shakes
the tufted orchards –
Einstein, tall as a violet

---

⁸⁷ William Curtis Swabey, 'Science and the Modern World by A. N. Whitehead', *The Philosophical Review*, 35, no. 3 (May 1926), 274; C. P. Steinmetz, *Four Lectures on Relativity* (New York: McGraw-Hill, 1923), 7.
⁸⁸ Peter Halter, *The Revolution in the Visual Arts and the Poetry of William Carlos Williams* (Cambridge: Cambridge University Press, 1994), 6.
⁸⁹ Steinmetz, *Four Lectures on Relativity*, 7.
⁹⁰ William Carlos Williams, *Paterson* (New York: New Directions, 1963), 9.

in the lattice-arbor corner
is tall as
a blossomy peartree

This stanza contains all the fragmentation of the first version condensed into a heavily fractured fourteen lines, and our awareness of the earlier version contributes to a reading of the poem as cubist collage. The collage is tangible in the way the lines are slotted together, like pieces of several differently cut puzzles of the same image. This is an act of contraction: lines which were once filled out, such as 'Sweet land of Liberty', become tightly condensed kernels in the later version, which offers only 'Sweet land!', atoms whose apparent obscurity invites them to be split and examined. Direct quotation of the song alluded to here introduces us to the fact that each aspect of the scene is a fragment, like the broken sentences of *Spring and All*, a paraphrase for the reader to elaborate and make whole. The parenthetic dashes, which we have seen in Williams to imply a linkage alongside visual disconnection between elements of poems like 'The Rose', here offer a bridge between what were previously separate representations of the same scene; the earlier version's stanzas are shuttered together, so that we are faced with a scene that holds a multiplicity of measures and frames of reference within each stanza.

What does this tell us about the thing itself? First, several 'things' are at play in Williams's poems: there is the scene described, which we have already attended to, and then there is the poem itself, a discrete, non-mimetic art object, akin to a cubist painting. As we have seen, structural experiment is at the heart of Williams's adaptations of art, and form is the key to understanding even his most plain-seeming poetry. In adopting new subject matter, Williams believed, the modern poet shifts the focus of the poem from its content to its form: 'it began to be noticed that there could be a new subject matter and that that was not the poem at all.'[91] This is key to his argument in 1948, where he urges us to hold 'the term reality as contrasted with phantasy and to [consider] that the *subject matter* of the poem is always phantasy – what is wished for, realized in the "dream" of the poem – but that the structure confronts something else.'[92] In parallel to Whitehead's account of the reality of bodies emerging from their interactions, Williams suggests the reality of the poem lies in the way it is structured.

The second version of 'St Francis Einstein' challenges our understanding of poetic structure both in its flexible and constantly changing form, and in the

---

[91] Ibid., 282.
[92] Ibid., 281. *Williams's emphases.*

way that it frames and condenses its content into a choppy flow of impressions, which the earlier version tells us emerge from different reference frames. Where the first version may be likened to a gallery of photographs taken from different angles and placed in series, the second version comes closer to a collage of these images pasted on a single canvas, an experience of the scene in a way that, like a cubist painting, induces multiple perspectives at a single view, as though steering the eye around a single object, rather than offering several renditions of it. As Paul Christensen asserts, 'Williams took from Whitehead what he thought was practical for poetry, amounting to a theory of perception which recognized the unavoidable distortions of linear thinking and called for cognizance of the object through multiple perspectives.'[93] But this rejection of linearity profoundly changes our experience of the poetic object. While the first poem allows us to choose our perspective by hovering in our preferred stanza, the later version denies an objective view more aggressively by bringing multiple frames together. This mashing together of previously disconnected viewpoints creates a more immediate and chaotic representation of the scene, but one which is arguably a refinement of Williams's original concept for a cubist-relativist poem. The poem, then, becomes a locus of relational possibility through which the reader must sift and find connections.

This jigsaw theory holds when the two parenthetic interjections are removed from the stanza; doing this reveals a visual pattern in the line lengths of the first half of the new stanza:

'Sweet land'
at last!
Out of the sea
freedom
for the daffodils!

While not a full-flowing sentence, this dissection of the poem shows the dramatic value of the shorter lines 'at last!' and 'freedom' which, relieved of company and left to breathe, expand to fill out the line. Positioned alone between positioning lines ('out of', 'for the') which tether them to the scene, the expansion of these lines reflects the relief both of Einstein, at finally arriving, and of America's anticipation of his arrival. Linguistically, these lines share a pattern of simple, mono- and duo-syllabic words, rising to a crescendo with *daffodils*. By contrast,

---

[93] Paul Christensen, *Charles Olson: Call Him Ishmael* (Austin, TX: University of Texas Press, 2014), 74.

the inserted fourth and fifth lines share a new register with more complex language, bringing back the allusive conjunction of the 'Venusremembering wavelets' with the first verb of the stanza:

> the Venusremembering wavelets
> Rippling with laughter –

The second interjection is equally, if not more dynamic, set against the smooth, exultant image of Einstein rising out of the sea:

> – in a tearing wind
> that shakes
> the tufted orchards –

The relationship between these sections created through the act of collage is to increase the energy of the stanza.

Williams's 1948 'attack... on *the rigidity of the poetic foot*' is a structural grapple with reality, designed to challenge poets to experiment with form to this end, and while the shifting feet of this stanza come closer to an example of the 'variable foot', foregrounding line-length to create a lattice of different speeds within the stanza, their success may seem to depend too much upon familiarity with the agenda of the earlier version of the poem.[94] This later version does, however, employ more technically several facets of relativity, as a step towards enacting and realizing a new theory of measure. As described by Steinmetz, lines are not unilateral or fixed; the only linear patterning in this version of the poem appears either within single lines or, as we have seen, through artificial extraction of individual frames of reference. By rejecting traditional notions of meter, Williams embraces 'the relativity of measurements', and attempts to render more closely relative experience on a line-by-line basis.[95] Thus, contraction and expansion within the line act as a tool for the poet to shape the perception of the modern subject in nuanced ways. In 'The Poem as a Field of Action', Williams seeks 'a new way of measuring that will be commensurate with the social, economic world in which we are living as contrasted with the past'.[96] By adopting a framework of relative measure, in which lines are freed from the constraints of uniformity and inflected by a system of metrics that respond to the perceived time-rhythm of their contents, Williams formalizes a theory of free verse which

---

[94] Williams, 'The Poem as a Field of Action', 289. *Williams's emphases.*
[95] Ibid., 283.
[96] Ibid.

accounts for line and line break, words and the breaks between them, in such a way as to more closely reflect the flux of modern experience. While this comes closer to its potential in his later poems, particularly *Paterson*, the 1936 version of 'St Francis Einstein' already offers a crude demonstration of this free expansion and contraction of a variable line to suit Williams's perspective and modern reality.[97]

'The only reality that we can know is MEASURE': Einstein in *Paterson*[98]

Williams's aspirations for the new form were ambitious. He saw a revolution in the poetic line as a step towards a better understanding of the 'complexities of the world about our ears [achieved through] a measure infinitely truer and more subtle than that of the past, … closer in its construction to modern concepts of reality'.[99] Indeed, he wrote to his friend John C. Thirlwall:

> It may seem presumptive to state that such an apparently minor activity as a movement in verse construction could be an indication of Einstein's discovery in the relativity of our measurements of physical matter … but such is the fact.[100]

However, Williams's pursuit of this 'truer' measure proved more elusive and difficult than this letter makes it sound.

With his final poem, the unfinished epic *Paterson* (1946–58), Williams attempted to discover what this new measure would look like. The opening sections integrate the language of equations and measurement, complexity and clarity, fittingly reminiscent of the 'complicated mathematics' of Einstein in 'St Francis Einstein of the Daffodils'. For instance, the 'thoughts' of the city manifest as the people who inhabit it, who 'alight and scatter' from the bus:

> Who are these people (how complex
> the mathematic) among whom I see myself
> in regularly ordered plateglass of

---

[97] Whether Williams ever truly solidified a workable relative measure for poetry is debateable. In one of his latest letters, he writes of his efforts in striving for the new measure: 'All the problems have not as yet been solved, but [*we need*] some sort of measure, some sort of discipline to *free* from the vagaries of mere chance and to teach us to rule ourselves again.' But he felt, as have many critics, that he came closest in *Paterson*. Williams, *Selected Letters*, 336.
[98] Williams, 'The Poem as a Field of Action', 283. *Williams's capitalization*.
[99] Williams, *Selected Letters*, 332.
[100] Ibid.

> his thoughts, glimmering before shoes and bicycles?
> They walk incommunicado, the
> equation beyond solution, yet
> its sense is clear.[101]

Here, the complex activity of the city's inhabitants, mirroring the complexity of the creative mind, and of the city itself, is figured as an insoluble equation. Each person, each thought, is isolated, 'incommunicado', and yet part of a much wider field of interrelation. Although one cannot pin down 'who' they are individually, sense can be found in the network they form: the city itself. This idea returns in the poem's second section, 'Sunday in the Park', where it is more explicitly aligned with concept of universal measurement. There, Williams presents the core message of 'The Poem as a Field of Action': the need for an intervention, a shift within the mind, within our understanding of the universe and within the poetic line:

> Without intervention nothing is well spaced,
> unless the mind change, unless
> the stars are new measured, according
> to their relative positions, the
> line will not change, the necessity
> will not matriculate: unless there is
> a new mind there cannot be a new
> line, the old will go on
> repeating itself with recurring
> Deadliness[102]

The mind, the universe and the poetic line are linked with rupture and change through the integration of relativity; this intervention, Williams implies, would amount a new school of poetry (the new line must 'matriculate'), where life is returned to poetry and words are restored to their previous power.[103] By establishing a setting filled with elements whose interactions are reinterpreted through the idea of a network of 'relative positions', Williams proposes a means of interpreting the poem – and the modern world – through analogy to Einsteinian measurement.

---

[101] Williams, *Paterson*, 9.
[102] Ibid., 50.
[103] Ibid.

It was not until he reached the third section of 'Sunday in the Park' that Williams felt he had found the solution: 'the passage from *Paterson* which prompted my solution to the problem of modern verse… is to be found in Book 2, p. 96, beginning with the line: "The descent beckons" … where the implications of the variable foot first struck me.'[104] The passage that leads into this section describes a hunt 'for the nul… the N of all / equations', an image of an abstract mathematical void-space 'that's past all / seeing', which leads to the Great Falls of the Passaic River. From here, with mathematics in mind, Williams introduces an experimental triadic line form, whose plasticity shows a descent which results in renewal and the discovery of 'new places' and 'new objectives':

The descent beckons
        as the ascent beckoned
                Memory is a kind
of accomplishment
        a sort of renewal
    even
an initiation, since the spaces it opens are new
places
        inhabited by hordes
heretofore unrealized[105]

Williams integrates spatial as well as verbal units into a verse-form characterized by what Oliver Southall terms 'a roughly isochronic interplay of line and pause'.[106] On the page, the visual is as important as the rhythmic, painting a stream of verbal fragments which tumble and reflect the descent itself. Williams suggests a way of understanding poetic time that relies not upon traditional temporal rhythm and standardized feet but rather a flexible and reactive rhythm based on the relationship between verbal and spatial units of variable size and length. This, in turn, creates a localized metric, loosely analogous to relative perception, in which lines and units expand or contract dependent upon the reader's position within the poem.

Although Williams identifies this passage as a manifestation of the 'variable foot', the links to Einsteinian measure would be easy to miss, were it not for the earlier, more explicit, experimentation of 'St Francis Einstein' and the exposition

---

[104] Williams, *Selected Letters*, 338.
[105] Williams, *Paterson*, 77.
[106] Oliver Southall, 'Desperate Measures: Williams's "new line" and the Poetical Economy of *Paterson*', *William Carlos Williams Review* 33, nos. 1–2 (2016), 221.

of 'The Poem as a Field of Action'. As Southall notes, Williams's gestures towards the actual form of the variable foot within 'The Poem as a Field of Action' are vague, and his applications of it in *Paterson* share in such a wide variety of analogies that it is at times difficult to pin down.[107] This is to be expected as part of the holistic integration of the measure into a poem whose subject is no longer art nor physics itself, but the representation of a more expansive sense of time, history and place. In this passage, the form becomes part of the fabric of Williams's reality, rather than its subject. The new measure partakes of and shapes the wider fragmentation and dissonance of *Paterson*'s reality, where a verbal collage of different verse and prose forms abut to create a poem which, though formally fractured, temporally disordered and technically incomplete, gains a strange, accretive totality around its core setting.

By 1948, then, Williams had crystalized a theory of poetics that prioritized measure above content, form above the represented object. As we have seen, the root of this lay in his engagement with the non-mimetic *avant-garde* of Cubism, which gradually became associated with relativity both in art criticism, and in Williams's own work. Whitehead foregrounded measurement when he posited that the single most important scientific advance across the turn of the century was the accelerated improvement in scientific instruments. Their ability to measure physical phenomena with greater precision than had ever been possible previously put measurement at the centre of all new physical advancements.[108] This is certainly the case; the validity of Einstein's time-shattering theories hung (and even in recent years, still hangs) upon the accuracy of measurement by Eddington's team in 1919.[109] Measurement from physics formed a basis for the variable foot, which in turn provided a formal justification for Williams to instil an American idiom, based on the spoken word, into poetry. The language of physics spoke to Williams as a means of articulating with certainty the outcomes of his cubist experiments. As by the 1940s a critical link had been formed by artists such as Moholy-Nagy and Laport, this transition became easier and more natural. Embracing the ideas about science and its applications found in Whitehead and Steinmetz, Williams pushed for new experimentation in poetic form, and felt with conviction that the embrace of physics and mathematics into new measures for poetry opened a new vista, in particular for American poets seeking a new, distinct means of expression.

---

[107] Ibid.
[108] Whitehead, *Science and the Modern World*, 143.
[109] Daniel Kennefick, 'Testing Relativity from the 1919 Eclipse – A Question of Bias', *Physics Today* (March 2009), 37.

Familiarity with science allowed Williams to assign his art, and the wider prosodic values of modern poetry, a scientific clarity. His conscious association of poetry with scientific values – developing an exacting, observational and measure-led poetics – began a reflexive engagement with science through which he sought to work out the implications of modern physics for literary practices, influenced by the innovations of Cubism's scientific approach to painting. Although Williams evokes a range of ideas, from Mendeleev's periodic table to the contemporary psychology of Freud, the prescription he offers to future poets is couched in terms from physics: to separate (subject) 'matter' from 'action', to seek a poetic constant ('Einstein had the speed of light as a constant – his only constant – what have we?') and to isolate and utilize the useful elements of poetic measure ('What we are at is to try to discover and isolate and *use* the underlying element or principle motivating this change').[110] His belief in a poetry influenced and sharpened by mathematics and physics only grew more cemented in his later years, and became a cornerstone of his later poetic practice. It reaches a peak in the collage of measures in *Paterson*, and their echoes can be felt distinctly in the work of the Objectivist poets, and were formative for Charles Olson's theories of 'composition by field'.[111] The concepts of relativity, its language and its implications for poetic structure presented Williams with a new form for poetry which he believed, like the vital springtime Einstein brought to the shores of New York, could generate a truly modern, relevant, and reinvigorated American poetics. 'Relativity gives us the cue,' he wrote later, 'So, again, mathematics comes to the rescue of the arts.'[112]

---

[110] Williams, *Paterson*, 281, 286, 291.
[111] Weaver, *William Carlos Williams*, 54; Margaret Glynn Lloyd, *William Carlos Williams's Paterson: A Critical Reappraisal* (Plainsboro, NJ: Associated University Presses, 1980), 147–50.
[112] Williams cited in Linda Funkhauser and Daniel C. O'Connell, '"Measure" in the Poetry of William Carlos Williams: Evidence from his Readings', *Journal of Modern Literature* 12, no. 1 (March 1985), 38–9.

2

Mina Loy's energy physics

In 1929, when *Little Review* editor Jane Heap asked Mina Loy, 'What do you look forward to?' The poet's answer was short and succinct: 'The release of atomic energy'.[1] Her life continues 'inevitably', she says, 'as time and space are an intellectual hoax'. Whether we take these comments as serious or ironic, both reflect an ongoing preoccupation with the new physics that can be seen in Loy's writing. The influence of physics can be felt throughout her work, from the startlingly scientific language of her earliest poems through to her much later reflections on the bombings of Hiroshima and Nagasaki.[2] In the latter, a short piece titled 'Tuning In to the Atom Bomb', she wrote vividly of a strange sense of guilt she felt:

> Serene, amid scintillas of sunlight gilding our narrow garden, writing of the danger induced by extracting force from Power, suddenly, seismically was I overcome by an eccentric sense of guilt; as though speared by an echo of some forgotten wisdom sunken in ancient time, forbidding all revelation of some perilous secret.
>
> Excentric guilt! I did not *know* the secret.[3]

Why should a female British expatriate poet feel personal guilt about devastation on the other side of the world? How could Loy be implicated in the deaths of over 200,000 people in an international conflict with which she was not directly involved? What could she be accused of?

To be sure, she could not have imagined in 1929 that her phrasing from the *Little Review* survey would be echoed by Einstein almost two decades later, when

---

Parts of this chapter have been published as Rachel Fountain Eames, '"Snared in an Atomic Mesh": Transcendent Physics and the Futurist Body in the Work of Mina Loy', *JLS* 13, no. 1 (2020), 31–49. Reproduced with thanks to the *Journal of Literature and Science* editorial team.

[1] Mina Loy, *The Little Review* (May 1929), 46.
[2] Sarah Hayden, 'Introduction', *Insel* (Brooklyn, NY: Melville House Publishing, 2014), xxxi.
[3] Mina Loy, 'Tuning in on the Atom Bomb', *Stories and Essays of Mina Loy* (Illinois & London: Dalkey Archive Press, 2011), 286.

he said in his first public statement after the bombs were dropped that 'The release of atomic energy has not created a new problem. It has merely made more urgent the necessity of solving an existing one'.[4] But perhaps Loy was looking back on the strain of physics that runs like a charge through her own work and the way her writings often idealized ideas of atomic dissolution. Notice the urgency and seriousness underlying Loy's characteristic punning language of ex-centricity in this piece, the contrast between danger thousands of miles away and the serenity of her garden and the drama of seismic, perilous energy and information. The subject is morbidly serious, and yet she cannot resist the pun – eccentric / *ex*centric – to imply the outward radiation of emotive experience from deep within, mirroring the sun's rays, in an almost cruel similarity to the nuclear explosions. Loy often draws on physics in this way, at the boundary of satire and sincerity, and I suggest that the thread running from the futurist and spiritualist roots of Loy's physics can offer insight not only into the currency of the new physics for Loy but also into its multiple role within wider modernist and avant-garde circles.

As she established her reputation, becoming the first poet to bring Italian Futurism to America with her 1914 manifesto 'Aphorisms on Futurism', Loy grew to value the new physics as a means of articulating her concerns. These were as varied and mercurial as the forms she used to convey them – she moved rapidly between critiquing avant-garde social circles, promoting female sexual liberation, and developing her own metaphysics, embracing different forms, poetry, prose, drama, painting and novel-memoir – but references to inter-atomic relations, high-energy physics and radioactivity remained in her work at every period of her life, occurring and reoccurring in different contexts with surprising regularity. Indeed, as Tara Prescott notes, Loy's playful use of language has a remarkable way of making technical scientific language 'appear natural in her poetry'.[5] Drawn from bellicose Italian Futurism and contemporary spiritualist discourses, Loy's writing often seems to reify atomic dispersal as the apotheosis of human evolution. I suggest that Loy found in the new physics a flexible, dynamic and authoritative framework through which to articulate her own experiences of modernity, allowing her to negotiate discourses of embodiment and spirituality in startlingly innovative ways. In particular, models drawn from the rapidly changing particle physics of the day offered her new ways of imagining the human body and its interactions.

---

[4] Albert Einstein, *Einstein on Politics*, ed. David E. Rowe and Robert Schulman (Princeton, NJ: Princeton University Press, 2007), 373.
[5] Tara Prescott, *Poetic Salvage: Reading Mina Loy* (2016), xxvii.

When Loy set out to start writing poetry, scientists were reimagining the invisible dominion of matter. In 1906, J. J. Thomson had been awarded the Nobel Prize for his discovery of the electron, the subatomic particle that had confirmed both that atoms were not the fundamental unit of matter, and that their behaviour was governed by electrical charges. Between 1909 and 1913 the orbital model, firmly situated at the heart of Classical dynamics, was integrated into particle physics to describe the shape of the atom. A growing understanding of radioactivity, the photoelectric effect, and experimentation with Röntgen rays (X-rays) had dislodged Thomson's popular 'plum pudding model' by suggesting atoms were more often unstable and reactive than stable. Thomson's atom would eventually dissolve or collapse. In 1911, Ernest Rutherford proposed a new model characterized by a dense nucleus orbited by a cloud of sparsely distributed electrons. This planetary model was revised in partnership with Niels Bohr by 1913 and came more closely to resemble a solar system, by affixing these electrons to concentric 'closed orbits'.[6] The Bohr-Rutherford model took energy radiation into account to present a new system in which equilibrium and radiant activity could be explained.[7] Bohr's previous work had shown that the 'spectra of the stellar nebulae and that of the solar corona' could be accounted for by a system of rings denoted by a consistent inverse square law; his vision of the electrons in an atom, which form set orbits around the nucleus, shares this model.[8] It demonstrated Einstein's mass-energy equivalence on an atomic scale; matter and energy became linked as 'a complex system of electrical charges in motion'.[9] As this chronology shows, contemporary ideas about subatomic particles were linked with emergent technological phenomena, electricity, X-rays and radio-waves, and radium, that quickly captured the public imagination.

Responding to these discoveries, Loy imagined the human body positioned at the intersection of active forces; the bodies described in her writings strive towards or break equilibrium, gaining electromagnetic force and gravity through dynamic atomic movement. Her most interesting and outrageous images are those of empowered (often sexual) bodies colliding and reacting with one another; her subjects 'tumble together', 'knock sparks off each other',

---

[6] Ernest Rutherford, 'The Scattering of α and β Particles by Matter and the Structure of the Atom', *Philosophical Magazine* 6, no. 21 (1911), 669–88; subsequently, Niels Bohr, 'On the Constitution of Atoms and Molecules', *Philosophical Magazine* 26, no. 1 (1913), 3, http://web.ihep.su/dbserv/compas/src/bohr13/eng.pdf [Accessed 27 August 2017].
[7] Ibid., 2–3.
[8] Ibid., 5–6.
[9] Isabella B. Threlkeld, 'The Emergence of Futurism in Italy: 1900–1916 – The Influence of Science on Art' (Unpublished MA Thesis, University of Nebraska, 1971), 4.

orbit and collide, blur and combine.[10] They are active and reactive, often figured in the language of the cosmos or the atom, sometimes both at once. The striking depictions of the sexual body in her early poetry, with its rough-edged descriptions of 'Pig Cupid', 'erotic garbage' and 'spermatozoa / At the core of Nothing', as well as the unflinching calls to action of her polemical 'Feminist Manifesto' (1914), have encouraged readings which foreground the poet as a 'sex-radical', battering down turn-of-the-century squeamishness, 'debunking phallocentric syntactic norms' in order to discuss the female body in terms fitting of the New Woman.[11] Readings by Rachel Blau DuPlessis and Steve Pinkerton, which discuss the wider implications of Loy's depictions of sexuality, have been valuable in addressing her importance as a commentator on female erotic autonomy, while others such as Ellen McWhorter have extended discussion of embodiment in Loy's work to include a gendered examination of intuition in a period in which technology 'could speak for the body'.[12] However, when we step away from the widely noted 'eroticism which revels in bodily functions, concentrating on skin, tissue, and fluids' to consider the function of atomic bodies in Loy's work, we can see the degree to which the physics informed her developing poetics, shaping her theories about the human body and its future.[13] By discussing Loy's use of 'the corporeal real world body, bodies of matter, and bodies of text', Jacinta Kelly offered a new way of reading Loy which attends to 'the body' beyond its gendered and sexualized permutations.[14] I wish to focus on the second of these – 'bodies of matter' – but I do so to point out that Loy's corporeal bodies are rarely presented without consideration of their position in the modern physical universe, where they exist simultaneously at the subatomic, corporeal and cosmic scales.

---

[10] Mina Loy, 'Songs to Johannes', *The Lost Lunar Baedeker*, 58–9.
[11] Ibid., 53, 56; Swathi Krishna S. and Srirupa Chatterjee, 'Mina Loy's Parturition and L'écriture Féminine', *The Explicator* 73, no. 4 (2015), 257; Rachel Blau DuPlessis, '"Seismic Orgasm": Sexual Intercourse, Its Modern Representations and Politics', *Genders, Races, and Religious Cultures in Modern American Poetry 1908-1934* (Oxford: Oxford University Press, 2001), 52, 61; Steve Pinkerton, 'Blasphemy and the New Woman: Mina Loy's Profane Communions', *Blasphemous Modernism: The 20th-Century Word Made Flesh* (Oxford: Oxford Scholarship Online, 2017); Loy established herself as a working model for the 'modern woman' type in an interview of 1917 for the *New York Evening Sun*, see: Christina Walter, 'Getting Impersonal: Mina Loy's Body Politics from "Feminist Manifesto" to *Insel*', *MFS Modern Fiction Studies* 55, no. 4 (Winter 2009), 663.
[12] Ellen McWhorter, 'Body Matters: Mina Loy and the Art of Intuition', *European Journal of American Studies* 10, no. 2 (Summer 2015), 3.
[13] Linda A. Kinnahan, *Poetics of the Feminine: Authority and Literary Tradition in William Carlos Williams, Mina Loy, Denise Levertov, and Kathleen Fraser* (Cambridge: Cambridge University Press, 1994), 56.
[14] Jacinta Kelly, 'Purging the Birdcage: The Dissolution of Space in Mina Loy's Poetry', *Limina* 18 (2012), 2.

Anyone wishing to trace Loy's intellectual development faces a number of challenges; the path of her ideas is a complex, non-linear one, marked by fleeting but often deeply assertive affairs with numerous movements and idealisms. Her work resists categorization. As Roger Conover says, 'Feminist and Futurist, wife and lover, militant and pacifist, actress and model, Christian Scientist and nurse, [Loy] was the binarians [sic] nightmare. She was a futurist, dadaist, surrealist, feminist, conceptualist, modernist, post-modernist, and none of the above.'[15] Her work is, in itself, fluid and non-uniform, 'marked by so many seeming contradictions, counter-allegiances, and inconsistencies that she was often considered unbalanced.'[16] This is further complicated by the fact that progression of her ideas is sometimes obscured by the complex publication history of her 'bodies of text'.[17] Loy published only two books in her lifetime – *Lunar Baedecker* (1923) and *Lunar Baedeker and Times-Tables* (1958) – and while her poems and pastiches appeared in era-defining periodicals including *The Little Review, The Dial, Others,* and *Camera Work* through the 1910s and 1920s, she seemed uninterested, particularly in her later years, in pursuing publication or building her reputation.[18] Many of the later works discussed here, such as her only novel, *Insel* (written 1930s, published 1991), were published only after her death; others, such as 'History of Religion and Eros', though now collected and published, are undated; and her fictionalized memoir 'Islands in the Air' (1936–) exists only as unfinished or oft-reworked archival fragments.[19] Throughout all of these, though, there runs a thread of physics which Loy evokes and manipulates variously to interrogate the aesthetic movements around her, to challenge through an equally masculine-coded lexicon the masculinist aesthetics of the avant-garde and to articulate her distinctly modern spirituality and the role of technology in humanity's future.

---

[15] Roger Conover, 'Introduction' to Mina Loy, *The Lost Lunar Baedeker* (Manchester: Carcanet, 1997), xiii.

[16] Ibid.

[17] For a good overview of the posthumous collection and publication of Loy's work, see Sara Crangle's introduction to Mina Loy, *Stories and Essays of Mina Loy* (Illinois & London: Dalkey Archive Press, 2011). Crangle states that *Insel* is no longer in print, but it has since been reissued and is available once more: Mina Loy, *Insel* (Brooklyn, NY: Melville House Publishing, 2014).

[18] At this time Loy's artistic attention had to be shared between her writing, her painting, and her business ventures with the establishment of her lampshade business (1917–30) and later work as a representative for her son-in-law, Julien Levy's New York Gallery (1931–). See Conover, 'Introduction', xii–xiii.

[19] Sara Crangle states that Carolyn Burke has dated 'History of Religion and Eros' to Loy's years in New York's Bowery District (1948–53); however, Burke does not attempt to date the essay. She merely writes that at this time 'Glimpses of this process [of reconciling her divided heritage] exist in [Loy's] unpublished essay "History of Religion and Eros," and in her scattered notes on various spiritual traditions'. Crangle, Kindle Location 101; Carolyn Burke, *Becoming Modern: The Life of Mina Loy* (New York: Farrar, Straus and Giroux, Kindle ed., 2012), 8865–7; Loy, *Insel*.

Loy drew upon a large range of popular appropriations of the New Physics to inform her '"fluctuant" conceptualizations of atomic energy'.[20] In order to demonstrate the breadth of her appropriations of physics, this chapter approaches Loy's work through the lens of two twentieth-century movements: Futurism and Spiritualism. I focus first upon Loy's engagement with futurist physics, particularly its ironic manifestations in her early satires of the movement's masculinist figures; I will then go on to demonstrate how 'Parturition', written concurrently to these, problematizes a purely ironic understanding of Loy's stance towards physics. This more sincere attempt at applying terms and notions from modern physics to modern embodied and psychic experience, I argue, makes it necessary to examine physics discourse in Loy's more esoteric sources, from Christian Science, Theosophy and modern Spiritualism. Loy's concern with spirituality grows more pronounced in her later works, and her religious views consistently partake in wider popular 'religio-scientific discourse'.[21] As such, physics offered a diverse and salient set of tropes, images and analogies through which Loy could address themes of artistic creativity, modern technological experience and spiritual and psychical research.

Parody physics: Loy's futurist satires

In 1908, F. T. Marinetti was looking to the future. Working on a manifesto titled 'Elettricimo' or 'Dinamismo', he wanted to shake the very foundations of modern art. This work became 'The Founding and Manifesto of Futurism', a dramatic statement of artistic intervention that exploded onto the front cover of the Paris newspaper *Le Figaro* on 20 February 1909. The Italian poet lambasted all art that had gone before, promoting a new artistic sensibility grounded in the technology, dynamism and the cutting-edge physics that shaped the modern world. 'Why should we look back', he asked:

> when what we want is to break down the mysterious doors of the Impossible? Time and Space died yesterday. We already live in the absolute, because we have created eternal, omnipresent speed.[22]

---

[20] Sarah Hayden, 'Introduction', *Insel* (Brooklyn, NY: Melville House Publishing, 2014), xxxi.
[21] Lara Vetter, *Modernist Writings and Religio-Scientific Discourse* (London: Palgrave Macmillan, 2010).
[22] F. T. Marinetti, 'The Founding and Manifesto of Futurism', in *Futurism: An Anthology*, ed. Rainey, Lawrence, Christine Poggi, et al. (New Haven, CT: Yale University Press, 2009), 51.

This hymn to the virtue of 'the habit of energy' and 'the beauty of speed', and its rhetoric of dynamism and motion conceived in technological and scientific terms, captured Loy's imagination as she and the Dadaist poet Frances Stevens pored over his work in the lead-up to the Great War.[23] It made waves among the expatriates Loy lived with in Italy in 1913 and 1914. During this time she made her publishing debut with 'Aphorisms on Futurism' (1914) which brought Italian Futurism to an American audience in Alfred Steiglitz's *Camera Work*, wrote numerous futurist satires and her famous 'Feminist Manifesto' (1914), and produced her first long poem, 'Parturition' (1914). This latter I will examine at some length later in this chapter, as it offers several typical examples of Loy's appropriation of physics. At this stage of her career, Futurism offered a means of shedding the flaccid experience of earlier art-forms in exchange for something more taut and transcendent. Marinetti's vision rested on the artistic potential of technology and science, the powerful machine and the electrified atom. Its aspirational language of challenging the impossible, taking control of the material world, and transcendent creation fascinated Loy; it sparked the most prolific creative periods of her life, leading to 'the most substantial literary response to Futurism ever made by a woman under direct influence of the movement'.[24]

Adopting Marinetti's favoured form, the manifesto, 'Aphorisms on Futurism' (1914) is charged with the same language of velocity, matter and collision:

> THE velocity of velocities arrives in starting.
> IN pressing the material to derive its essence, matter becomes deformed.
> AND form hurtling against itself is thrown beyond the synopsis of vision.[25]

For both writers, physics offers a pulsing language of movement and dynamic activity, expansion and contraction, that perfectly embodies their desire to smash through old ways of thinking and revivify the arts. To utilize physics is to take control of the universe. 'WHAT can you know of expansion, who limit yourself to compromise?' writes Loy, 'the smallest person, potentially, is as great as the Universe.' Mirroring the tenet of Einsteinian relativity that the faster a moving object comes to the speed of light the more compressed it appears, the second and third lines above play with the idea of material (and artistic) forms being complicated by the addition of modern force and velocity. Futurism is the

---

[23] Ibid; Lucia Re, 'Mina Loy and the Quest for a Futurist Feminist Woman', *The European Legacy* 14, no. 7 (2009), 801.
[24] Julie Schmid, 'Mina Loy's Futurist Theatre', *Performing Arts Journal* 18, no. 1 (January 1996), 1.
[25] Mina Loy, 'Aphorisms on Futurism', *Camera Work* 45 (1914), 149–52. All other quotes of 'Aphorisms' are from the same source.

means of unlocking that potential, unleashing a creativity that dominates time and space itself: 'TIME is the dispersion of intensiveness. / THE Futurist can live a thousand years in one poem.' An untitled poem from the same year condenses these ideas into a neat but evocative formula:

> There is no Space and Time
> Only intensity,
> And tame things
> Have no immensity.[26]

Where Williams embraced relativity to shape his poetic form, this poem shows Loy beginning to integrate physics as part of a wider intellectual inquiry. Aware of the dynamism of the Futurist project, Loy relates 'intensity' and 'immensity' – force and scale – in a way that mirrors both the power of Marinetti's speed and Einstein's revolutionary notion of mass-energy equivalence ($E = mc^2$). This tension between the intense and the dispersed would become an ongoing concern for Loy in later works, taking on wider spiritual connotations, but here as in 'Aphorisms', it is taken as one of the fundamental laws of the Futurist universe, a universe that is primarily physical, defined by its 'activity', the perpetual motion of material bodies, their power, dynamic interaction, and emissions. These are the forces the Futurists wanted to enlist and control, but already Loy notices a potential contradiction in this plan: if you cannot tame something without diminishing it, how can the Futurist take hold of universal force without neutralizing its creative power?

Control is central to Marinetti's language in the 'Founding and Manifesto of Futurism', and the idea that science seeks knowledge in order to bring the universe to heel is one which has inspired (and plagued) scientists for centuries. Marinetti places the artist in the role of scientist, steering humanity towards a more powerful future. In language that evokes planetary physics and engineering, Marinetti writes: 'We intend to hymn man at the steering wheel, the ideal axis of which intersects the earth, itself hurled ahead in its own race along the path of its orbit.'[27] At the intersection of plastic art, technology and literature, his movement was to be grounded in an aesthetic sense transformed and revivified by science: 'Futurism is based on the complete renewal of human sensibility

---

[26] Mina Loy, 'There Is No Life or Death', *The Lost Lunar Baedeker*, ed. Roger L. Conover (Manchester: Carcanet, 1997), 3. As Conover recounts, this poem, submitted to Alfred Stieglitz's *Camera Work* in 1914 would have been Loy's first published poem were it not for delays with the issue, which allowed 'Café du Néant' to appear earlier.

[27] Marinetti, 'The Founding and Manifesto of Futurism', 51.

that has occurred as an effect of science's major discoveries.'[28] In 'Destruction of Syntax – Radio Imagination – Words-in-Freedom' (1913), Marinetti's call to integrate the concepts of science into a new literature is not limited to the natural field of perception but pushes beyond into a new world only recently made visible by scientific instruments. Literature, he says, must take into its scope 'the infinite smallness that surrounds us, the imperceptible, the invisible, the agitation of atoms, Brownian movements, all the thrilling hypotheses and all the dominions explored by high-powered microscopes'.[29] Futurists must become scientists, and futurist science is a practice of exploration and dominion. But Marinetti does not simply want to adopt a scientific approach at the cost of the artistic, rather he seeks a synthesis: Futurist as artist-scientist, free to draw upon either mode of exploration to create innovative work. 'I want to introduce infinite molecular life into poetry not as a scientific document, but as an intuitive element. It should be mixed in with art works... since the fusion of both constitutes the integral synthesis of life.'[30] Marinetti weds the biological and the physical: the human driver is a manifestation of atomic dynamism and human intention, of man's ability to manipulate matter through technology and human will, while 'infinite molecular life' is fused with human artistic intuition. This welding of scientific observation of artistic intuition figured in the experimental language of synthesis and integration presented a path for art that was distinctly suited to modern experience.[31]

But Loy had an uncomfortable relationship with Futurism's power dynamics. While 'Aphorisms' revels in the Futurist's self-assurance, 'leap[ing] from affirmative to affirmative' to arrive 'THROUGH derision of Humanity as it appears – / TO... respect for man as he shall be – ', she was troubled by the unashamedly masculinist and misogynist frame of the Futurist movement.[32] Living among the Futurists in Italy, discussing their theories of art in the circles of Paris and Florence, and forming close bonds with their key thinkers, Marinetti and Giovanni Papini, she was adopted as the 'exceptional' woman, a term whose implications she both mocked and wrestled with in her work. In many ways

---

[28] F. T. Marinetti, 'Words-in-Freedom', in *Futurism: An Anthology*, eds. Rainey, Lawrence, Christine Poggi, et al. (New Haven, CT: Yale University Press, 2009), 143.
[29] Ibid., 147–8.
[30] Ibid.
[31] Notions of 'synthesis' had been popularized by the flurry of attempts in biology to find a synthesis of Darwinian and Mendelian theories of evolution and heredity, a central concern for biologists throughout the first half of the twentieth century. As we have seen, the term was also adopted for the second phase of Cubism.
[32] Loy, 'Aphorisms on Futurism', 150, 152.

this hypocrisy and the grandiose claims of Futurism, delivered in Marinetti's distinct, pyrotechnic style, invite satire. Loy found much to enjoy and to mock in the behaviour of these bombasts, and many of her early works lampoon the masculinist pseudo-intellectual exchanges she overheard in Florence. The futurist circle was a vibrant intellectual environment which openly attested to its own 'contempt for woman', a ferment of ideas in which Loy, as Marinetti's 'exceptional woman', stood as both insider and outsider.[33] Although, as Lucia Re has pointed out, Futurism's complex relationship with women and 'the feminine' was not limited to Marinettian misogyny, it is this particular aspect Loy fell into direct contact with and critiques in her satires.[34] In poems such as 'Three Moments in Paris' (1914), Loy often parodies her role as a woman being subjected to, rather than taking part in, these conversations. Here, she affects the bovine lethargy Marinetti objected to in the female influence:

> And sleepily I sat on your chair beside you
> Leaning against your shoulder
> …
> As your indisputable male voice   roared
> Through my brain and body
> Arguing dynamic decomposition
> Of which I was understanding nothing

Loy introduces us to the male-dominated world of the futurists, where she is passive and lethargic, but then, using the language she would later use to characterize the sum of Marinetti's influence on her, she wakes up:

> But you who make more noise than any man in the world when you clear
> your throat
> Deafening   woke me
> And I caught the thread of the argument
> Immediately assuming my personal mental attitude
> And ceased to be a woman

The tension here between intellect and lethargy, masculine and feminine. Her exasperation is obvious as male voice after male voice boom across

---

[33] F. T. Marinetti, 'Contempt for Woman' (1911), *Futurism: An Anthology*, 86; Burke, *Becoming Modern*, 2324.

[34] For a wider discussion of the female in Futurism, see Lucia Re, 'Mina Loy and the Quest for a Futurist Feminist Woman', *The European Legacy* 14, no. 7 (2009), 801.

each other, and her own involvement boils down to flippant, knowing self-dismissal – 'Anyhow who am I that I should criticize your theories of plastic velocity?'[35] But it was perhaps this exasperation, and the playfulness with which Futurism laid out its tools of war machines, technology, and physical decomposition, that kept Loy interested in working with futurist themes long after she claimed to have disavowed it.

One of the several ironies of 'Three Moments in Paris' is that Loy herself understood far from nothing of what she was hearing, and almost immediately as she joined the futurist circle, she began responding to what she heard. It appears that Loy was happy to co-opt Marinetti's scientific influences on her own terms, and her work clearly bears relation to his concerns about the representation of bodies of matter in literature. 'Be careful,' Marinetti warns:

> not to assign human sentiments to matter, but instead to divine its different governing impulses, its forces of compression, dilation, cohesion, disintegration, its heaps of molecules massed together or its electrons whirling like turbines. There is no point in creating a drama of matter that has been humanized.[36]

Loy adopts this aesthetic of dynamic movement but applies it specifically to deeply human experiences. Her poetry thereby turns the futurist mechanism of atomic dynamism inwards as a means for exploring the relationship between physical and psychic states, their boundaries and their overlap. In 'Songs to Joannes' (1917), the bodies of Loy's lovers read like humanized matter, imbued with human motivation and urgency, orbiting, attracting, fusing and reacting with one another to dramatize the physical and psychological liberation of female sexuality, its tensions and its resolutions. Take, for instance, the microcosm of attraction and repulsion in section VIII:

> Keep away from me   Please give me a push
> Don't let me understand you   Don't realise me
> Or we might tumble together
> Depersonalized
> Identical
> Into the terrific Nirvana
> Me you – you – me[37]

---

[35] Mina Loy, 'Three Moments in Paris', *The Lost Lunar Baedeker*, 15.
[36] Marinetti, 'Technical Manifesto of Futurist Literature', *Futurism: An Anthology*, 122.
[37] Loy, 'Songs to Joannes', *The Lost Lunar Baedeker*, 58.

or the way that the 'impact of lighted bodies' sends sparks into chaos in section XIV:

> Today
> Everlasting passing apparent imperceptible
> To you
> I bring the nascent virginity of
> – Myself for the moment
> No love   or the other thing
> Only the impact of lighted bodies
> Knocking sparks off each other
> In chaos[38]

Although the interaction of these bodies mirrors Marinetti's 'governing impulses' of matter, these remain love poems concerned with human romantic and sexual forces. Marinetti's particular example of rejecting the 'smiles and tears of a woman' in favour of brute construction materials makes Loy's use of physics for poems deeply grounded in female sexual experience all the more striking and ironic.[39] Contrary to Marinetti's suggestion, Loy's foregrounding of the body's material interactions generates poems charged with futurist motion and energy, and Loy develops a futurist poetics in which the female experience Marinetti rejects is centre stage.

By contrast, her futurist satires often seek to flatten male experience into parodic dramas of matter governed not by masculine will but by the inevitable forces of the physical world. If physics proved useful for the exploration of complexity in human relationships, it also offered an alternative, systematic understanding of the world that could be employed for comic effect. These 'simplifications of men', as Loy would call them, move through space like atomic marionettes, slaves to the forces they adulate.[40] Loy's response to Marinetti's call to arms was a vision of the world in which human bodies are characterized by their atomic nature, viewing the body as a site of thermodynamic and interatomic interaction. The dramatic reduction of Marinetti to a 'Man of absolute physical equilibrium' in 'Sketch of a Man on a Platform' (1914), for example, uses analogy to thermodynamics to strip the futurist of his power rather than reinforce it.[41] Loy directly satirizes her relationships with Marinetti, presenting

---

[38] Ibid., 58–9.
[39] Marinetti, 'Technical Manifesto of Futurist Literature', 122.
[40] Mina Loy, 'Human Cylinders', *The Lost Lunar Baedeker*, 40.
[41] Mina Loy, 'Sketch of a Man on a Platform', *The Lost Lunar Baedeker*, 19.

him as he invited himself to be presented, as an embodiment of his movement.[42] A stark inversion of the futurist ideal, in which man takes full mastery of his physical environment, in 'Man on a Platform' Marinetti and his movement act like free particles, pushed and pulled around by forces beyond their control. Contradicting the high speed of Marinetti's machine aesthetic, in which stasis and 'contemplative stillness' is anathema to the futurist agenda, Loy depicts the futurist as a massy object with strong gravity, rooted but inherently attractive:

> Among the men you accrete to yourself
> You are more heavy
> And more light
> Force being most equitably disposed
> Is easiest to lift from the ground

The process of accretion described here connotes a unified idea of both planetary and material growth, the massive object accumulating more and more particles through gravitational or inter-atomic attraction.

Throughout the poem, Loy satirizes the idea of physical force at the heart (both conceptually and literally) of Futurism. Marinetti's body takes on the properties of a nucleus, exerting field of force which draws men, like electrons, into an 'equitably disposed' orbit around him.[43] The final two lines above suggest that artistic movements, as they grow, must inherently diminish the individual dynamism of their central figure. In order to get Futurism off the ground, the ideas which enthuse Marinetti and make him singular must be adopted and employed equally by his followers. Thus, the very fact that the 'Man of absolute physical equilibrium' takes root anywhere means he risks becoming a danger to his own agenda. The crux, perhaps, is that Marinetti's embodied charisma – 'Your genius / So much less in your brain / Than in your body' – might eclipse any deeper theoretical purpose in his work.

Of course, Loy was not herself immune to Marinetti's attractions. They were lovers when this poem was written and, though mocking, the lines are underpinned by sexual tension, leading a section that compares Marinetti's combativeness with his sexual force. Poems like this show that Loy was deeply attentive to the deceptive power of Marinetti's charisma, but while it might be tempting to think that her resistance to the egos lying at the heart of Futurism

---

[42] Loy's other satires of Futurism can be found in Mina Loy, 'Futurism x Feminism: The Circle Squared (Poems 1914–1920)', *The Lost Lunar Baedeker*, ed. Roger L. Conover (Manchester: Carcanet, 1997), 3–46.
[43] Burke, *Becoming Modern*, 198.

allowed her to draw upon its analogies without endorsing its ideologies, this is not quite true. Conover writes that while 'it is doubtful [Loy] would have agreed with [Marinetti's] characterization of war as "the world's only hygiene", she fully embraced his enthusiasm for war and his antipathy toward pacifism'.[44] She was quick to volunteer as a nurse when war broke out in 1914, and her letters to Carl Van Vechten record her misgivings about not being able to go to the front herself. 'My masculine side longs for war', she admitted, and elsewhere protested at the lack of 'some sort of military training [for] women who want it'.[45] In her letters this 'war fever' is infused with Marinetti's influence, war seen as a virile aesthetic experience of explosive sounds and morbid delight. Loy worked, assisting surgeons, she told Van Vechten,

> entirely devoid of sentiment – entirely on the chance of getting near a battlefield & hearing a lovely noise! … You have no idea what fallow fields of psychological inspiration there are in human shrieks & screams… I will write a poem about it – & you should hear what a tramp calls the Madonna when he's having his abdomen cut open without anesthetic.[46]

The guns of war, 'the lightning agitation of molecules in the mouth of a howitzer' and 'tides of screaming faces and arms' were the vision and soundscape of Futurism as envisaged by Marinetti, for whom the developments in electrical and communication technologies driven by physics were intrinsically linked with warfare.[47] Yet these descriptions blur the line between reportage and self-fashioning, as Loy turns her thoughts to turning the scenes into poetry, linking them directly with her futurist aesthetics.

Electromagnetism and atoms, technology and machines, were the harbingers of an explosive and exciting future for humanity. Most explicitly, Marinetti's 1911 piece 'Electrical War' describes a 'haunting vision of the future' in which the world 'will be wholly revived, shaken up, and bound together by the new electric forces!'[48] The text fuses images of biological and electrical power with the assertion of a wireless future, using the image of technology's penetration of the body as a means towards positive evolution:

---

[44] Connover, *The Lost Lunar Baedeker*, 179.
[45] Cited in Ibid.
[46] Burke, *Becoming Modern*, 4018–24.
[47] F. T. Marinetti, 'Geometrical and Mechanical Splendour and the Numerical Sensibility', *Futurism: An Anthology*, 176.
[48] F. T. Marinetti, 'Electrical War', *Futurism: An Anthology*, ed. Lawrence Rainey, Christine Poggi, et al. (New Haven & London: Yale University Press, 2009), 101.

> Penetrating into every muscle, artery, and nerve of the peninsula, the energy of distant winds and rebellions of the sea have been transformed by man's genius into many millions of kilowatts, spreading everywhere yet needing no wires, their fecundity governed by the control panels, like keyboards, throbbing under the fingers of the engineers.[49]

In Marinetti's deeply masculinized world, the act of penetration is unambiguously positive and vitalizing. This is a future in which the will of *man* is liberated by *his* total mastery of the physical environment: 'Because heat and coolness and ventilation are regulated by a flick of the hand, they [the people of the future] finally know the fullness and resistant solidity of their willpower.'[50] It is a bio-electrical utopia in which electrical energy is not only restorative and fecundating but also a proponent of hastened biogenesis:

> Every car carries a gigantic steel arm on its roof that ... spreads the fecundating seed in all directions. And it is electricity that hastens its sprouting. All the atmospheric electricity hanging over us, all the incalculable electricity of the earth, has finally been harnessed ... By means of electrolysis and the multiple reactions it sets off, everywhere electricity stimulates vegetal cells ... and directly excites vegetative energy.[51]

In her 1914 play, 'The Sacred Prostitute', Loy's caricature FUTURISM mimics an auctioneer, selling a vision of the Future 'in all its sublime invisibility' to an audience of awe-stricken men who take him as 'a prophet':

> FUTURISM: Gentlemen – The FUTURE
> ... I offer you a magnificent Future – entirely constructed on speculation.[52]

The character FUTURISM interrupts a group of men's discussion about women with an explosion of gunpowder, shouting nonsense abuse reminiscent of Marinetti's famous sound poem *Zang Tumb Tuum* (1912–14); his 'every gesture propounds vulgarity intensified to Divinity', characterized by ironic adverbs 'pathetically', 'martially', 'magnificently'.[53] The female characters in the play echo the speaker of 'Three Moments in Paris', resigned in the face of FUTURISM's dogged energy, and Loy evokes the augmented futurist's 'x-ray

---

[49] Ibid., 101.
[50] Ibid., 102.
[51] Ibid.
[52] Mina Loy, 'The Sacred Prostitute', *Stories and Essays of Mina Loy*, ed. Sara Crangle (Illinois & London: Dalkey Archive Press, 2011), 193–5; accessible online at *Triple Canopy* https://www.canopycanopycanopy.com/contents/the_sacred_prostitute.
[53] Ibid., 193, 197.

eyes' and 'ears of steel' to suggest not only the vulgarity of Futurism's applications of technology – the idea that X-rays could allow vision beyond the realm of common decency was among the first popular jokes and concerns about the technology – but also the way it might blind the futurist to natural beauty:

> FUTURISM. But you have just the sort of body I like – suave.
> LOVE. (smoothing down her formless roseate garment) How do you know?
> FUTURISM. The Futurist has x-ray eyes, and ears of steel – He can see everything without looking at it, and stand any amount of noise – the evening breeze no longer reaches me, but the gentle vibrations of the *mitrailleuses* are still audible.[54]

The penetration of X-ray vision allows the futurist to ascribe a rigid bodily form to the 'formless', fluid feminine, while the sound of guns drowns out any hope of appreciating the romantic evening breeze.

To the popular imagination of the 1910s, Marinetti's futures may not have sounded inherently farfetched. One event that gestured towards the potential for an electrical future was the popular decision to award the 1909 Nobel Prize to the Italian electrical engineer Guglielmo Marconi for his achievements in the development of wireless telegraphy. As John J. White writes, the discovery and public use of telegraphy 'clearly excited the public imagination' and its potential as a new approach to communication and, by extension, poetry was of particular interest to the futurists.[55] From Italy to Russia, Futurism embraced the creative potential of wireless communication, with Marinetti championing 'lirismo telegraphic' and one Russian futurist, Velemir Khlebnikov, extolling the idea of radio as 'the main tree of consciousness', a unification of the innovations of 'the works of the artist of the pen and the artist of the brush, the discoveries of the artists of thought (Mechnikov, Einstein)'.[56] Khlebnikov's use of natural imagery here may seem uncharacteristic for the futurists; reminiscent of Darwin's 'tree of life', however, it gestures to the evolutionary imperative many futurist artists, including Loy, felt in embracing new technologies.[57] This inspiration was both conceptual and formal; for Marinetti much of the awe of this new technology was its ability to pass messages wirelessly. In 'Electrical War', Marinetti presents

---

[54] Ibid., 198.
[55] John J. White, *Literary Futurism: Aspects of the First Avant Garde* (Oxford: Clarendon Press, 1990), 148.
[56] Khlebnikov cited in White, 149; this image recalls Darwin's 'tree of life', gesturing to an evolutionary imperative behind Futurism's embrace of new technologies.
[57] For a discussion of the history and usage of the 'tree of life' metaphor, see: David P. Mindell, 'The Tree of Life: Metaphor, Model, and Heuristic Device', *Systematic Biology* 62, no. 3 (May 2013), 479–89.

wireless communication as the crowning achievement of future humanity: 'the energy of distant winds and the rebellions of the sea have been transformed by man's genius into many millions of kilowatts, spreading everywhere yet needing no wires'.[58] This vision translated into a call for poets to unlock the 'wireless imagination', freeing language and revealing its essence by removing the 'connecting wires' of traditional syntax.[59]

We saw in the last chapter that Williams's poetry reacted to modern geometries through a radical, cubistic stripping down of form. For Loy and the futurists, 'lirismo telegraphic' invited a similar, scientifically inflected form of fragmentation, in which typography, space and shape on the page held as much value as the language itself. Contemporary reviewers, such as *Poetry*'s Harriet Monroe, were often bemused by Loy's 'telegraphic' style, but telegraphy offers an example of modern physics' tangible effect upon modern day-to-day life, and of its potential application to new forms of poetry.[60] The fracturing of syntax in Loy's poetry, with its reduced punctuation and line spacing, exemplifies many of the virtues Marinetti suggests might be gained through telegraphic lyricism:

> Condensed Metaphors. – Telegraphic images. – Sums of vibrations. – Knots of thought. – Closed or open fans of movement. – Foreshortened analogies. – Color Balances. – The dimensions, weights, sizes, and velocities of sensations. – The plunge of the essential word into the water of sensibility, without the concentric eddies produced by words. – Intuition's moments of repose. – Movements in two, three, four, five different rhythms. – Analytical explanatory telegraph poles that sustain the cable of intuitive wires.[61]

This extract captures the breadth of concepts taken by the futurists from the new science: the language of condensers, telegraphy, wave theory, optics and dynamics is blurred with colour theory, musical movements, language and artistic intuition. Marinetti's theory of 'words-in-freedom' encouraged immediacy of sensation by 'brutally destroying the syntax of... speech', rejecting conventional word order and punctuation in favour of an 'assault' designed to 'render all the vibrations of [the artist's] "I"'.[62]

But in attempting to inject an 'I' into literature through the stripping back of individual stylistics or, as he puts it, 'destroying the canals of syntax',

---

[58] My emphasis.
[59] Marinetti, 'Words-in-Freedom', 145.
[60] Harriet Monroe, *Poetry*, 96, YCAL MSS 6/5, Folder 129.
[61] Marinetti, 'Words-in-Freedom', 147.
[62] Ibid., 145.

Marinetti might open up a production-line of Futurist carbon-copies, whose individual 'I' is lost along with the connecting wires. Certainly, Loy's nameless futurist figures are usually obvious stereotyped forms of Marinetti. Although Loy found value in words-in-freedom's ability to form connections through juxtaposition of nouns (for example in lines like 'Desire Suspicion Man Woman' from *Songs to Joannes*), and use of line fracture, she also used it to paint parodies of Futurism with broad strokes. 'Two Plays', published in the August 1915 issue of *Rogue*, following 'The Man on the Platform' earlier that year, parody Futurist performativity at its most stereotypical, adopting the telegraphic style that is absent from 'The Sacred Prostitute' to blur stage direction and monologue. Spanning just two pages of the journal, these mini-dramas give a brilliantly distilled example of Loy's futurist parody, her characterization of the futurist male, his ego, and his language. Here, we find a clear manifestation of the futurist utopian vision, which brings into dialogue many of the images and concerns we have discussed. The first play, 'Collision', employs Marinetti's words-in-freedom in its disjunctive language and fractured syntax, which begins in the stage directions but continues into the solitary character's speech.[63] The play opens:

> Huge hall – disparate planes, angles – whiteness – central arc-light – blaze
> Emptiness –
> But for one man –
> A dependant has shut the door –
>
> Man: 'Back! Bang door! Succession – incentive – ejection – idea – space – cleared of nothings –   leaves everything – material – exhaustless creation!'[64]

The set description brings together typically futurist features we have seen elsewhere in Loy's work; the disjunction of emptiness and dynamic angles with a central electric light that forms the core of the drama, while the fragmentation of words into small chunks on the page, devoid of syntax, gives a sense of quanta – these are the particles that make up the scene, particles which gain meaning through their juxtaposition rather than syntactical coherency. What might initially seem a shorthand list of elements on stage is complicated as the telegraphic style continues into the Man's speech, a 'succession' of words and

---

[63] Schmid, 'Mina Loy's Futurist Theatre', 4.
[64] Mina Loy, 'Two Plays', *Rogue* (August 1915), 15.

clauses drawn from the futurist register of energy, motion and dynamic creation. Drawn to the radiant electric heart of the scene, the man 'stares blankly into arc-light' before pressing an 'electric button' that instigates a series of dramatic mechanical sound and lighting effects to create a kaleidoscope of 'disharmony'.[65] This 'pandemonium' calms him as, through his engagement with electricity, he approaches a state of utopian electromagnetic transcendence:

> Man: 'At last – vibration is intensified to the requisite ratio – for every latent conscious and subconscious impulse to respond to automatically – completely – virility ceases to be implicated in disintegrant auto-stimuli – leaving the nucleus free for self-activity –
>
> Expansion – Extension – Intension –
>   CREATION – '[66]

This speech is dense with the multi-connotative language of futurist science: physical vibrations join with psychological, particularly Freudian, impulse; the language of the scientist's meticulous measurement meets automatic action; virile multiplication and growth meets disintegration; and these contradictions and collisions, 'modes of DISHARMONY', as Loy puts it, lead to an ultimate act of creation.[67] But for all its explosiveness, the futurist's success is short-lived. The play ends almost immediately after this statement with a jarringly sombre repetition:

> Out of the attained unison – a new tremor produces itself – as it graduates to the primary celerity – in a secondary Inception – the curtain falls – the curtain falls – [68]

In all this, the futurist is not so much the catalyst as a passive (if loud) voice-box for technology, acting under the trance-like inspiration of the electric light, overshadowed by the technological pyrotechnics of the moving stage machinery around him, flickering electric light, 'vari-colored shafts of lightning', 'the floor worked by propellers', and occasional explosions' threaten to swallow the willing futurist up.[69] These techniques, however, appear elsewhere in Loy's work with a much less parodic purpose, as we see when we look at 'Parturition'.

---

[65] Ibid.
[66] Ibid., 14.
[67] Ibid.
[68] Ibid.
[69] Ibid.

Physics without parody: 'Parturition' (1914)

In her long poem 'Parturition', Loy embraces the new physics to explore a more serious subject. One of the first poetic depictions of childbirth from the female perspective, 'Parturition' affords a depth to the female experience that is absent from Loy's depictions of Marinetti, in part fostered by its first-person viewpoint and lack of satire, but also by its attention to the psychic as well as physical realms of experience, which are emphasized through the 'hard, clinical, scientific, visceral, first-person description of a woman's elevated consciousness during childbirth'.[70] An in-depth reading of the poem draws out the continuities and disjunctures between Loy's use of physics and that of her futurist colleagues, demonstrating that Loy saw a deep link between physics and emotional and spiritual experience. Here we will see that physics informs 'Parturition' on several levels: the formal, the visual and the conceptual. The poem may be read as a more serious engagement with the atomically transcendent aspects of Futurism, more in line with the theories of Italian Futurism's most prolific theorist, Umberto Boccioni, than those of Marinetti. I suggest this poem lays the groundwork for many of Loy's later spiritual ideas, using physics to engage with serious contemporary concerns around new medical technologies, gendered anxieties about materiality and penetration, and the relationship between psychic and embodied experience.

'Aphorisms on Futurism' (1914) made Loy an ambassador for the movement in America when it appeared in Alfred Steiglitz's journal *Camera Work*, but already her concerns differed from those of Marinetti. Presenting a movement known for its kinetic fervour, many of 'Aphorisms' images are typically futurist, including an invitation to 'Leap into [the Future] – and it EXPLODES with Light.'[71] However, they differ from Marinetti's technological vision by apparently shifting the focus away from mechanism and modern technology towards a vision of human capacity and psychic potential, depicting a 'crisis of consciousness' resolved in terms of absorption, expansion, emotional disintegration and mental amplitude. The first-generation futurists assumed a shift of focus from human experience towards a mechanized vision of the modern world and its inhabitants as bodies of matter subject to external and internal forces. Marinetti calls for writers of 'futurist literature', therefore, to 'Destroy the "I" in literature [and] Substitute, for human psychology now exhausted, the lyrical obsession with matter'.[72] Though

---

[70] Prescott, *Poetic Salvage*, 33.
[71] Loy, 'Aphorisms on Futurism', 13–15
[72] Marinetti, 'Technical Manifesto of Futurist Literature', 122.

Loy consistently embraces electromagnetic, as well as chemical and biological, imagery, in poems like 'Parturition' she transforms them into a means of exploring rather than rejecting experiential and psychological states. 'Aphorisms on Futurism' shows some of Loy's discomfort with the futurist rejection of mind in its emphasis on 'egotism', 'mind' and 'consciousness', but her criticism is not absolute, and her writing on these themes often integrates futurist techniques and ideas.[73]

By 1914, futurist painters like Sandro Boccioni and Giacomo Balla had adapted techniques from physics into their geometry; combining the 'lines of force' found in Faraday's electromagnetic experiments with dynamic geometries of concentric circles and intersecting planes, they sought new modes of representation 'constructed on laws from science illuminated by our intuition, sensitive to new conditions of life created by scientific discoveries' which suggested that 'all is movement'.[74] The circle offered them a shorthand for the depiction of light as wave emission, and the pattern of concentric circles at the opening 'Parturition' evokes Bohr's model of the atom and the solar corona that inspired it. Loy introduces the labouring body of her speaker-subject as the radiant heart of a forcefield of pain:

> I am the centre
> Of a circle of pain
> Exceeding its boundaries in every direction
>
> The business of the bland sun
> Has no affair with me
> In my congested cosmos of agony[75]

The strength of this pain is such that the sun is 'bland' by comparison, and the speaker creates her own microcosm for which, later stanzas indicate, the birthing body is the 'pinpoint nucleus'. This sense of contention, of microcosm battling with microcosm, is mirrored in the one of Futurism's most famous depictions of electric light, Balla's *Street Light* (*Figure 3*). Symbolizing the superiority of the modern and industrial over the natural, the painting draws its techniques of representation from contemporary physics, depicting a vibrant electric light formed both of concentric circles and of lines of force, waves and particles. Electric light was reified in the futurist canon as an essential icon of the energy

---

[73] Mina Loy, 'Aphorisms on Futurism', *The Last Lunar Baedeker*, 150–1.
[74] Boccioni cited in Threlkeld, 'The Emergence of Futurism in Italy', 48.
[75] Mina Loy, 'Parturition', *The Last Lunar Baedeker*, 4–8. All references are to this edition.

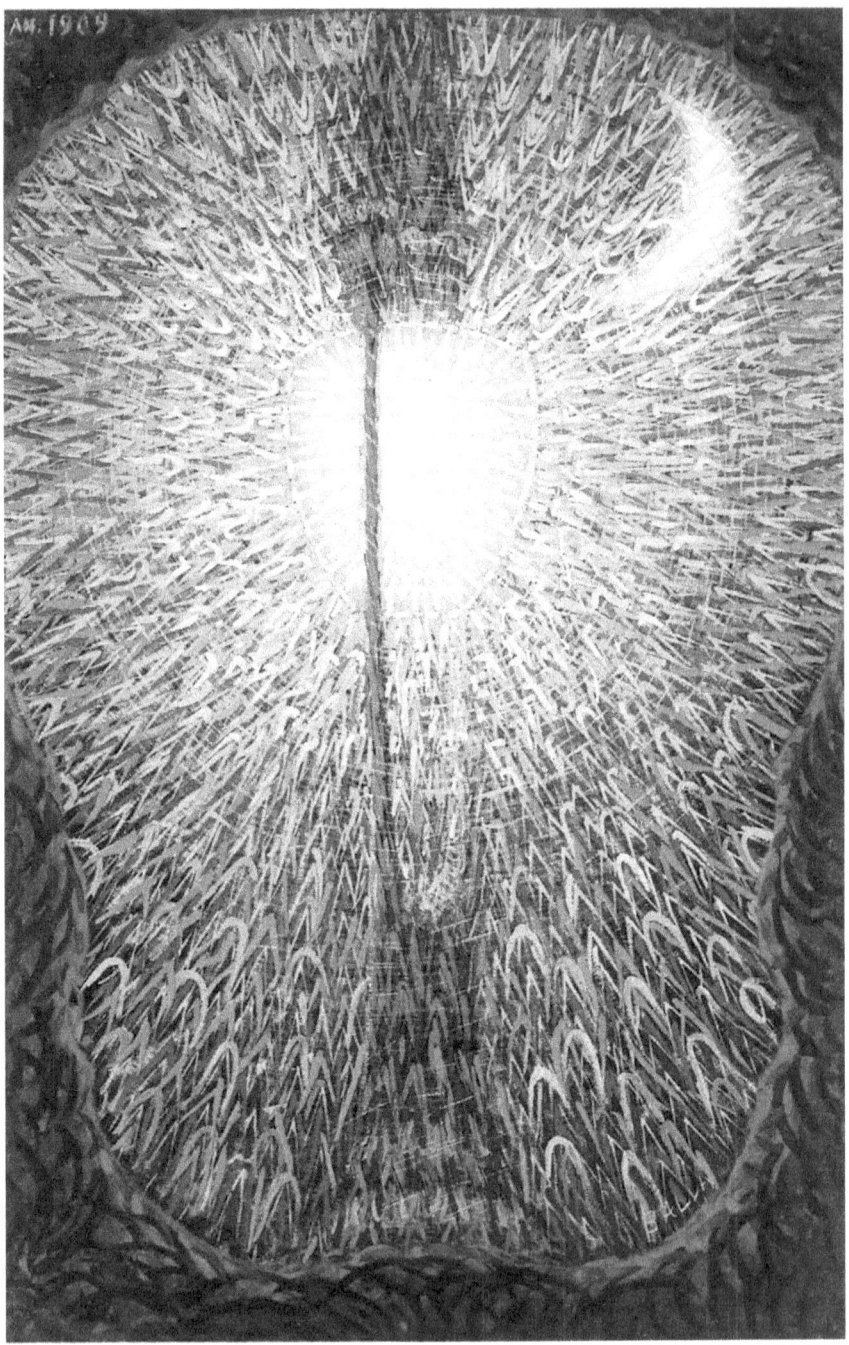

Figure 3 Giacomo Balla, *Street Light* (c. 1910–11), oil on canvas, 174.7 × 114.7 cm, The Metropolitan Museum of Art, New York, 7. 1954.

of modern life, and here the explosion of light energy from the foregrounded streetlamp subjugates the natural cosmic light of the moon. This tension, which Laura Wittman has called 'Futurism's assault on the moon', is distinctly gendered.[76] In 'Let's Murder the Moonlight' (1909), Marinetti's ecstatic call to arms, 'the carnal moon, the moon of warm beautiful thighs' is a dangerously feminine figure, 'dripping with the intoxicating milk of acacias' who brings with her the seductive anathema of tiredness and lethargy.[77] The (male) futurist's solution is to murder her with electricity, rigging electromagnetic turbines so that 'three hundred electric moons, with rays of blinding chalky whiteness, canceled [sic] the old green queen of love affairs'.[78] Loy, whose first book of poetry would be framed as a guide to the moon, subverts this opposition; challenging Marinetti's bravado, the personal, female experience in 'Parturition' eclipses the masculine sun and forms a powerful cosmos of its own. Julie Gonnering Lein has drawn attention to the heterosexual implications of electricity's reliance on the unification of opposing poles; her reading of section XII of 'Songs to Joannes' posits Loy's interest in electrical light, particularly arc light streetlamps as 'fascinating but ultimately limited models for human interaction'.[79]

In this context, the curious shadowed outline of Balla's painting, which disrupts the concentric circles of the light, might be read as the 'monstrous vulva' Marinetti describes in 'Let's Murder The Moonlight', at once a receptacle for and a challenge to the 'terrific spasm' of futurist supremacy.[80] Although the misogyny of the futurist movement posed a significant challenge for Loy, and would eventually lead her to distance herself from Marinetti's ideals, this poem offers a corrective to the futurist reduction of womanhood by engaging with the language, geometries and core images of Futurism to create a deeply layered depiction of a necessarily feminine experience. Prescott's reading of 'Parturition' attends to the gendered nature of the scientific language Loy embraces here, proposing that its use in a poem about distinctly female experience offers means of transcending gender binaries. Marinetti's hypersexualized 'monstrous vulva' finds its match in the clinical description of the dilating cervix of Loy's birthing mother.[81] She is preoccupied with the pain of parturition, rather than matters of

---

[76] Laura Wittman, 'Introduction to Part Three', *Futurism: An Anthology*, 414.
[77] Marinetti, 'Let's Murder the Moonlight', 58–9.
[78] Ibid., 59.
[79] Julie Gonnering Lein, 'Shades of Meaning: Mina Loy's Poetics of Luminous Opacity', *Modernism/modernity* 18, no. 3 (September 2011), 621–3.
[80] Marinetti, 'Let's Murder the Moonlight', 61.
[81] Prescott, *Poetic Salvage*, 35.

sun and moon, masculine and feminine. Where Loy's futurist satires challenge the hypermasculine futurist perspective by flattening it, 'Parturition' does the opposite for the female futurist.

Loy's personified and hostile cosmology fuses the interplanetary and atomic scales with the biological function of pain-receptive nerves:

> In my congested cosmos of agony
> From which there is no escape
> On infinitely prolonged nerve-vibrations
> Or in contraction
> To the pinpoint nucleus of being

Unifying physics and biology, Loy transforms the body into a microcosm of feeling, with the shift in scale mirroring the radiant pulses of the body at its centre, outward then inward to the 'pinpoint nucleus'. The image of the 'nucleus' joins the cellular and atomic diction of biology and physics, bringing the biological processes of the nervous system in line with a wider universal system, connecting the human body with the universe. This sensation eclipses solar radiation, lifeless by contrast with immediate and vital nervous experience. Interestingly here, time is subject to spatial expansion through the extension of wave vibrations. The prolongation of the 'nerve-vibrations', electrical impulses running from the point of pain to the brain where it is processed and perceived, is mirrored in poem's formal choices, with long vowels and polysyllabics 'infinitely prolonged nerve-vibrations', becoming the longest line of the stanza, before snapping back in the shortest with sudden contraction.

By 1914, the concept of the physical vibration had accrued a multitude of connotations. As Enns and Trower have shown, the distinctions between various manifestations of vibration in the modernist period – in the fields of physics, biology and spiritualism – had become increasingly blurred.[82] Linguistic elision contributed to this blurring, with 'vibration' and 'wave' used interchangeably in many circles, so that analogies which crossed between fields and forms were common. Light waves and sound waves met with brain waves and nerve vibrations in the popular imagination, gaining rapid ubiquity. 'Experiments in physics and physiology,' as they describe, 'also revealed the existence of vibrations beyond the threshold of human perception, such as X-rays and radio waves, and people suddenly became aware that the environment around them was saturated

---

[82] Anthony Enns and Shelley Trower, *Vibratory Modernism* (London: Palgrave Macmillan, 2013), 2.

with invisible and inaudible vibrations.'[83] For the futurists, vibrations symbolized the perpetual motion of matter on a scale imperceptible to the human eye, a scale to be reached for by the artist seeking new realms of representation, as Marinetti writes: 'We want to [...] scatter [the "I"] into the universal vibration and reach the point of expressing infinitely miniscule entities and molecular movements.'[84] This adulation of the vibratory world of atomic matter appears throughout Marinetti's futurist writings and formed the basis of Boccioni's foundational theories of futurist art. As I will discuss later in this chapter, vibratory physics seemed to offer scientific validity to occult phenomena, from astral projection to telepathy, drawing the attention of eminent physicists and intrigued laypeople alike. For Loy, the vibration provided a rich analogy that brought together contemporary ideas from physics, biology and spiritualism, with the idea that 'different forms or frequencies of vibration were [...] exchangeable variations of a singular universal form of energy'.[85] Perhaps influenced by her reading on the 'Theory of Vibrations' and 'Vibratory Mechanics', many of her works (including 'Parturition', 'Islands in the Air' and *Insel* discussed in this chapter) describe a fluid movement between these different frequencies, often focussed on the relationship between the human body and an external, ethereal universe.[86]

In 'Islands in the Air', birth is a process of restriction and containment: the 'winged perception ... snared in an atomic mesh'.[87] This image of embodiment as a trap is, I argue, central to Loy's understanding of the body, and usefully informs our reading of her wider desire for 'the release of atomic energy'. Using the common image of the soul as a bird, Loy gestures to the vibratory soul's resistance to embodiment: 'although it [the soul] has been ensnared in our atomic mesh, it persists as an untethered sensibility.'[88] Vibrations passing beyond the body through time and space, envisaged as a bio-electric transmission of energy, restore a lost sense of cosmic connectivity, allowing the mind to reach beyond its 'atomic mesh' and find peace and unity in a space between wavelengths. In 'Parturition', the speaker's desire to reach beyond the material into the ethereal bliss of a disembodied reality is blocked by her corporeal body: her nerves have

---

[83] Ibid., 2.
[84] Marinetti, 'Geometrical and Mechanical Splendor and the Numerical Sensibility', 176.
[85] Enns and Trower, *Vibratory Modernism*, 2.
[86] Loy's archive includes a series of notes and references to her own research and reading about vibratory mechanics, including its role in the production and transition of sound and the function of the human eye. See: YCAL MSS 778/5, Folder 158; Loy, 'Islands in the Air', 'Hurry', YCALMSS 6/4, Folder 58, 5.
[87] Mina Loy, 'The Bird Alights', 'Islands in the Air', YCALMSS 6/4, Folder 59, 9.
[88] Loy, 'The Bird Alights', 3.

their own vibrations which expand and contract, making her pain inescapable. Loy's nerve-vibrations offer a form of unification, bringing together the pulsing waves of vibratory consciousness and the bodily experience of uterine contractions to examine a unity between the psychic and physical experiences of birth. The tension between the material, biological body and wave-mind here resembles Bergson's description of psycho-physics. In *Time and Free Will* (1910), Bergson suggested that '[E]very state of consciousness corresponds to a certain disturbance of the molecules and atoms of the cerebral substance, and that the intensity of a sensation measures the amplitude, the complication or the extent of these molecular movements'.[89] Even the mind, then, cannot escape the 'atomic mesh'. A theory which fused biology and physics in an attempt to explain human consciousness, psycho-physics reinforced the idea that the body is constrained by the conditions of its own atomic structure. Fortunately for Loy, however, theories of vibration as energy emission offered hope for the expansion of human potential beyond the body, encouraging imagined futures in which the human body might function as a radio receiver for extrasensory vibrations.[90]

The constant fluctuation and dissolution of atomic matter in Loy's work figure the potential for the self to reach beyond the body alongside serious contemporary anxieties about embodiment that had been sparked by new medical technologies. For Loy, ideas of X-ray penetration and electrical stimulation of the body held simultaneously invigorating and disturbing connotations, both in medicine and in the matter of individual psycho-spiritual evolution. Rays moving in and out of the body as easily as light through air had revealed – to public astonishment – a view of the corporeal body that differed considerably from that seen with the naked eye. In the 1910 'Technical Manifesto of Futurist Painting', Boccioni was the first to draw links between X-rays and avant-garde art, particularly considering the potential of the futurist X-ray vision that Loy often parodied for the serious representation of the body in art: 'Who can still believe in the opacity of bodies... ?' He asked, 'Why should we forget in our creations the doubled power of our sight, capable of giving results analogous to the X-ray?'[91] By 1910, Röntgen rays had been used to reveal the foetus in the womb, and electrotherapies had been used to induce contractions in order to

---

[89] Henri Bergson, *Time and Free Will* (London: George Allen & Unwin Ltd., 1910), 6.
[90] Linda Dalrymple Henderson, 'Vibratory Modernism', in *From Energy to Information: Representation in Science and Technology, Art, and Literature*, ed. Bruce Clarke and Linda Dalrymple Henderson (Redwood City, CA: Stanford University Press, 2002), 128–31; Enns and Trower, *Vibratory Modernism*, 1–5.
[91] Umberto Boccioni, Carlo Carrà, Luigi Russolo, Giacomo Balla, and Gino Severini, 'Futurist Painting: Technical Manifesto', *Futurism: An Anthology*, 65.

'overcome ... atony and inertia of the uterus', blurring the previously unavoidable physical barrier between within and without, and altering the birth experience forever.[92] The X-ray's 'radically new way of seeing [broke] down the barrier that skin had always represented between outer and inner.'[93] Loy's description of conflicting forces acting upon (and within) the birthing body fuses the medical diction of the X-ray examination with modern psychology to create a complex matrix of associations.

> Locate an irritation without
> It is within
> Within
>
> It is without
> The sensitized area
> Is identical   with the extensity
> Of intension

The pressure described is both internal and external, with the medicalized language of 'Locate an irritation', 'The sensitized area', depicting a struggle between scientific clarity and the impossibility of pinpointing the location of the pain itself, which seems to pass through the body, at once inside and outside. The use of 'without' instead of 'outside', however, allows the states of 'without' and 'within' to be direct inversions of one another, forming an image of wave-like oscillation and reinforces the idea of loss and negation. Loy's use of technical terms from psychology ('extensity', 'intension'), rather than the more straightforward 'external' and 'internal', emphasizes the treatment of this section as a medical procedure treating both body and mind as 'identical'. Thus, the dissolution that follows is naturally psychic as well as bodily.

Marinetti's manifestos had encouraged a positive reception of disintegration, inviting futurists to view absolute motion as 'the result of the inherent volatility of matter with its whirring electrons and propensity to "disaggregate".'[94] The futurists suggested that blurred boundaries between previously distinct objects in space: 'Our bodies penetrate the sofas upon which we sit, and the sofas penetrate our bodies.'[95] However, the popular writings of the French

---

[92] Mihran Krikor, *Röntgen Rays and Electro-Therapeutics: With Chapters on Radium and Phototherapy*, 2nd ed. (Philadelphia & London: J. B. Lippincott & co., 1910), 362, 106.
[93] Linda Dalrymple Henderson, 'Cubism, Futurism, and Ether Physics in the Early Twentieth Century', *Science in Context* 17, no. 4 (2004), 448.
[94] Poggi, 317.
[95] Boccioni, Carrà, Russolo, et al.,'Futurist Painting', 65.

interdisciplinarian Gustave Le Bon caused public alarm by underscoring the potential for types of matter not traditionally considered radioactive to fragment and disperse, describing the 'almost universally adopted' scientific conclusion that the 'dissociation of matter – this radioactivity as it is now called – is a universal phenomenon as widely spread throughout the universe as heat or light'.[96] According to Le Bon, 'Matter is an enormous reservoir of energy,' a 'new form of energy […] intra-atomic energy', whose instability accounts for most forces in the universe: 'Matter represents a stable form of intra-atomic energy; heat, light, electricity, etc., represent instable forms of it.'[97] Consequently, however, 'Matter, hitherto deemed indestructible' was now subject to a state of continuous dematerialization.[98] For the futurists, who relished the insecurity of perpetual motion, matter was a reservoir of untapped potential and perpetually moving electrical energy. Boccioni and his colleagues were happy to declare 'that movement and light destroy the materiality of bodies'.[99] This revelation offered just the 'complete renewal of human sensibility' Marinetti described. For others, however, it offered a disturbing image of a world on the brink of atomic decay. This new threat of dissolution was persistent and vivid enough in Loy's imagination that she would go on to write 'perhaps, according to atomic physics, there is no actual flesh'.[100] The confusion of 'in' and 'out' in 'Parturition' can also be seen to dramatize the instability of other conflicting dichotomies of hope and anxiety. For instance, Loy depicts the liminal state that the birthing mother experiences through the balance between gain and loss: between life and death; peace and pain; between the doubleness of pregnancy and singularity of motherhood; between the gain of a child – a new, distinct body – and the loss of the bodily unity of the pregnant woman. This emotional experience is treated ambiguously throughout the poem so that rather than offering an unbridled celebration of new life, Loy problematizes the emotional, psychic and physical consequences of childbirth through a series of conceits that draw together and interrogate, rather than resolve, this matrix of physical and biological anxieties. These complex binaries form part of the poem's wider matrix of unified polarities, most obviously captured in terms of physics at the moment of 'climax'.

---

[96] Gustave Le Bon, *The Evolution of Matter*, trans. F. Legge (New York: Water Scott Publishing Co., 1907), 7.
[97] Ibid., 9.
[98] Ibid., 8.
[99] Boccioni, Carrà, Russolo, et al., 'Futurist Painting', 65.
[100] Mina Loy, 'History of Religion and Eros', *Stories and Essays of Mina Loy* (Ilinois & London: Dalkey Archive Press, 2011), 248.

As we have seen, the mother's body is a centre of radiant action, an epicentre at once central and outward reaching which, like Marinetti's futurist soldiers in 'Let's Murder the Moonlight', is threatened by loss of energy and movement. The act of creation is simultaneously an act of self-evacuation: if Marinetti's energy is depleted by his birth of a movement in 'Man on a Platform', Loy's new mother undergoes a far more profound experience of loss. The climactic moment of birth results in total self-negation:

> There is a climax in sensibility
> When pain surpassing itself
> Becomes exotic
> And the ego succeeds in unifying the positive and
> negative   poles of sensation
> Uniting the opposing and resisting forces
> In lascivious revelation
>
> Relaxation
> Negation of myself as a unit
>   Vacuum interlude

But beyond contrasting psychological depth of this experience and that of the male futurist in Loy's work, I suggest that the psychic and bodily dissolution experienced here gestures towards later Futurism's increasingly abstract spirituality, a strain of futurist thought that applied what Boccioni termed 'material transcendentalism' to the human subject. A student of the scientifically rooted divisionist school, an offshoot of Impressionism that sought vibrance in painting through the dissolution of colours into individual but optically interacting dots, Boccioni was the leading art theorist of the futurist movement. The fragmentation of the subject into dots or points has obvious analogies to the atom, and such a technique seemed to Boccioni and his colleagues central not only to vibrant painting, but to the continuation of painting as a medium: 'painting cannot exist today without divisionism,' they wrote, 'Divisionism, for the modern painter, must be an innate complementariness, which we deem essential and necessary.'[101] The living 'mist' created by impressionist and neo-impressionist techniques encouraged the depiction of new, scientifically appropriate perceptions of experience; in order to create art appropriate to modern experience, this suggests, one must dissolve the subject into its

---

[101] Boccioni, Carrà, Russolo, et al., 'Futurist Painting', 65.

constituent parts. Doing so opens up new possibilities. Writing on futurist sculpture, Boccioni described a hunt for forms which, by pushing beyond the emptiness of the atmosphere, might uncover new aspects of reality in previously empty space:

> The [impressionist] mist was already a step toward an atmospheric plasticity, toward a physical transcendentalism which, in turn, is another step toward the perception of analogous phenomena that have hitherto remained hidden from our obtuse sensibilities. These phenomena include perceiving the luminous emanations of our bodies […] which are reproduced in photographic plates.[102]

For artists, the X-ray had 'definitively demonstrated the inadequacy of the human eye, which detects only a small fraction (i.e. visible light) of the much larger spectrum of vibrating electromagnetic waves then being defined'.[103] In response to this shift of perception, Boccioni visualized matter as a stream of 'endless lines and currents' which 'emanate from our objects, making them live in the environment which has been created by their vibrations'.[104] As in Loy's poetry, where physical bodies intersect, collide and gain radiant influence beyond their own boundaries, the futurists' attention to the 'scattering and fusion of details' assimilates contemporary physics into a deeply atomic vision of the modern world, its experiences, its people and its interactions.

Boccioni shared Loy's concern with modern psychology, emphasizing 'states of mind', an intuitive, rather than technical, apprehension of modern science, and the synthesis of concrete and mental experience. As such, the attempt in 'Parturition' to bring a feminine 'cosmic' voice to futurist physical analogies is not as uncharacteristic of the movement as her satires might suggest. Loy's depiction of consciousness as a system of physical states is mirrored in the female futurist Maria Ginanni's 'Variations' (1917), which shares Loy's language of 'physical transcendentalism' as an expanded mode of human experience:

> I have found absolute completeness by grabbing onto your loose consistency, firefly air! Dissociating, totally scattering the atoms of my brain with your seething pullulation you bring it complete rarefaction, the perfect destruction of all exact limitations. I set sail for regions perfectly devoid of consistency – I dissolve into complete absence, Nothing. And through the abolishment of all consciousness,

---

[102] Umberto Boccioni, 'The Plastic Foundations of Futurist Sculpture and Painting', *Futurism: An Anthology*, 141.
[103] Henderson, 'Cubism, Futurism, and Ether Physics in the Early Twentieth Century', 448.
[104] Boccioni, 'The Plastic Foundations of Futurist Sculpture and Painting', 141.

of all exactitude, through this reduction of my thinking forces to their minimum,
I can instead grasp the essence of the all: the Infinite.[105]

Here, as in 'Parturition', scattering and dissolution lead to transcendence. For Loy dissolution of the self as a unit through giving birth brings a disappointing plateau of the emotions and a sense of confusion as to why the mother lives on: 'I should have been emptied of life / Giving life', followed by a sudden and immediate opening up, in which the speaker gains access to a wider plane of evolutionary understanding.[106] Just as the acquisition of followers makes Marinetti 'more heavy' (larger) and 'more light' (with less work to do, personally, as the weight is spread across the group as a whole), the radiative force of the birthing mother's experience spreads out beyond her in this moment, dissipating to leave only a 'Scarcely perceptible / Undulation', waves of new life following revelation.[107] In this moment, the 'unit' nucleus-body dissolves, becoming immaterial, pure wave-form. For Loy, as for Ginanni, the moment of transcendence is coupled with 'complete absence' and 'the abolishment of all consciousness'. The idea that physical dissolution and psychic transcendence could be brought about by bio-electromagnetic fluctuations became a recurrent and fundamental subject of Loy's metaphysics and evolutionary theories throughout her life.

Bohr's atoms were essentially unstable bodies whose primary activity was to seek balance and 'settle down in a stable state of equilibrium'; the transfer of energies, however, is an ongoing process of electron radiation and equilibrium rarely lasts, making atomic physics a much closer analogy to the restlessness of futurist perpetual motion than Marinetti's analogies to machinery.[108] For Loy, this manifests in the ability of the body to pass through and take on the behaviours of multiple states over the course of a text. 'Parturition' shows the body manipulated through a series of physical and chemical experiments: birth becomes a process of radiation, 'crystallization' and metaphysical 'intensifying', with the body at turns becoming a crystallized solid and an 'undulating' liquid, threatened with dissolution through the 'Blurring of spatial contours'.[109] The intense physical experience of giving birth is rendered as a psychological battle of the ego 'unifying' the 'positive and negative', 'opposing and resisting' forces of sensation.[110] The unification of forces here is a manifestation of Loy's play

---

[105] Maria Ginnani, 'Variations', *Futurism: An Anthology*, 467.
[106] Loy, 'Parturition', 6.
[107] Ibid.
[108] Bohr, 'On the Constitution of Molecules and Atoms', 4.
[109] Loy, 'Parturition', 5–6.
[110] Ibid., 6.

with 'contraction' in this poem, expressing the experience of a dilation and contraction moving beyond the immediate uterine action into a transcendent psychic and spiritual sphere. While the technicality of her language might be expected to distance the reader from her experience, Loy's free association between these many touchpoints from physics, medicine, chemistry, psychology and sense experience lends a scientific authority to the female experience at a time in which hard scientific language was presumed to be masculine.[111]

The changing states in 'Parturition' correspond with a shift from particle to wave form; from being the centre of a circle, the speaker gradually embraces the 'undulations' and 'waves' of the birth experience, and in doing so gains the X-ray vision of the futurist without concession to modern technology. In this poem, which so frequently alludes to the new states of contemporary physics, direct references to machines and technology are noticeably absent; the enlightenment which allows the speaker, in the aftermath of birth, to see

> Each woman-of-the-people
> Wearing a halo
> A ludicrous little halo
> Of which she is sublimely   unaware

is not the result of man-made X-ray goggles, but a natural result of the organic process of birth. As we have seen, the world of inter-atomic forces offers Loy a means of expressing deeper emotional states of 'consciousness in crises', of bodies thrown into flux by physical or affective forces.[112]

In depicting the apex of psychic and physical crisis, Loy embraces linguistic and metrical experimentation, turning her poem into its own 'ego-laboratory'. At its peak, language and perception begin to break apart as her speaker rapidly accretes knowledge in a flurry of extrasensory revelation:

> Stir of incipient life
> Precipitating into me
> The contents of the universe
> Mother I am
> Identical
> With infinite Maternity
>   Indivisible

---

[111] For a discussion of Loy's use of the masculinized scientist in opposition with the intuitive female, see: McWhorter, 'Body Matters', 13–18.
[112] Loy, 'Parturition', 8.

>   Acutely
>   I am absorbed
>   Into
> The was – is – ever – shall – be
> Of cosmic reproductivity

The fracturing of lines into single words, indented so they seem to float in space on the page, conveys at once a struggle to express a transcendent state, and the simultaneous dissolution and multiplicity Loy describes. She is both identical and infinite, gaining by her absorption into the cosmic order as she becomes aware of her participation in 'evolutionary processes' which transcend time and species.[113] Marinetti went so far as to suggest that 'only the unsyntactical poet who unlinks his words is able to penetrate to the essence of matter'.[114] Loy's formal unlinking of this choppy enjambment coalesces in the hyphenation of the liturgically inflected line that follows: 'The was – is – ever – shall – be', which contracts past, present and future into a single, almost religious, revelation of belonging.

Loy's atomic spiritualism

The non-satirical tone of 'Parturition' emerges from its links with Loy's wider spirituality which, as we will see, was no less inflected by notions of contemporary physics than were her Futurist influences. The year that Marinetti sought to convert the world to Futurism, Loy underwent a conversion of her own. Following the death of her first child, she became a Christian Scientist, a conversion that formed the base of her developing interest in spirituality and metaphysics. In 1913, Loy turned to Christian Science as a solution to her own ill-health and that of her daughter, Joella, adopting the movement's doctrines in a 'nontraditional form'.[115] A hugely popular American offshoot of Spiritualism, Christian Science emerged from the writings and teachings of Mary Baker Eddy in the second half of the nineteenth century. As Vetter explains, 'Christian Science seemed to Loy a philosophy that successfully wedded the scientific and the spiritual, and she was not alone. To the progressive thinker at the beginning

---

[113] Ibid., 6.
[114] F. T. Marinetti cited in White, *Literary Futurism*, 173.
[115] Virginia Kouidis, *Mina Loy: American Modernist Poet* (Baton Rouge: Louisiana State University Press, 1980), 7.

of the century, Christian Science was not seen as an odd religious sect but as a trendy spiritual philosophy.'[116] By the time of Loy's conversion, the movement had gained momentum to become among the fastest-growing denominations in the United States, with growing influence in Britain and Europe.[117] As Frank Podmore explains in his useful account of the history of the movement, the central tenets of Christian Science included a focus on the mind and 'the non-reality of disease, sin, matter' as according to Eddy's teaching 'these are all illusions of "mortal mind," itself having no real existence'.[118] Tied up with ideas of healing through 'mental work', Christian Science, like many of the technologies we have discussed and Loy's concern with the female body in 'Parturition', was rooted in its approach to medicine and the relationship of the human body to its atomic/material environment. Schreiber has noted the seriousness of Loy's spirituality and its increased importance in shaping her work from the 1920s onwards:

> it seems safe to say that sometime during the early 1920s Loy suffered something like a religious crisis, or a crisis of the spirit which required her to renegotiate the terms of her relationship to poetic production.[119]

Schreiber makes a convincing claim for the widespread influence of spirituality in Loy's work, noting that, as with all of her pools of influence, the poet spread her net wide, 'dipping into Christian Science, metaphysics (Bergson), theosophy, and non-denominational versions of mysticism', and freely draws on discourses from across this spectrum.[120]

Loy's cosmology embraces science's perceived links with spirituality, combining contemporary understandings of subatomic particles and electromagnetism with scientifically defunct, but still popularly espoused, ether theory. If, as John J. White suggests, 'the telegraphic dissemination of the new word of science became the technological equivalent of spreading the Gospel', it also became a wellspring for new interpretations of religiosity itself.[121] Loy's adoption of a

---

[116] Lara Vetter, 'Theories of Spiritual Evolution, Christian Science, and the "Cosmopolitan Jew": Mina Loy and American Identity', *Journal of Modern Literature* 31, no. 1 (Fall 2007), 49.
[117] According to Claire Gartrell-Mills, 'The percentage increase in the movement between 1906 and 1936 in the U.S.A. outstripped that of most other established denominations. Between 1906 and 1926, the movement grew from 635 churches to 1,913, an increase of 200 per cent, compared with a national average for all denominations of 9.4 per cent during the same period.' Claire F. Gartrell-Mills, 'Christian Science: an American Religion in Britain, 1895–1940' (unpublished doctoral thesis, University of Oxford, 1991), 34.
[118] Frank Podmore, *Mesmerism and Christian Science: A Short History of Mental Healing* (Cambridge: Cambridge University Press, 2011), 283.
[119] Meera Schreiber, 471.
[120] Ibid., 469.
[121] White, *Literary Futurism,* 148.

wider discourse of atomic physics in her spiritual writings may be read as a way of negotiating or reconsidering Christian Science's rejection of material reality in favour of something more complex and nuanced. In many ways, it was ripe for reinterpretation. Christian Science's doctrine, primarily mediated by Eddy, was largely formulated in the 1870 and 1880s, prior to the quantum discoveries that made an empirical unification of science and spirituality seem plausible. Its validity as a 'science' was easily questionable, manifesting in what Podmore identifies as 'the curious use of "Science" to connote all that other religions signify by "faith"'.[122] However, turn-of-the-century physics appeared to many to have injected an 'air of mystery, ineffability, and abstraction into scientific ways of seeing the world, overturning the nineteenth-century mechanistic, deterministic "old" physics and inviting religious interpretations of science.'[123] This fusion of science with spirituality leads Loy's Christian Science to share in what Vetter characterizes as a widespread 'Religio-Scientific Discourse' that held currency across the spectrum of esoteric spiritualisms.[124] Notions of atomic matter, energy transfer, electrical transmission, and radioactivity came to be frequently cited in spiritualist texts and journals, and as Mark Morrisson notes, 'the Theosophical society... carefully followed the experimental and theoretical works of scientists such as Crookes, Ramsay, Röntgen, Thomson, Soddy, Rutherford, and the Curies.'[125]

Many of these spiritual sources 'presented their theories in dazzling arguments couched in a pseudo-scientific terminology which were claimed to be empirically provable'.[126] The developments expounded by these physicists sparked numerous claims by spiritualists that science could not only challenge, but also *justify* occult phenomena. By the time of Loy's conversion, the complex navigation of the scientific in psychical research was nothing new. Simone Natale points out that 'throughout the nineteenth and early-twentieth century... psychical research was extraordinarily receptive to the wonders of modern technology', and as such Loy entered a spiritual environment in which psychic research and physical science shared a common language.[127] The fertility of contemporary physics for generating consecutive new and episteme-shattering technologies

---

[122] Podmore, *Mesmerism and Christian Science*, 285.
[123] Vetter, 'Theories of Spiritual Evolution, Christian Science, and the "Cosmopolitan Jew"', 1.
[124] Ibid.
[125] Mark Morrisson, *Modern Alchemy: Occultism and the Emergence of Atomic Theory* (Oxford: Oxford Scholarship Online, 2007), 67.
[126] Gartrell-Mills, 'Christian Science', ix.
[127] Simone Natale, 'A Cosmology of Invisible Fluids: Wireless, X-Rays, and Psychical Research around 1900', *Canadian Journal of Communication* 36, no. 2 (2011), 272.

was held up as justification for a continued interest in occult theories: 'If transatlantic telegraphy, electrical lighting, or airplanes were believed impossible just a few years before their invention, then, reasoned the supporters of psychical research, why could not phenomena such as clairvoyance, telepathy, and spirit communication be the scientific discoveries of tomorrow?'[128] Spiritualists took the ability of X-rays and telegraphy to reveal the invisible and communicate in defiance of previously understood physical models as a precedent through which to challenge those who would deny the validity of interest in psychical media such as spirit photography and telepathy. An invisible subatomic world had been illuminated so that, in Henderson's words, '[t]he existence of invisible realms just beyond the reach of the human eye was no longer a matter of mystical or philosophical speculation; it had been established empirically by science'.[129]

Loy addresses what she saw as a hypocrisy of belief in scientific over psychical research in her essay 'History of Religion and Eros', where she protests that

> While modern science successfully harnesses intangible phenomena inducted from the invisible Universe, the layman unquestioningly accepts the astounding results. Presented with any claim of mystic science his faith immediately reverses. He behaves as if he had never even *heard* of anything but solids.[130]

Although this is a late text, dating from the 1940s, it provides a valuable context for many of the less theorized examples of Loy's earlier atomic spirituality. This essay, unpublished during her lifetime, is Loy's most complete description of the model of metaphysics around which she bases many of her atomic images and concepts. Explicitly fusing physical, biological and spiritual being into the notion of the 'electro-life', Loy describes the way in which a person might liberate themselves from their biological constraints, breaking through the 'atomic mesh' to reach a higher state of being. She notes, too, the value of using scientific frameworks to justify and validate unorthodox views, acknowledging how the scientific context of Freud's work opened up the potential for subjects such as eros and spirituality to be taken seriously. As we will see in Chapter 3, these frameworks also offered the Baroness a similar means to explore the inner vestiges of human physical and psychic experience and articulate her own unorthodox fusion of Christianity, nihilism and materialism.

At the end of her 'History', Loy likens her own explorations of 'psychological terrain' to those of Freud who 'aided by the scientific aegis' made eros 'fashionably

---

[128] Ibid.
[129] Henderson, 'Cubism, Futurism, and Ether Physics in the Early Twentieth Century', 447.
[130] Loy, 'History of Religion and Eros', 245.

polite to mention. Clearing a way out for inhibition'.[131] This passage, in which Loy lays out her 'law' of metaphysics and the function of the modern mystic, is exemplary of the way in which Loy establishes her own scientific aegis, as multiple threads of physics infuse her spirituality with scientific authority:

> Subject to his new potency in spirit [the mystic] found the *etheric* transposal set him free from *the pull of gravity*; permitted *accelerated locomotion* without muscular effort. He gained *control of his own electric system, experimented* with its use, *the electronic transfer of his person through space*, the *projection* of his mental perceptivity to a distance, etc.: Released from the *vibrational* circumscription of the concrete whose *laws* are subordinate to *the dominant law of the Power-Universe*, he came to understand that law by which the functioning of our usual universe may be modified,
>
> (1) The *structure of matter* rearranged
> (2) The materialising function of power
> (3) The *nature of the elements* overruled by Power
> (4) Electric life reconducted within the body.[132]

I have added emphasis to highlight the sheer frequency of terms from physics used here, which I hope to tease out in this section. We will return to some of Loy's claims in due course, but for now I want to emphasize how her language of motion and velocity, mastery, control and experiment, matter, elements, vibration and electricity come together to create a fully *physical* representation of spirituality that emerged from numerous scientific, artistic and occult sources. The tone of these writings is non-satirical, and although Loy would have been aware of the considerable aspiration behind these spiritual ideas, the relative consistency of such references in her religious writings and practices does not suggest that she approached them with the irony of her earlier work. Importantly, the mastery discussed here diverges from the futurist ideas of Marinetti; though considered in terms of locomotion and electric systems, its focus is not technological or mechanical but biological and spiritual. It is allied with the self-dispersal and essential release of Loy's 'Aphorisms', situated in the deeply personal and psychic realm of the self figured in 'Parturition', and is seen as the source of a utopian future humanity, in which the species will free itself from the 'atomic mesh' through astral projection and wireless communication.

---

[131] Ibid., 251.
[132] Ibid., 241–2. My emphasis.

As I have intimated, spiritual interpretations of physics during this period were not limited to non-scientific converts. The continued perception of psychical research's validity in the popular imagination was in no small part due to the work of some of the most eminent physicists and science popularizers of the time, most notably Sir Oliver Lodge, J. J. Thomson and William Crookes. The authority of these top-tier scientists was assured by the vital roles they had each played in the development of the very technologies that had revealed the subatomic realms spiritualists hoped to investigate. Lodge was widely respected for his contributions to radio physics, including the near-simultaneous independent discovery of the radio wave at the same time as Hertz; Thomson had been awarded the 1906 Nobel Prize for Physics for the discovery of the electron; and Crookes's cathode-ray experiments were fundamental in the earlier development of atomic physics that led to this discovery. Furthermore, both Lodge and Crookes were publicly committed to scientific spiritual investigation. They both served, at different times, as President of the Society for Psychical Research, and Lodge in particular used his professional reputation and popular science writings to further arguments for the validity of psychic phenomena, including telepathy, spirit mediums and the sustained validity of the ether well into the 1930s.[133] Lodge's writing and lectures contributed a great deal to the authority and perceived validity of psychical research, and ether theory retained currency among these groups throughout the early twentieth century as a result of its retention and dissemination by such respected figures. Indeed, a retained belief in ether theory was central to Lodge's hopes for psychical research; in *The Ether of Space* (1909), for instance, he stated plainly: 'If any one thinks that ether, with all its massiveness and energy, has probably no psychical significance, I find myself unable to agree with him.'[134]

For Loy, the ether retained value as an aesthetic medium for bio-electric transmission, carrying the weight of psychic connotations it had accrued through late-nineteenth-century Spiritualism, and which was sustained by these scientists. As Henderson has described, theories of vibration, wireless transmission and a retained confidence in ether theory offered modernist writers and artists a seemingly fresh and authoritative means of explaining and exploring ideas of the ineffable.[135] Work like Lodge's gestured towards the infinite,

---

[133] Morrisson, *Modern Alchemy*, 81.
[134] Oliver Lodge, *The Ether of Space* (New York: Harper & Brothers, 1909), 123.
[135] Linda Dalrymple Henderson, 'Vibratory Modernism', *From Energy to Information: Representations in Science and Technology, Art, and Literature*, ed. Bruce Clarke and Linda Dalrymple Henderson (Stanford: Stanford University Press, 2002), 126–30.

presenting authoritative, seemingly scientific conjecture about the spiritual potential of an ethereal cosmos. In 1904, Lodge drew comparison between the atomic cosmos of the human mind and the movement of the planets, positing a model for the mind of God:

> just as the corpuscles and atoms of matter, in their intricate movements and relations, combine to form the brain cell of a human being; so the cosmic bodies, the planets and suns and other groupings of the ether, may perhaps combine to form something corresponding as it were to the brain cell of some transcendent mind.[136]

Lodge argued that the 'Mind may be incorporate or incarnate in matter, but may also transcend it', a process he linked with the dissolution and resolution of atomic matter into ether:

> A multitude of things obviously perish, thereby showing themselves to be trivial or accidental arrangements according to our hypothesis. A flame is extinguished and dies, a mountain is ultimately ground into sand by the slow influence of denudation, a planet or a sun may lose its identity by encounter with other bodies. All these are temporary collocations of atoms; but it appears now that an atom may break up into electric charges, and these again may some day be found capable of resolving themselves into pristine ether.[137]

Loy wrote of her own birth in similar terms: when it comes into being, her mind is disembodied. It is a

> sheer existance [sic] when matter scarcely perceptible and ether not entirely invisible together formed a cosmic vapour [...] The scattered currents of my mind diverted from uneasy channels united in the expectant peace of concentration when the ray of vision is about to fuse with the ray of sound.

She is an electromagnetic being formed of 'scattered currents' waiting to be resolved.[138] The elision of 'light' here in favour of 'vision' may relate to the understanding put forward by Lodge that 'Light is an electromagnetic disturbance of the ether. Optics is a branch of electricity'.[139] Vision, which resolves electromagnetic waves of light into images, therefore, might be a closer analogy for Loy than 'ray of light'.

---

[136] Oliver Lodge, '"Mind and Matter": A Criticism of Professor Haeckel (1904)', *The Hibbert Journal* 3 (New York: Harper & Brothers, 1905), 325–6.
[137] Lodge, 'Mind and Matter', 325, 322.
[138] Mina Loy, 'Islands in the Air', 'Hurry', YCALMSS 6/4, Folder 58, 1, 5.
[139] Oliver Lodge, *The Ether of Space* (New York: Harper & Brothers, 1909), 11.

This passage offers an interesting example of the way in which the boundaries of vibrational language became blurred in the popular imagination: waves and rays are elided as part of the same spectrum, allowing a surreal synaesthesia which elevates the disembodied spiritual aspects of the text. 'Ether is being found to constitute matter,' Lodge argued, quoting Thomson's formula that 'all mass is mass of the ether; all momentum, momentum of the ether; and all kinetic energy, kinetic energy of the ether.'[140] If matter is seen as a series of etheric vibrations, then sound, generated by vibrations, might be easily – if not scientifically – absorbed into the spectrum. Birth and becoming in 'Islands in the Air' is a process of restriction and containment: the 'winged perception… snared in an atomic mesh'.[141] Using the common image of the soul as a bird, Loy adds that, 'although it [the soul] has been ensnared in our atomic mesh, it persists as an untethered sensibility.'[142] As Lodge suggested, despite their embodiment, Loy imagined that the incarnate mind retains its transcendent potential.

This potential, achieved by radio-projection and re-polarization of the bio-atomic body, was heavily theorized by theosophical investigators in the first half of the twentieth century. As Morrisson discusses, occult thinkers committed thousands of hours to producing new 'scientific' models for occult phenomena and, in particular, the work of Annie Besant and Charles Leadbeater offered a popular example of these religio-scientific theories. Their 1908 study, *Occult Chemistry*, went through many editions during the period of Loy's writing and is still in print today.[143] The authors cited Crookes's research and claimed for themselves not only the ability to directly perceive 'the mechanical interactions among subatomic particles', but the 'ability to break down chemical compounds into their constituent elements and then to break apart atomic structures merely by the power of their trained and purified minds'.[144] In a claim similar to the medical miracles of mind-work seen in Christian Science doctrine, these superhuman abilities could be imagined simply as an extension of the kinds of experimental work showcased by contemporary atomic physics, where atoms were being fractured and dissected, rearranged and dissolved by scientists. 'The structure of matter rearranged' and 'the nature of elements overruled by Power' posited by Loy in her 'History', then, were not merely imaginary possibilities – from the seemingly alchemical development of commercial

---

[140] Ibid., 11.
[141] Mina Loy, 'Islands In The Air', 'The Bird Alights', YCALMSS 6/4, Folder 59, 9.
[142] Ibid., 3.
[143] Morrisson, *Modern Alchemy*, 68.
[144] Morrisson, *Modern Alchemy*, 83, 69.

electroplating in the 1850s to the generation of new synthetic elements like technetium (1936) and curium (1944), and of course the atomic bomb in 1945, scientists and engineers had been manipulating the elements in more and more alarming ways – but the notion of achieving similar effects through psychic intervention had become a growing focus for the spiritualist community.

As early as 1914, Loy had evoked mind-controlled electromagnetism to describe how 'the ego succeeds in unifying the positive and / negative poles of sensation / Uniting the opposing and resisting forces'. The invention of the radio presented Loy and others with a fruitful technological analogy to the processes of the mind and its wave emissions. Lodge was keen to promote the idea that human sensory organs were simply 'instruments for the ready appreciation of ethereal ripples', and the idea that this mechanism might be unlocked and employed for mystical purposes had held sway in occult and spiritualist circles for several decades.[145] In *Clairvoyance* (1889), Leadbeater had adopted language of the telephone, telegraph, and telescope, as well as conceiving astral perception as a 'polarization, by an effort of human will, of a number of parallel lines of astral atoms reaching from the operator to the scene which he wants to observed'.[146] In 'Parturition', as in Loy's later work, the brain is seen as 'an instrument of reception and transmission', which acts like a radio receiver, resolving conflicting forces into a unified state in the same way that a radio-set transforms incoming waves into clear sound.[147] During birth, this experience of reunification has the bio-electrical sensation of an orgasm, leading to 'lascivious revelation', offering superhuman insight. The eventual ability of the ego to overcome and to balance the bodily force of pain prefigures Loy's later image of the 'ego laboratory' in 'History', in which the mind-body make-up of the human individual allows the mystic-scientist to become a channel for a higher consciousness.[148] By harnessing the 'electro-life', she suggests in an image similar to Lodge's, a highly evolved mystic might engender an 'etheric transmutation of the mind's instrument' in which it is subject 'no longer to air' but to 'something comparable to ether, which, interpenetrating its atomic structure, liberate[s] his organism from biological law hitherto unsurmountable'.[149] She goes so far as to

---

[145] Enns and Trower, *Vibratory Modernism*, 3.
[146] Cited in Morrisson, *Modern Alchemy*, 75.
[147] Loy, 'History of Religion and Eros', 244; In a late poem, 'Brain' (1945), she explicitly figures the brain in these terms: 'Radio pulp / stacked with [myriad] microscopic / recordings of consciousness'. YCAL MSS 6, Box 5, Folder 80.
[148] Loy, 'History of Religion and Eros', 238.
[149] Ibid., 241.

suggest, in distinctly Marinettian terms, that this potential has been elicited by the conditions of American modernity: 'The man of flesh phase in evolution is giving way to the "man of electric vitality" largely through the accelerated life tempo of the United States.'[150] Energy physics therefore is not simply brought into analogy with biology, but considered a fundamental aspect of modernity and futurity, heralding human evolutionary advancement.

Extending the scope of these discoveries in physics to the human body, Loy suggests that evolution has led to some humans being born with exceptional sensitivity to 'vibrational stimuli beyond the standard gamut... A simple, rational, electrical extension endowing them with quirks of perception comparable to telepathy, television'.[151]

> It is not prohibitive to man, as the complete microcosm, to train his intelligence on his components and gain control of their potentialities. To avail himself of his resources, akin to the atomic, electronic etc. in order to transcend the restrictions of his overt senses.[152]

As Loy advanced her metaphysics, she imagined multiple visions of the future characterized by an embrace and unlocking of the potential of physics – particularly rays of varying frequencies – for spiritual expression. The quote above is characteristic of Loy's vision for the expansion of human potential. Her conception of psychophysics continued to manifest in physical terms around the 'vibratory zone of consciousness', a rippling model of spatial movement within and beyond the mind, through which the mind is able to exert itself upon the 'concrete' outside world.[153] She envisaged a mystical application for the sciences of vibratory energy, with implications for the individual and the future evolution of the species as a whole.[154] The notion of projected, often utopian, futures was a common thread of Futurism and, as Poggi notes, 'An interest in science (and pseudo-science) was common... satisfying the desire to embrace the latest forms of knowledge, and to acquire extrahuman and even psychic powers.'[155] Loy's continued interest in futurist ideas draws upon this utopian aspiration which, fused with her own religious leanings, led her to develop her own theory of electromagnetic mysticism.

---

[150] Ibid., 248.
[151] Ibid., 239.
[152] Ibid.
[153] Loy, YCAL MSS 6/7, folder 191.
[154] For a discussion of Loy's theories of human evolution, see: Vetter, 'Theories of Spiritual Evolution, Christian Science, and the "Cosmopolitan Jew"'.
[155] Poggi, 310.

The outcome of Loy's 'History', then, is a utopian future superhumanity. It presents a liberated vision of a future that shares the ascension of human will shown in Marinetti's 'Electrical War', where 'Free human intelligence reigns everywhere'.[156] Like Loy, Marinetti's human intelligence extends to complete mastery over the new physics:

> All the laws of electricity in rarefied gases have been catalogued [sic]. With surprising ease, scientists govern masses of docile electrons. The earth, which we have long known to be entirely composed of tiny electrified particles, is now regulated like an enormous Ruhmkorff generator.[157]

Loy postulates man's ability to train himself to control his own material components in order to reach a transcendent, electrical state of being.[158] For Loy, the mystic's awareness of and ability to harness the potential of his or her 'electro-life' enables access to an additional plane of existence, one in which super-sensitivity, 'absolute presence' and clairvoyance are possible. Under these conditions, the physical body transcends biological norms, becoming subject to the wave-fluctuations of the controlling electro-life, pictured as the ability of the mind to emit and receive electromagnetic 'rays'. Humanity has not only gained mastery over the new physics through technology, but by reconceptualizing their relationship with their own biology.

The final aspect of atomic spirituality I want to turn to here is the notion of atomic release. The rhetoric of dispersal and 'dynamic decomposition' seen in Futurism has mirrors in Loy's spiritual discourse, which grants deeper meaning to the 'depersonalized', intermingling and dispersed bodies in her writing. As we saw in the introduction to this chapter, the notion of the 'release of atomic energy' has especial and, I suggest, non-satirical significance for Loy that emerges from the spiritualization of physics discussed here. If we take Loy's term 'release' as a reference to the 'atomic mesh' described in 'Islands in the Air', it might refer to the dispersal and freeing of atomic and spiritual energies otherwise constrained. Throughout Loy's work, there is a sense of danger and discontent around ideas of constricted energy, whether atomic, electrical, sexual or, as often in her writing, a combination of these. In 'History', Loy discusses the importance of 'electrical release' as a kind of erotic safety valve; interestingly, she draws upon the planetary model of the atom as a backdrop for her comparison:

---

[156] Marinetti, 'Electrical War', 103.
[157] Ibid.
[158] Loy, 'History of Religion and Eros', 239, 237–53.

Even as there exist scaled approximations in the universe, such as a once-assumed structural similarity of astronomic constellations to the invisible atom, so, comparable to the mystic's electrical suffusion by the infinite élan, Eros is also an electrical release.[159]

The infinite élan – or energy of the infinite – disperses and spreads through the mystic as the mystic disperses and spreads through the universe. Mirroring Besant and Leadbeater, Loy's mystic is involved in 'identifying the microcosmic with the macrocosmic in the energy of the atom'.[160] Atomic dispersal through astral means is central to achieving this higher state, and indeed, as Schreiner notes of Loy's later work, 'Loy maintains that brokenness is the ultimate state of being.'[161] So here we see Loy celebrates three forms of interconnected diffusion – diffusion of energy through space; dispersal of the conscious mind through the universe and release of electrical energy through sexual activity. I suggest that she also has in mind a fourth form, linked with the creative dispersal of the artistic genius.

Loy's experimentation with concepts from physics was informed not only by her engagement with Futurism, but also with her own interpretation of spirituality, which came to figure spiritual liberation and transcendence in atomic terms. In the next section of this chapter, I want to discuss these dispersals, and the way in which Loy negotiates the more serious spiritualist and satirical futurist uses of physics in depiction of the artistic genius and the 'process of creative revelation' in her only novel, *Insel*.[162]

The man of electric vitality: *Insel* (1933–6)

Whenever I let him in he would halt upon the threshold drawing the whole of his luminous life up into his smile. It radiated round his face and formed a halo hovering above the rod of his rigid body. He looked like a lamppost alight.[163]

Thus enters Insel, the eponymous 'organically surreal' protagonist of Loy's only novel, whose life and state of being become the central and obsessive focus of her narrator, Mrs Jones.[164] Based on the German surrealist artist, Loy's friend,

---

[159] Ibid., 249.
[160] Ibid., 246.
[161] Schreiber, 475.
[162] Loy, 'History of Religion and Eros', 245.
[163] Mina Loy, *Insel* (Brooklyn, NY: Melville House Publishing, 2014), 31.
[164] Ibid., 178.

Richard Oelze, Insel is a radioactive puzzle, variously dissipating, reforming, dissolving and projecting throughout the text, a figure who is 'so at variance with himself [that] he exist[s] on either side of a paradox'.[165] In a distinctly futurist image, Insel appears in the doorway at once radiant and attractive; his body is a site of atomic interaction and transfer, drawing energy through it like charge through an electromagnetic field; and like the atoms of the modern age, he is a figure whose very form relies on the act of being observed. The density and range of analogies to atomic physics in Loy's conception of Insel mean that he might be seen as the apotheosis of her engagement with physics; indeed, throughout the novel, Insel's multivalent physics address most of the angles, anxieties and interests I have discussed, bringing together physics, biology, spiritualism, embodiment and artistic creativity. Set among the 1930s Parisian avant-garde, Insel is a complex novel whose tone is sometimes difficult to pin down. While its narrator shows no scepticism about the validity of Insel's electro-psychic abilities, Insel is peppered with moments of apparent hyperbole and humour. As is typical for her, Loy creates a character who is ethereal and difficult to pin down; indeed, Insel's very unfathomability is a central concern of the novel, as Jones tries (and fails) to observe, record, and map Insel's fluctuations. Throughout Insel, as I will show, Loy complicates aspirational understandings of atomic dissolution as she plays with its potential both for artistic creation and physical destruction. This section will explore the text's echoes of Loy's earlier writing, and examine the dramas of energy, electromagnetic representations of the body and the manipulation of space-time in the novel.

Composed during her acquaintance with Oelze in Paris (1933–6), Insel was originally conceived as a section of 'Islands in the Air', then developed into a novel. Echoes of 'Islands' near the beginning indicate the immediate, if unlikely, affinity between the novel's central characters. Jones's immediate impression of Insel is that 'he only looked like an embryonic mind locked in a dilapidated structure'.[166] Recalling Loy's soul trapped in an atomic mesh, this image shows a continuity in Loy's conception of the link between soul and bio-physical body. Insel's 'embryonic' mind and Loy's description of him as a 'primordial soft machine', is significant both in its suggestion of potential for growth and in its potential for variance: as Catriona Livingstone has observed, contemporary biology assigned significance to the embryo as a point of departure and a symbol of 'the

---

[165] Ibid., 16.
[166] Ibid., 3.

multiplicity of human identity', linked to evolution by recapitulation theory.[167] Like the uncertain particles of quantum mechanics, the embryo's unfixed, plastic nature made it a reservoir of potentiality, gesturing to many possible future (and past) states at once. In this Insel is a manifestation of late-Futurism's infinitely multiplied personality, which Laura Wittman, drawing quotes from Marinetti, describes as 'becoming a "harmony of electronic systems," that is, an analogical "scattering," that can "deny the distinction between spirit and matter"'.[168] Insel, an embryonic mind in a dilapidated body, is a continuation of Loy's concerns in 'History', where the tension between flesh and the 'energy of the atom' pose obstacles to the would-be mystic, that can only be overcome through astral self-dispersal.[169] Insel, the 'truly congenital surrealist', may be seen as the archetype of the mystic-artist, a figure whose constant fluctuation, variance and seeming inability to hold to any one physical state is at once the source of his magnetic and artistic power, and the root of his fleshly body's self-abnegation.[170]

Insel combines two dramas of energy: Insel's electro-psychic emission and his bodily consumption. He is at once intensely cerebral and unavoidably carnal; sitting at a restaurant, Jones muses on the conflicting impulses she feels towards the artist, in terms of polarity familiar to Loy's readers from her poetry:

> In sitting so close to Insel at the small terrace table all the filaments of what has been called the astral body, that network of vibrational force, were being drawn out of me towards a terrific magnet, while I sat unmoved beside the half-rotten looking man of flesh. My astral inclination, withheld by counteractive physical repulsion, could not gain its presumable end of flying onto that magnet – It was as though he had achieved an impossible confusion of his positive and negative polarity.[171]

Jones mirrors his variance, struggling to pin down her attraction to Insel. Moments like this become charged with a deep spiritual and emotional significance, but as they stretch into greater Surrealism invite a more ironic and humorous reading. The narrative, like the narrator, seems to be at war with itself, frequently returning to remind us of Insel's earthiness – his body which, like the boneless meat he insists on eating, is flaccid and frightening, his emaciated skull

---

[167] Ibid., 7; Catriona Livingstone, '"Embryo Lives": Virginia Woolf and Recapitulation Theory'. BSLS 13th Annual Conference, Oxford Brookes University, 6 April 2018.
[168] Wittman, 'Introduction to Part Three', 413.
[169] Loy, 'History of Religion and Eros', 246.
[170] Loy, *Insel*, 44.
[171] Ibid., 38.

resembling a death's head – while simultaneously gesturing beyond Insel's flesh towards an inner genius of 'unbelievable magnetism'.[172]

Although pushed to surrealist extremes, the root of many of Loy's analogies in the novel can be traced back to her earlier futurist experimentation; the foregrounding of electromagnetism, light and radiation, and X-rays all draw from Loy's earlier source material, so that Insel may be considered almost as organically futurist as surrealist. Insel embodies Marinetti's projections, particularly of the sensory organs as receptors for waves and electrical signals that allow X-ray insight. Describing a crowd gathered in a Paris hotel, Insel says: 'I can see right into these people... I know exactly what they are; I know what they do.'[173] In moments like this, the novel slips back towards Loy's earlier satirical handling of the avant-garde genius figure. As though with the 'x-ray eyes' of Loy's futurist parodies, Insel gains a supra-sense here it is greeted with knowing irony by the narrator:

> And that was all.
>
> As if by his sense of insight, he needed not to perceive anything specifically, his mind exposed these people as brightly illuminated 'whats.' A reaction he accepted for entire comprehension.
>
> His conceptions were like seeds fallen upon an iron girder. I noticed that I received them very much in the guise of photographic negatives so hollow and dusky they became in transmission, vaguely accentuated with inverted light –.[174]

Insel's pronouncements mirror the grandiose generalizations of the futurists: a flattened acceptance of omnipotence, which suggests that Insel's luminance is not inherent, but in part a projection or creation by the more creative narrator. The observation goes both ways: like the female figures of Loy's futurist plays and poems, Jones sees through Insel in turn, but her response is less scathing than Loy's earlier satires, offering the opportunity for a coruscating display of her own wit. The superficial, 'brightly illuminated "whats.",' likely a pun on watts as a unit of electrical power, suggests a kind of automatism behind Insel's insight, decisions made in a flash but just as easily as negatives distorted mid-development by light effects. The image of the iron girder and seeds, reminiscent of Marinetti's fecundating machines of 'Electrical War', offers a sense of natural potential (for embryonic life, for the flourishing of true insight) facing interference from the

---

[172] The significance of the death's head image is emphasized in the novel's original working title, *Der Todtenkopf*; Loy, *Insel*, 45.
[173] Ibid., 44.
[174] Ibid.

industrial landscape, an external manifestation of the dichotomy between free soul and atomic mesh.

Insel might be read as a rendering of Loy's 'man of electric vitality'; like the agricultural machines in 'Electric War' which draw down the 'all the atmospheric electricity hanging over us', he acts a lightning conductor, thrilling with energy:

> He seemed to collect electricity from the air (in the afternoon there was a violent storm). This crackling electricity flashed so nearby without attaining to me. It was as if I were *almost* leaning up against a lightning conductor.[175]

The central manifestation of Insel's artist-mystic abilities is his radiation of '*Strahlen*' or 'rays', electromagnetic psychic emissions which attenuate him to the wider universe, deepening his ability to communicate, and connecting him to a wider artistic vitality. These *Strahlen* link Insel directly with Loy's scientist-mystic allowing him access to a realm of electromagnetic and vibratory transmissions beyond the usual remit of human perception. Marking him as transcendent, Insel's *Strahlen* are the one thing which makes him palatable to Jones ('Insel was unpleasant bereft of his radiance') and are great source not only of awe, but of anxiety within the novel, their unreliability and susceptibility to interference and dissolution reflecting the creative flow of the surrealist's artistic genius. This anxiety manifests first when Jones threatens to clean Insel's suit in gasoline, Insel objects vehemently and she immediately attributes his fear to his state as an electromagnetic being:

> 'Are you afraid,' I asked, in a sudden concern for his 'rays,' 'that it would interfere with your *Strahlen*? – I'm not going to wash it. You can't short-circuit'.[176]

At the very end of the novel, this anxiety centres on the collapse and dissolution of their relationship:

> I longed to get even with Insel, to say 'I have absorbed all your *Strahlen. Now what are you going to do?*'
>
> I said nothing of the kind... for one thing one feared as above all else menacing Insel was some climax in which his depredatory radioactivity must inevitably give out.[177]

The terms of this anxiety, applied to artistic production, are similar to Loy's theories of sexual bio-physics depicted in 'Songs to Joannes' and discussed in

---

[175] Ibid., 73.
[176] Ibid., 87.
[177] Ibid., 154.

her 'History of Religion and Eros'. Loy's suggestion that sexual release acts as a 'safety valve' mirrors the danger in *Insel* of short-circuiting through a surplus build-up of electromagnetic energy within the body; the process is reminiscent of that seen in 'Parturition', where the exorbitant pain of birth is relieved by the polar unification of the charged nervous system.[178] Here, as Julie Gonnering Lein says of 'Songs to Johannes', Loy 'complicates the common modernist electro-sexual metaphor by emphasizing technology's capacity for depersonalized danger and by critiquing its rapturous aura'.[179] Analogies to the short circuit, alongside other physics metaphors of interference and communicating vessels, were popular among the surrealists, with Freudian connotations these images became favoured metaphors of disequilibrium and creative overload.[180] There is a clear coherence between these ideas and those Loy had been developing since her involvement with Futurism. Andre Breton's 'Second Manifesto of Surrealism' (1930), for instance, placed a similar rhetoric of electrical transcendence through the unification of electrical poles at the heart of the surrealist agenda:

> Just as in the physical world, a short circuit occurs when two 'poles' of a machine are joined by a conductor of little or no resistance. In poetry and in painting, Surrealism has done everything it can and more to increase these short circuits.[181]

Connecting electromagnetic behaviours with the workings of the mind, Surrealism provided a fitting context for Loy's pre-existing concerns with psychic and physical states, with natural affinities for many of her metaphysical ideas. But the representation of these ideas remains critical; in *Insel* short-circuiting is above all dangerous, connected with madness, artistic lethargy and death.

Jones develops a scientific fascination with Insel's suprahuman abilities, and her hypotheses about their source share the ideas of electro-evolution found in Loy's earlier writing. In 'History', Loy wrote of the evolutionary extension of man's ability to detect and respond to vibrations, the mystic tuning himself like a radio receiver to 'a unique current', gaining 'control of his own electric system'.[182] This is a process of 'lightening the body, ... an etheric transmutation of the mind's instrument [which] liberated that latent faculty of the mind for

---

[178] Loy, 'Parturition', 6.
[179] Lein, 'Shades of Meaning', 621; see here also for a compelling examination of Loy's electrical eros as figured in 'Songs to Joannes' and its relation to her lampshade making business ventures.
[180] Roger Shattuck, 'Love and Laughter: Surrealism Reappraised', *The History of Surrealism* (London: Penguin Books, 1978), 23.
[181] Andre Breton, 'Second Manifesto of Surrealism', in *Manifestoes of Surrealism*, trans. Richard Seaver and Helen R. Lane (Ann Arbor, MI: University of Michigan Press, 1969), 161–2.
[182] Loy, 'History of Religion and Eros', 239.

reception of a transcendent form of radio transmission'.[183] Jones considers how Insel's body might have adapted to allow such transmissions:

> Perhaps they were transmitted by his hair. I have always presumed that hair with its electric properties will not remain unutilized in a future evolution of the brain.[184]

The speaker in 'Parturition' experiences transcendent connectedness, tied up with visions of her place in the wider chain of evolution: 'For consciousness in crises races / Through the subliminal deposits of evolutionary processes'.[185] Here she feels an evolutionary connection to animals, to a 'feathered moth / laying eggs', 'a cat with / blind kittens among her legs … I am that cat', 'small animal carcasses / Covered with blue-bottles', which all share 'that same undulation of living'.[186] While here the speaker's deep connection to the natural world distances the poem from the futurist project of celebrating man's evolutionary and mechanical pre-eminence, Loy's later work on the 'electro-life' in 'History' and its manifestation in *Insel* suggest her preoccupation with a more anthropocentric adaptation of evolutionary theory, shaped by an understanding of the body as an electromagnetic organism, whose future manifestations embrace technology to attain a mode of being less situated in the biological body than in the charged air around it.

The final aspect of Insel that links him with the futurist vision of man's supremacy over his physical environment is his ability to generate and manipulate the energy-mass equivalence. Echoing Loy's earliest poem ('There is no Space and Time / Only intensity'), seen at the beginning of this chapter, Jones observes the way in which Insel 'contracted time into intensity'.[187] As Sarah Hayden notes, this capacity to generate an 'idiosyncratic time zone, applying himself variously in the novel to accelerate, decelerate and stop time', is mapped onto the strength of his electromagnetism at any given moment in the text.[188] Loy gestures to the futurist tension between aspiring to perpetual motion and the consequences of time dilation inherent in speeding up: 'He told me he had found the secret of perpetual motion if only he had the money to buy the stuff. To me it seemed he had rather discovered a slow time that must result in eternity'.[189] General

---

[183] Ibid., 241.
[184] Loy, *Insel*, 93.
[185] Loy, 'Parturition', 6; original spacing.
[186] Ibid., 6–7.
[187] Loy, *Insel*, 75.
[188] Hayden, xxvi.
[189] Loy, *Insel*, 84.

Relativity states that clocks run slower in accelerated reference frames and under the influence of gravitational fields; Insel, whose fluctuating material state also incurs a fluctuating gravity, exemplifies the exaggerated physical laws to which Loy subjects the human body. In this, we see a similar physical distortion to that created by Williams in his descriptions of Einstein's fluctuating size in the last chapter, where surreal effects were generated imposing Einsteinian spatial principles at a human scale. Like the futurist, who can challenge Time's 'dispersion of intensiveness' and 'live a thousand years in one poem', Insel's presence distils the moment and extends it into eternity.[190] He slows time, so that Jones perceives her experience with Insel as 'the longest period of [her] life', and the Einsteinian language is blended with Bergsonian reflections on memory, perceived time and *durée*: 'It is almost impossible to recover the sequence or the veritable simultaneity of the states of consciousness one experienced in the company of this uncommon derelict.'[191] Mechanistic time dissolves too, until its role in governing behaviour becomes increasingly irrelevant: 'With some effort, having breakfasted all night, we conceived the idea of going to "lunch".'[192]

Loy's drafts, held at the Beinecke Rare Book and Manuscript Library, show that despite the presence of Einsteinian distortions in her first conception of the novel, she sought to make the reference more obvious in later drafts. A scrap containing the scene below sits separate from the manuscripts with a note stating that it is to be added in the second draft:

> As I was also engaged for dinner, I asked the time. Insel who was sitting on a wooden stool stretched out his arm – it reached much further than its actual length would warrant.
>
> Behind the curtain in the corner, carefully secreted under empty boxes, neatly stacked, was his wristwatch. He did not *bring* it out – his arm seemed in some Einsteinian contraction to shorten the necessary distance for focusing the hands.[193]

This addition suggests the centrality of Einsteinian elements to Loy's conception of the character; Insel's ability to distort space and time around his physical body as it fluctuates between states of embodiment and dissolution foregrounds his atomic nature as a body of matter. As the 'man of electric vitality', he can subsume and harness physical forces as a manifestation of the 'ultimate self', of ultimate

---

[190] Loy, 'Aphorisms on Futurism', 150.
[191] Loy, *Insel*, 43.
[192] Ibid., 68.
[193] Mina Loy, YCAL MSS 6/2, Folder 31; *Insel*, 113.

modernist becoming.[194] Jones realizes that the 'prolongation of time I so often experienced in the company of Insel' manifests in moments of this ultimate self-realization where 'there was no aquarium diffusion, none of that virtually giggling attainment to Nirvana. No x-ray excursion nor any fractionation. His mediumship concentrated in a sole manifestation. This interference with time'.[195] This moment carries multiple echoes of Loy's earlier scientific language, from the collapse of cosmic macrocosm and personal microcosm, the brain as electromagnetic receiver and the soothing influence of the bio-electrically achieved absolute awareness:

> I could not make out whether the cause was a shift in the relative tempos of a cosmic and microcosmic 'pulsation,' whether *my* instant–the instant of a reductive perceiver–passed through some preponderant magnifier and enlarged, or whether a concept (became gnarled in one's brain through restriction to the brain's capacity) unwinding at leisure, was drawing my perception – infinitely soothed – along with it.[196]

Though derived from visions of a utopian future humanity, Insel's apprehension of the absolute manifest in his *Strahlen*, his powers of perception, spatio-temporal manipulation and artistic genius is by no means idealized. He is a vagrant, unattached and seemingly unattachable to the world around him, and demonstrates the stakes of higher consciousness. He does, however, represent the apotheosis of Loy's engagement with physics, bringing together the material and psychological applications of the concepts of physics seen in her earlier writing to manifest in the full-fledged Surrealist *par excellence*, an embodiment of humanized matter whose self-realization enables him to engage the full power of his being and access transcendent artistic insights.

Back to the bomb: Rethinking atomic dissolution

Returning to the question with which we started this chapter: How does Loy's conception of 'the release of atomic energy' inflect her struggle to resolve contradictions at the time of the atom bomb? An 'eccentric sense of guilt' comes over her as she is writing about 'the danger induced by extracting force from Power'. The action described in the title of the piece, 'Tuning in on the Atom

---

[194] Loy, *Insel*, 148.
[195] Ibid.
[196] Ibid.

Bomb', makes the affinity between Loy's spiritual writing, in which '[p]ower' refers to the atomically enmeshed spirit, and the extraction is a wilfully induced release of its contained energies, and the bombs' release of devastating energy through nuclear fission, palpable. 'Tuning in' is a short, but convoluted, text, only recently published in Sara Crangle's collection of Loy's works, and as such has not received any critical attention. However, I suggest its concern with practical atomic physics challenging Loy's understanding of reality, a reality she had conceived on the grounds of albeit spiritually mediated physics, highlights the value Loy placed on physics as a means of interpreting the modern world. In turn, the destruction atomic energy had wrought challenged her own conception of atomic release as a liberating and spiritually powerful experience.

Watching atomic dissolution play out, albeit from a safe distance in the newspaper headlines, casts a new and devastating light on one of the foundational concepts of Loy's lifelong philosophy.[197] The guilt she feels, I suggest, is concerned less with the human impact of the bombs as with their effect on her own spiritual quest, and her enjoyment in theorizing about it:

> Longing to regain serenity I struggle to regain serenity, to refocus a tremulous perception, to recapture my easeful surroundings – to see 'Nature' as before my inexplicable shock? explosion blast? despite a dawning premonition it might no longer prove to be enjoyable – – ... My usual warm appreciation of the concrete world disintegrated in a global disappointment – – continued in endless chain-reaction of terror transpiercing me. I could feel the former ulcer in my body revert to its origin, a sensate sore in cerebration – nauseous nucleus of fear.[198]

In some ways, 'Tuning in' portrays an extreme case of the unease with atomic dissolution seen in *Insel*; the continuous prose style, peppered with atomic language, is similar here, as are many of the surrealist effects. The difference is that the event it is attached to is fully realized and not speculative; where her earlier work ruminated on atomic *potential*, the outcome of the atomic bomb is destructive, seemingly without potential for anything more than destruction. There are echoes of Loy's earliest work in this piece – most notably, for instance, her fear manifests in medical and atomic terms as an 'ulcer' (Loy had been diagnosed with an ulcer in 1940), 'a sensate sore in cerebration', a 'nauseous nucleus of fear', reminiscent of 'Parturition's 'pinpoint nucleus' at the centre of its speaker's 'circle of pain'. Loy's guilt leads to a religious vision of evacuated

---

[197] Mina Loy, 'Mi and Lo', *Stories and Essays of Mina Loy*, 281.
[198] Loy, 'Tuning in on the Atom Bomb', 286.

space, challenged faith and dissolution; the atomic release of the bombs, far from encouraging extrasensory vision, plunges her into confusion, terror and spiritual blindness. It is also a moment of realization, that despite years of theorizing and trying to articulate her atomic-physical universe, Loy 'did not *know* the secret'.[199] Where in works such as 'Parturition' and 'History' she held atomic dissolution as a source of ultimate Power and perception, the horror of this later text is Loy's struggle with the contradiction of this realization, and the emotional reaction it evokes, with her earlier views. She faces a 'dawning premonition' that, in the wake of the atomic bomb, perceiving and writing about spirituality in the thoroughly atomic way she previously had might not be enjoyable or authoritative.

The text may be seen as an earnest struggle with faith in the face of an international crisis, but its tone remains uneven and slippery, from the punning language of the 'eccentric' and 'excentric' I discussed in my introduction to the ironic moment in which Loy determines to continue 'dropping smiled "darlings" to [her] daughter who responded, "What makes you always so damned cheerful?"' even as she insists her misery and block are baseless.[200] The latter, a thread which runs through the piece, is particularly troubling in light of the political and human devastation that triggers her reflections. Although they never slip into complete irony, these moments give the piece strange emotional disconnect, which though it might reflect the blacking out of Loy's spiritual engagement, leads to ethical questions about where, precisely, Loy's guilt comes from. Without the anchors of faith in the atomic spiritualism she has developed, the text floats about between Loy's favoured discourses of physics, psychology, biology and religion without a solid mooring, until it cuts off abruptly, with a bathetic, mid-sentence ending similar to her futurist satires:

> For weeks, I resisted, a misery so mysteriously baseless, slowly reducing to tremulous fear the terror that appeared to invade me from something endlessly surrounding me – till it faded to the annoyance of neurosis – – – – – – this lessening.[201]

The notion of loss through physical interaction runs through Loy's work, from the self-abnegation of 'Parturition' to the plateau of energy in 'Man on a Platform'. Where there is energy, Loy's work seems to say, there is also a risk of losing it. This 'lessening', material, psychological and spiritual might then seem a fitting end to Loy's experimentation with physics.

---

[199] Ibid.
[200] Ibid., 288.
[201] Ibid., 289.

As we have seen, physics offered a flexible and cutting-edge language through which Loy could characterize and make sense of the world. The connotations of energy physics in avant-garde and spiritualist circles during the period of her writing allowed her to appropriate terms and analogies for diverse purposes from caustic satire and social critique to much more serious interrogations of modern spirituality. As her interest in the spiritual evolved, so did her use of physics, becoming, into the 1940s, one of the primary models she used to interpret the world around her. The porosity of early-twentieth-century discourses of physics, the rapid development of new theories and technologies, their dual application to aspirational views of human evolution and status as a source of numerous contemporary anxieties gave Loy an ongoing, multivalent source of ideas and analogies that inflected the development her theories of art and spiritual development, and the formal texture of her writing throughout her life.

Loy's engagement with physics filtered through multiple artistic and philosophical movements; where Williams engaged with physics as an ordering principle, seeking to introduce some of its clarity and structure to the poetic line, Loy's relationship with physics was more personal, becoming entangled with her social networks, ideas about artistic creativity and her spirituality. A calling-card for modernity, scientific language and reflexive use of its concepts to open up possibilities for representing the human body as a 'body of matter' were as provocative as her unfettered descriptions of female sexuality. Together they positioned Loy at the heart of the avant-garde. This interest in transforming the concepts of physics into literary matter, present from her earliest poetry to her later autobiographical and philosophical writing, underlies her final, dramatic reaction to the atomic bomb.

For much of Loy's career, the concept of atomic dissolution held largely positive connotations of hope, creation, reproduction, expansion and transcendence. Extolled as a means of self-enlargement and power by the futurists, the new physics offered her a multivalent language of atomic bodies, radiation, force and interaction as a means to explore the complexities of modern sexuality and female experience. She saw in the systematic world of science an opportunity to lampoon the hyper-modern rhetoric of the futurists while developing her own psycho-physical cosmology, fusing scientific ideas with spiritual ideals. By contrast, the 'shattering terror' of the atom bomb demonstrated a dramatic inversion of the aspirational values Loy had long ascribed to atomic dispersal. This 'inexplicable shock', the ultimate end, perhaps, of Marinetti's trajectory of bellicose dominance over matter, rather than bringing Loy insight or control, brought 'an endless chain-reaction of terror transpiercing' her body, transforming her, in language reminiscent of 'Parturition', into a 'nauseous nucleus of fear'.[202] Having been complicit in the embrace of physics as a useful, utopian tool of modernity, the much-anticipated revelation of the atom's 'secret' – its potential for untold and inhuman destruction – jarred with Loy, forcing a reassessment of the aspirational values she and many others had previously ascribed to subatomic phenomena.

---

[202] Ibid., 286, 281.

3

The Baroness Elsa Von Freytag-Loringhoven's physical systems

During a period of convalescence in a German psychiatric hospital in the mid-1920s, the Dadaist poet and proto-performance artist Baroness Elsa von Freytag-Loringhoven wrote to her lifeline, Djuna Barnes, of her trials and aspirations. One of these sprawling, unpublished letters contains a curious suggestion that the Baroness's life – defined by its embodiment of love, art and performance – might yet take a new path:

> Oh – Djuna – how I should love-love-love- to <u>devote</u> myself to science – <u>abstract</u> science[1]

But why would a celebrated Dadaist, known for her erratic behaviour and performative irrationality, devote herself to science? The eccentric Baroness poet, made famous by her exploits in New York's Greenwich Village during the 1910s, was not the sort of person whose work one might expect to be concerned with science, abstract or otherwise. Her dramatic, maddening displays of outrageous costuming, boundary-crossing behaviour and openly demonstrative sexuality led her to be branded a madwoman more often than a genius during her lifetime. Indeed, most scholarship on the Baroness to date has focussed on the details of her life as an expatriate German, consummate New Woman, and forerunner of later-twentieth-century performance art. Such studies tend to foreground anecdotes that demonstrate her position as the embodied performance of Dada and her exceptionalism as the woman Jane Heap called 'the only one living anywhere who dresses Dada, loves Dada, lives Dada'.[2]

---

[1] Loringhoven Papers, Series II, Box I, Folder 6, 8.
[2] Jane Heap, 'Dada—', *The Little Review* 8, no. 2 (Spring 1922), 46; Such essays include: Linda Lapin, 'Dada Queen in the Bad Boys Club: Baroness Elsa von Freytag-Loringhoven', *Southwest Review* 89, nos. 2–3 (2004), 307–19; Paul Hjartarson, 'Living Dada', *ESC* 30, no. 2 (June 2004), 151–60; others have approached her through an art historical lens, focusing primarily on her role in Dada without consideration of her writings; see Eliza Jane Reilly, 'Elsa von Freytag-Loringhoven', *Woman's Art Journal* 18, no. 1 (Spring–Summer 1997), 26–33.

Although many of her poems include scientific terminology, with titles like 'Atom', 'X-Ray', 'Cosmic Chemistry' and 'Perpetual Motion', few studies of her work have attended to her poetry in any depth, and none approach her interest in science with the seriousness it deserves. Indeed, as this chapter will show, the Baroness engaged with scientific ideas throughout her career, and this letter to Barnes marks a turning away from her earlier scepticism about science towards a greater embrace of scientific ideas in her poetry.

There are a number of reasons for the relative lack of work on the Baroness: the transience of her performances, the destitution which prevented her from publishing, the impenetrability of some of her poetry and the fact that, unlike some of her contemporaries, she left only a minimal paper trail for us to work with. Paul Hjartarson and Amelia Jones have both highlighted the challenges faced by scholars who work to collage together the 'fragmented and usually hyperbolic' sources around the Baroness's work. Her poems are often dense, obscure and ecstatic, seemingly written in a fervour of passion, threading together diverse sources from reported speech to advertising slogans, ancient myths to scientific images, creating a space in which the gamut of modern experience flows freely, often without clear syntactic division. However, in focusing on her 'performative dada', scholars have not yet given sufficient attention to the contents and formal aspects of what is available in the many drafts and redrafts of her literary work.[3] With the publication of her autobiography (1992) and Irene Gammel's cultural biography of the Baroness (2002), as well as the more recent edited collection of many of her poems (*Body Sweats*, 2011), some scholars have begun to consider her poetry in its relation to translation, feminist embodiment and Dada performance.[4] Yet Robert Reiss's call in the mid-1980s for a reassessment of the Baroness's importance, in particular his insistence that 'the Baroness's output of poetry alone... is staggering [and] worth attentive reconsideration today', still stands.[5]

This chapter seeks to trace back the references to physics and scientific methodology in the Baroness's writing through a legacy of Dadaist 'playful

---

[3] Amelia Jones, *Irrational Modernism: A Neurasthenic History of New York Dada* (Cambridge, MA: MIT Press, 2004), 30; Paul Hjartarson, 'Living Dada', *ESC* 30, no. 2 (June 2004), 159.
[4] Elsa von Freytag-loringhoven, *Baroness Elsa*, ed. D.O. Spettigue and Paul I. Hjartarson (Ottawa: Oberon Press, 1992); Irene Gammel, *Baroness Elsa* (Cambridge, MA: MIT Press, 2002); Elsa von Freytag-loringhoven, *Body Sweats: The Uncensored Writings of Elsa von Freytag-Loringhoven*, ed. Irene Gammel and Suzanne Zelazo (Cambridge, MA: MIT Press, 2011); Julie Goodspeed-Chadwick, 'Reconsidering the Baroness Elsa von Freytag-Loringhoven and Kay Boyle: Feminist Aesthetics and Modernism', *Feminist Formations* 28, no. 2 (Summer 2016), 51–72.
[5] Robert Reiss, '"My Baroness": Elsa von Freytag-Loringhoven', *New York Dada*, ed. Rudolf E. Kuenzli (New York: Willis Locker & Owens, 1986), 85.

physics' that anticipated the kind of acausal thinking that emerged in physics in the mid-1920s.[6] Drawing upon ideas of cross-cultural transfer, I suggest that the scientific symbolism manipulated by the Dadaists was part of a wider cultural turn away from causality in the post-war period, which predated, and perhaps shaped, the epistemological crisis in formal theoretical physics. Dadaist works emerge in this period as laboratories of the imagination, through which artistic, social and scientific values and systems are critiqued, torn down and overwritten. In particular, I want to suggest that the Baroness's later poetry, written in English during her exile from her Dadaist compatriots during her time in Weimar Berlin, offers a fascinating insight into the wider environment of interwar Germany, a country shaped by a 'culture of crisis', where political, social and scientific tensions came to a head. In order to trace the thread of scientific thought that emerges in the Baroness's later work, I will consider first the proliferation of scientific imagery and methodologies she was exposed to as part of New York's avant-garde. We will see that explicit appropriation of science's language of systems was combined here by Dada practitioners with a wider set of anti-causal values, which later come to feature highly in the development and exposition of Quantum Mechanics in the mid-1920s. I will then go on to discuss the contents of the Baroness's poems from her Berlin period, showing how ideas from physics allowed her to construct new systems of order during a period of her life in which all 'sense-laws' appeared to be under threat.[7]

Dada's cult of indeterminacy

Before we can understand the Baroness's attitude to science, we must first examine the stance of the Dadaists towards determinist physics as an underlying system of modern cultural values. For some, the desire for indiscriminate destruction was clear. Tristan Tzara, one of the founders of the movement in Zurich, addressed by the Baroness as 'dadaboss', claimed he was 'against systems' and that 'the most acceptable system is on principle to have none.'[8] Dada's relationship to science, like its relationship to most organized systems of values,

---

[6] Linda Dalrymple Henderson, 'The *Large Glass* Anew: Reflections of Contemporary Science and Technology in Marcel Duchamp's "Hilarious Picture"', *LEONARDO* 32, no. 3 (1999), 113.
[7] Elsa von Freytag-Loringhoven, 'Selections from the Letters of Elsa Baroness von Freytag-Loringhoven', *Transition* (February 1928), 26.
[8] Gammel, *Baroness Elsa*, 298; Tristan Tzara, 'Seven Dada Manifestos', *The Dada Painters and Poets: An Anthology*, ed. Robert Motherwell (Cambridge, MA: Harvard University Press, 1989), 79.

is often perceived in terms of its negations.[9] Tzara delighted in his movement's supposed freedom from theories, academies and laboratory work.[10] 'Those who are with us,' he declared, 'preserve their freedom. We recognize no theory. We have enough cubist and futurist academies: laboratories of formal ideas.'[11] These negations betray an ambivalent relationship with the experimental and 'scientific' pretensions of modernist art which, though superficially rejected, are embraced in the Dadaists' continued use of the language of the laboratory, theories of equivalence and variation, and their critique of objective truth. Indeed, the systematic rationale of doubt that resonates throughout the Dada manifestos may be seen as an extreme, mocking reflection of the scepticism that characterizes scientific practice.

Dada grew out of the 'mass fratricide and widespread carnage' of war which, John Wrighton argues, 'unsettled the sedimentary morality of scientific determinism, institutionalised religion, [and] industrial and historical progress'.[12] It was a social as much as an artistic movement, steeped in the very systems of thought it rejected; its practitioners, particularly in the United States, engage all levels of culture with an attitude of equivalence, handling street-side toothpaste adverts with the same lack of respect as academic textbooks of non-Euclidean geometry.[13] Their art and poetry was characterized by the bombastic freedom of its subject matter, form, and materials; for the Dadaists, everything was fair game and nothing was safe. Given this, I argue that Dadaist appropriations of science offer more insight into contemporary scientific culture than might at first be apparent, and that, as Stephen Forcer points out, although

> Dada rails against rational, Positivist science and against the pseudo-progressive ends to which science is put, [it may also be seen as] a cultural adjunct and manifestation of apparently irrational experimental developments in the non-linear non-Euclidean theorization and understanding of physics and cosmology that begin to take off in the 1920s and 1930s.[14]

In fact, as we shall see, the Dadaists often positioned themselves on the fringes of science in culture, appropriating its discourses as a means of satirizing its

---

[9] Raihan Kadri, 'Dadaist Poker: The Body and the Reformation of Form', *Dada and Beyond: Vol. 1, Dada Discourses*, ed. Elza Adamowicz and Eric Robertson (New York: Rodopi, 2011), 145.
[10] John Rodker, 'Dada and Else von Freytag-Loringhoven' [sic], *The Little Review* (Summer 1920), 34.
[11] Tzara, 'Seven Dada Manifestos', 77.
[12] John Wrighton, 'The Textual Ethics of Dada: A Case Study', *Textual Practice* 31, no. 1 (2017), 118.
[13] See: Elsa von Freytag-Loringhoven, 'Subjoyride', *Body Sweats*, 99–102; Marcel Duchamp, *Readymade Malheureux* (1920); Suzanne Duchamp, *Marcel Duchamp's Unhappy Readymade* (1920).
[14] Stephen, Forcer, *Dada as Text, Thought and Theory* (Oxford: Legenda, 2005), 106.

values: science's assumed objectivity, the nature of observation and modern physics' perceived shift towards theoretical, rather than practical, questions, all come under attack in Dada, whose works claim to set fire to the whole pantheon of modern culture in favour of gratuitous chaos and irrationality.

The surrealist and art historian José Pierre noted that although 'the term [Dada] was invented in Zurich, the Dada spirit first became evident in New York', and it was here that Dada's concern with science was most evident; the proto-Dada of New York freely engaged modern technology and the theoretical sciences as a vital component in their anti-art creations.[15] Distanced from the political/actual devastation of Europe, these artists inhabited the bustling urban centre of New York, developing works which responded to the industrial machines and structures of the city, while they critiqued the increasingly commercialized art world. Indeed, Dadaist critic and writer Gabrielle Buffet Picabia characterized this period in New York by its 'ebullience of invention, of exploration beyond the realm of the visible and the rational in every domain of the mind – science, psychology, imagination'.[16] True to this, the Baroness's work was varied, freely traversing the boundaries of painting, collage, poetry, costume design, performance art and sculptural engineering. Alongside Marcel Duchamp, Man Ray, Francis Picabia and Marius de Zayas, her work shows a paradoxical tendency towards *construction*; amid the tearing down of existing norms, there is always a delight in making something new. De Zayas wrote in Alfred Steiglitz's magazine *Camera Work* that the death of art 'is not absolute but relative, and that every end is but the beginning of a new and fresh manifestation'.[17] Seeing art as invention, in 1920, the Baroness compared herself to James Joyce (beside whose controversial *Ulysses* her works were published in the *Little Review*) as an artist and 'proud engineer', and went further to declare the freedom of the artistic genius' voice to proclaim 'what scientist can only say in impersonal detached dignified quietness'.[18] As Dikran Tashjian says, 'experimentation [in New York] was not meant to be an end in itself but rather to lead to new empirical laws which, in turn, would facilitate artistic discoveries'; whether in developing new photographic techniques, reconstituting what should

---

[15] Willard Bohn, 'The Abstract Vision of Marius de Zayas', *The Art Bulletin* 62, no. 3 (September 1980), 434.
[16] Cited in Linda Dalrymple Henderson, *Duchamp in Context* (Woodstock: Princeton University Press, 1998), xx.
[17] Dickran Tashjian, *Skyscraper Primitives: Dada and the American Avant-Garde, 1910–1925* (Middletown, CT: Wesleyan University Press, 1975), 25–6.
[18] Elsa von Freytag-loringhoven, 'The Modest Woman', *The Little Review* 7, no. 2 (Summer 1920), 37, 40.

be considered art or engineering new modes of experiential performance, the Dadaists' experimentation tended towards a pattern of creative destruction.[19]

As she developed her poetic style, the Baroness also brought spontaneity and performance to the streets of Greenwich Village, presenting through elaborate costumes constructed from the detritus of the city streets and a shameless tendency for shoplifting, hypersexual antics and experimentation with found objects as sculpture, a subversive image of the living artist influx. By dramatically transforming her appearance with make-up, incorporating postage stamps, red hair lacquer and home-made costumes, including a tin-can bra, birdcage, spoons and a taillight, the Baroness challenged contemporary perceptions of womanhood and female sexuality, and made herself into an embodiment of the rapid transformations of the modern city. In this, she embodied the fluid essence of the artist seen in Loy's *Insel*. As Amelia Jones has noted, 'flux – in its tendency to overflow the bounds of rationalism – was highly threatening to modern masculinity, even, apparently, in its avant-garde guises.'[20] Before we examine the Baroness's turn towards developing a system of 'sense-laws' in her later poems, we must appreciate how the flux of her performance and sculpture intersects with emergent notions of an increasingly 'irrational' modernist science.[21] The Baroness's practice was part of a wider culture of irrationality which, in some aspects, prefigured the popular perception that, after relativity, physicists left 'rational' logic and comprehensibility behind. In this section, we will see that the core conceptual interests of New York Dada introduced the Baroness to a system of artistic value that later came also to characterize the new physics; her contemporaries' engagement with a 'scientific spirit' in art offered a foundation for the Baroness's later interest in 'abstract science'.

In 1915, when he arrived in New York, Duchamp predicted the increased presence of the 'scientific spirit' in art, suggesting that 'the twentieth century is to be still more abstract, more cold, more scientific.'[22] By the mid-1920s, this prediction had gained ground across a range of fields, as physics too became increasingly remote from concrete human experience. Nineteenth-century concerns with thermodynamics gave way to the discussion of cold, statistical notions of impossibly tiny quantum particles whose behaviour seemed to hold little regard for the scientists who attempted to describe it to a wider public. In New York's proto-Dada we see an art whose ideas and values prefigured

---

[19] Tashjian, *Skyscraper Primitives*, 31.
[20] Jones, *Irrational Modernism*, 13.
[21] Forcer, *Dada as Text, Thought and Theory*, 105.
[22] Marcel Duchamp cited in Tashjian, *Skyscraper Primitives*, 49.

these later developments in natural science and spun them into a strange world of contradictions, irrationality and a new mode of aesthetics that regularly impersonated the trappings of science to critique modern ideas about positivism, causality and the scientific method.

This 'scientific spirit' manifested in the 1910s in the writing and caricatures of Marius de Zayas, the New York–based Mexican artist whose criticism in *Camera Work* captured the 'intellectual substructure of the Dada spirit'.[23] De Zayas pioneered a pseudo-scientific, quantifying approach to visual representation. He developed an abstract, cubist-inspired system of portraiture which represented the subject's essence rather than their appearance, through a visual 'analysis' of them grounded in algebraic formulas, 'geometrical equivalents', force and trajectory.[24] By appropriating the values and linguistic tropes of contemporary science and mathematics, with the incorporation of equations and gestures to physical forces, de Zayas developed a complex system which sought to apply the 'scientific method to modern aesthetics'.[25] His abstract caricatures of Steiglitz (Figure 4) and Agnes Meyer integrate geometric forms reminiscent of futurist 'lines of force', wave imagery and algebraic equations, to create an image full of motion and the scientific flavour of modernity. Adapting the trend for projective geometries and notions of the fourth dimension popular among the cubists, de Zayas hoped to gesture towards the imperceptible realities revealed by modern physics and mathematics as a means of conveying the abstract essence of his personalities.[26] While an outspoken devotee of scientific positivism, and a self-described 'cause-and-effect speculator', de Zayas's work had an influential effect upon the particular profusion of pseudo-scientific systems that emerged in Dada.[27] His assessment that 'art is dead', and that 'its present movements are not at all indications of vitality; they are the mechanical reflex of a corpse subjected to a galvanic force', implied the need for more than a jolt if Art was to be revived.[28] Dada would step up to offer that revival; linked with ideas of force, mechanism and electricity from the start, Dada brought with it a maelstrom of variations on the theme of the mechanical corpse and the forces that governed it.[29] The

---

[23] Tashjian, *Skyscraper Primitives*, 16.
[24] Bohn, 'The Abstract Vision of Marius de Zayas', 439–40.
[25] Ibid., 440.
[26] For a wider discussion of Cubism and its interests, see Chapter One.
[27] Marius de Zayas, 'What 291 Means to Me', *Camera Work* XLVII (January 1915), 7.
[28] Marius de Zayas, 'The Sun Has Set', *Camera Work* (1911) cited inTashjian, *Skyscraper Primitives*, 25.
[29] Evident throughout the work of Picabia and Duchamp, Haussman, Ernst, and later the *cadavres exquis* of the Surrealists. See, for instance: Francis Picabia, *Fille née sans mère (Girl Born without a Mother)* (1915); Max Ernst, *Anatomie als Braut (Anatomy as Bride)* (1921); and Marcel Duchamp, *The Bride Stripped Bare by Her Bachelors, Even (La mariée mise à nu par ses célibataires, même)* (1915–1923), the latter of which I discuss later in this chapter.

Figure 4 Marius de Zayas, 'Abstract Caricature of Alfred Stieglitz,' *Camera Work* 46 (1914), 41.

Baroness toyed with this concept in her performances, attaching an electric battery light to her bustle and parading herself as a hybrid woman-machine; her early writing buzzes with references to electricity as the driving spark of sexual passion, attempting to 'collapse the rationalizing conception of the body as a machine'.[30]

In its desire to overthrow systems of order, by the late 1910s Dada had come strangely to encompass a number of themes that had become prevalent in the fluctuating world of modern physics: doubt, uncertainty, non-linearity, ambiguity and the influence of the observer upon reality. In typical contradictory fashion, these values emerged in the first instance from a denunciation of scientific logic in all its forms. Writing his 'Seven Dada Manifestos', Tzara declared war on the

---

[30] Irene Gammel and John Wrighton, '"Arabesque Grotesque": Toward a Theory of Dada Ecopoetics', *Interdisciplinary Studies in Literature and Environment* 20, no. 4 (Autumn 2013), 802; Jones, *Irrational Modernism*, 126.

tyrant Logic, 'an enormous centipede' whose 'chains kill'.³¹ He expressed disgust at the ordered world of the sciences, a world he did not recognize in his day-to-day experience:

> Science disgusts me as soon as it becomes a speculative system, loses its character of utility – that is so useless but is at least individual. I detest greasy objectivity, and harmony, the science that finds everything in order. Carry on, my children, humanity… Science says we are the servants of nature: everything is in order, make love and bash your brains in.³²

Passages like this suggest that although, as Forcer says, some of the shared ground between Dada and the sciences may not have been intended by the artists themselves, an awareness of and desire to contest modern science permeated Dada discourses not only in the New York experiments but also in Europe.³³ Tzara's rejection of speculative systems, objectivity and 'the science that finds everything in order' was perhaps more timely than inflammatory, written alongside the appearance of headlines about Einstein's Relativity that asserted the destruction of order and hitherto accepted harmony in the physical world. *The Times*, for instance, declared with confidence in 1919 what Dadaist works like Duchamp's measure-manipulating *3 Standard Stoppages* (1913) had already playfully suggested: 'a new image of the measure of length' in which there appears 'no difference between straight and crooked'.³⁴ Indeed, the backlash against Einstein's discoveries – 'a gross affront to common sense', – could often as easily be applied to the results of the Dada project as to the new science.³⁵ Flux had become a mainstay of the modern image of the universe, and by the early 1920s it seemed unlikely to be resolved, as reporters argued: 'Long ago the solid earth disintegrated beneath our feet into atoms; then we learnt that the atom is not the bedrock for which the weary mind longs in a world of flux; and now we are assured that space itself is not what it seems but "warped"'.³⁶ Reading popular articles like these, a member of the public might easily have

---

[31] Tzara, 'Seven Dada Manifestos', 80.
[32] Ibid.
[33] Forcer, *Dada as Text, Thought and Theory*, 105.
[34] Duchamp cited in Rhonda Roland Shearer and Stephen Jay Gould, 'Hidden in Plain Sight: Duchamp's *3 Standard Stoppages*, More Truly a "Stoppage" (An Invisible Mending) Than We Ever Realized', *Toutfait* (2019), https://www.toutfait.com/hidden-in-plain-sight-duchamps-3-standard-stoppagesmore-truly-a-stoppage-an-invisible-mending-than-we-ever-realized/ [Accessed 2 March 2020]; 'Einstein on His Theory', *Times* (28 November 1919) cited in Price, 26.
[35] *The Times*, cited in ibid., 27.
[36] 'Unpopular Science', *Daily News* (8 November 1919), 6.

been encouraged to think that, even in the ordered world of science, Logic's 'enormous centipede' was on its last legs.

Dada performance manifested flux in its rejection of binaries in favour of ambiguity and complementarity; the Baroness and Duchamp, for instance, challenged gender binaries with their displays of androgynous costume. The Baroness presented America with a new, subversive vision of the modern woman who embodied power, frenetic movement, and an aggressive and open sexuality that shocked a majority of her more conservative contemporaries. In fact, the first many heard of the Baroness was a salacious headline in the *New York Times* on 17 September 1910 describing her arrest for blithely venturing onto Pittsburgh's Fifth Avenue in a man's suit, smoking a cigarette. Her crime? The reporter put it simply: 'She Wore Men's Clothes.'[37] Duchamp likewise transformed himself into a living piece of gender-bending art through the creation of his feminine alter-ego, Rrose Selavy, in 1920. Selavy embodied passion, eros and femininity, as a subject, muse, artistic interlocutor and an artist in her own right (several of Duchamp's works are signed with her name rather than his), and captured the same ambiguity and genderplay the Baroness brought to New York.[38] With a maelstrom of possible readings – 'Rose, *c'est la vie*!' or '*Eros c'est la vie*!' or '*La vie en rose*' or '*arroser la vie*' – even Selavy's name embodied the love of wordplay, puns and multivalence central to Dada.

For both the Baroness and Duchamp, the unification of artist and subject, man and woman, formed part of a wider conceptual performance in which the Dadaist body was able to hold multiple and contradictory meanings: 'old/new, erotic/grotesque, European/American, human/technological, ancient/modern', becoming, as Irene Gammel has put it, 'an assemblage of paradoxes embodied in one body.'[39] If, as Tzara wrote, 'Dada places before action and above all: *Doubt*', these multivalent performances of gender fluidity challenge and inspire doubt in even the most well established of cultural systems: '*Dada* doubts all.' The Baroness and Duchamp both 'dealt more in doubt than in certainty', consciously demanding their audiences asked questions, without supplying them ready answers.[40] Provoking scepticism through playful manipulation and subversion of the viewer's expectations, costume allowed the artists to embody all-encompassing identities which not only satirized the social mores of the

---

[37] Anon, 'She Wore Mens Clothes', *The New York Times* (17 September 1910), https://home.cc.umanitoba.ca/~fgrove/bio/ill_pittsbNYTsep1910.html [Accessed 2 March 2020].
[38] See for instance Duchamp, *Why Not Sneeze, Rrose Selavy?* (1920); Duchamp, *Fresh Window* (1920).
[39] Gammel, *Baroness Elsa*, 193.
[40] Andrew Hughill, *Pataphysics: A Useless Guide* (London: The MIT Press, 2012), 160.

period but also provided a space for complete freedom of expression unbounded by any single set of ideologies. Doubt led to experimentation, which in turn led to shocking and innovative artistic discoveries that demanded a continued interrogation of accepted terms and definitions.

Dadaist doubt also questioned the seriousness of Art more widely, challenging categorical boundaries and forcing the public to re-assess what made a creation 'art'. When the Baroness's poem 'Mineself – Minesoul – And – Mine – Cast-Iron Lover' was published in the *Little Review* in 1919, it sparked debate not only about the sanity of its author but about the category of art itself. The poet-critic Lola Ridge wrote in, outraged, to demand an explanation from the editors: 'Are you hypnotized, or what, that you open the *Little Review* with such a retching assault upon Art ("The Cast-Iron Lover")?'[41] Since the establishment of Cubism, non-representational works had begun to challenge the viewer to create their own understanding of a work, and the New York Dadaists pushed this to extremes. Their non-representational sculptures, such as the Baroness's *Portrait of Marcel Duchamp* (1919), a cocktail glass loaded with feathers, metal spirals, wires and *objets trouvés*, and the mounted plumbing trap readymade she provocatively named *God* (1917), offered a profusion of possible readings.[42] They shared the quality Katherine Dreier notes of Duchamp's *Fountain* that "There are those who anxiously ask, 'Is [the artist] serious or is he joking?' Perhaps he is both! Is it not possible? ... It puts it rather up to you.'[43] *God*, photographed by the Baroness's collaborator Morton Schamberg, is a striking example of Dada's irreverent titles, creating a powerful disjunction of the aesthetic and conceptual. In naming the plumbing trap, mounting it, photographing it and declaring it art, the Baroness and Schamberg demonstrate both the absurdity and pretentiousness of the art market, and the beginnings of conceptual art which have transformed the practice ever since. For the viewer, the authorial intention of the artist is designed to direct and affix meaning to the work, signposting its relevance and directing the mind through a maze of conflicting possibilities. These works sought to push Art kicking and screaming out of the realm of representation and into a higher space of abstraction. While, as Michael Leja argues, 'discrepancies between a thing and its label initiated a particular response mechanism in many New

---

[41] Lola Ridge, 'Concerning Else von Freytag-Loringhoven', *The Little Review* 6, no. 6 (October 1919), 56.
[42] Elsa von Freytag-Loringhoven, *Portrait of Marcel Duchamp*, photograph by Charles Sheeler. The Bluff Collection.
[43] Rudolf Kuenzli and Francis Naumann (eds.), *Duchamp: Artist of the Century* (Cambridge, MA & London: MIT Press, 1996), 78.

Yorkers in 1913 – a humbug alert – that precluded aesthetic appreciation and led automatically to doubts about truthfulness',[44] moving away from descriptive titles allowed a layer of abstracted meaning to be imposed upon a piece, gesturing not to the work itself but rather to the conceptual space *around* it, challenging the viewer to question their definition of art, its purpose, and even the existence of meaning at all. Denial of the truth of these works as 'Art', paradoxically, may have been exactly the reaction the Baroness and Duchamp were aiming for.

The Baroness's critics' desire to expel her work from categorization as 'art' established her as a fascinating outsider, at once a household name, acknowledged 'legend' of Greenwich Village's avant-garde scene, and a subject of satire, confusion and repudiation. By November 1919, her work was being derided and, by some, forcibly removed from its category as Art. This was precisely the same time Einstein's theories broke out into public discourse, demanding of the interested public the same kind of urgent reconsideration of the category of Science as it moved beyond the publicly demonstrable experimental proofs of the past towards a heavily conceptual, mathematically abstract basis. As physics moved away from easily visualizable models, it too came under fire as Einstein's critics vehemently 'denied the status of a theory of physics to the theory of relativity'.[45] As we shall see, scientists seeking to engage their colleagues and the public with the new physics faced 'a counter-discourse [which] questioned the axioms of modern physics and simultaneously asserted specific demands on what constitutes science'.[46] When Oswald Spengler sat down to characterize the trend of post-war physics, doubt and the destabilization of preordained categories was at the forefront of his mind; 'Western European physics – let no one deceive himself – has reached the limit of its possibilities', he wrote, 'this is the origin of the sudden and annihilating doubt that has arisen about things that even yesterday were the unchallenged foundation of physical theory', a doubt that 'extends to the very possibility of natural science' and was beginning to manifest in the 'rapidly increasing use of enumerative and statistical methods, which aim only at the probability of results, and forego in advance the absolute exactitude of the laws of nature, as one understood it in hopeful earlier generations'.[47] For

---

[44] Michael Leja, *Looking Askance: Skepticism and American Art from Eakins to Duchamp* (London: University of California Press, 2004), 226.
[45] Milena Wazeck, *Einstein's Opponents: The Public Controversy about the Theory of Relativity in the 1920s*, trans. Geoffrey S. Koby (Cambridge: Cambridge University Press, 2014), 8.
[46] Ibid.
[47] Oswald Spengler, *The Decline of the West*, cited in Paul Forman, 'Weimar Culture, Causality, and Quantum Theory, 1918-1927: Adaptation by German Physicists and Mathematicians to a Hostile Intellectual Environment', *Historical Studies in the Physical Sciences* 3 (1971), 122.

some, it seemed that Science as well as Art was 'dead'. Indeed, by 1919–22, some theoreticians had begun to lose their certainty, expressing 'annihilating doubt' about the ultimate veracity or value of their discipline.[48] Built on a foundation of fanciful thought experiments, increasingly abstract mathematics and replacing the certainties of the past in favour of a bizarre new world of bent light and ambiguous atoms, it may have seemed to some that Physics was going the way of the Dadaists.

Dada was also fascinated by ideas of intentionality and chance; it acknowledged chance as a governing principle of lived experience and adopted it into new, aleatory working practices. Indeed, an interest in chance and probability may have provided more impetus for artists' interest in science than is often acknowledged. Maurice Raynal, art critic and friend of Picasso, for example, wrote of the appeal of the new science's emphasis on chance even upon artists who had no formal grounding in the sciences: 'If... science was a favoured subject, this was not due to any special interest in new inventions... but rather to the emphasis laid on the mysterious operations of Chance, and all that these impelled.'[49] The incorporation of chance into creation led to several of New York Dada's most influential advances, including the advent of the 'readymade'. The Baroness and Duchamp allowed the world around them to provide chance discoveries which they could transmute into art; *objets trouvés* such as *God* and *Enduring Ornament* (1913) – a 3½-inch rusted metal ring the Baroness claimed to have found on her way to marry Baron Leo von Freytag-Loringhoven at New York's City Hall – are iconic early examples of the *avant-garde* practice of unifying artistic intention and chance discovery. A symbol of marriage, *Enduring Ornament* predates Duchamp's first 'readymade', *Bottle Rack,* by a year.[50]

Both artists laid themselves open to chance as a guiding principle of their art and its extension into performance. Reflecting on Duchamp's influence on the 'modern spirit' in art, Breton offered an evocative clue to the epistemological importance of chance for the artist: 'I have seen Duchamp do an extraordinary thing, toss a coin up in the air and say "Tails I leave for America tonight, heads I stay in Paris".'[51] Breton emphasizes not the artist's wishes – '*No* indifference about

---

[48] Ibid.
[49] Maurice Raynal cited in Friedman & Donley, *Einstein as Myth and Muse*, 22.
[50] The provenance of the ready-made and Duchamp's *Fountain* have been brought into question by Gammel's autobiography and recently come under public discussion. See: Siri Hustvedt, 'A Woman in the Men's Room: When will the Art World Recognise the Real Artist behind Duchamp's Fountain?', *The Guardian* (2019), https://www.theguardian.com/books/2019/mar/29/marcel-duchamp-fountain-women-art-history [Accessed 10 December 2020].
[51] André Breton, 'Marcel Duchamp', *The Dada Painters and Poets: An Anthology*, 210.

it, it is certain that he infinitely preferred to stay or go' – but rather the magic of the 'interval', the moment of suspension and absolute uncertainty, during which the coin might fall either way.[52] In this moment, with all possibilities available, complete apprehension is possible: 'Ah! if the coin could take a month or a year to fall, how well everyone would understand us.' The process of the coin-toss then, like the interval during which the strings fell to produce *3 Standard Stoppages*, or the spontaneous walk around Greenwich Village that produces a readymade, becomes a vital aspect of the artwork itself. Dada as performed by Duchamp and the Baroness, therefore, pivoted on radical questions about the roles of certainty, uncertainty, determinism and chance in the modern world, questions which came to dominate the physical sciences by the mid-1920s. After all, within a decade of the Baroness deciding that her chance discovery, *God*, was art, Schrödinger and his colleagues would have proven – against all common sense – that chance was a foundation of the very universe, and the scientific world faced a new, disturbing interval-reality 'where nothing is any longer really certain, everything is possible and at the same time every possible position is also maintained'.[53]

Each of these concerns – overthrowing old systems; embracing ambiguity, complementarity and chance; interrogating intentionality and adopting omnipresent doubt as a method of innovation – represents part of the *zeitgeist* of the interwar period, whose influence was reflexive and transformative across cultural domains. The currency these ideas gained among artists during this period created conditions in which the Baroness could continue to explore the implications of the new physics for the aesthetic sphere. To say that science is influenced by the culture around it is as true as the fact that the art of a period is intimately informed by the contemporary understandings of the universe science describes. Indeed, 'the understanding that science is produced locally in particular cultural and social settings has become widely accepted, almost to the point of hardly requiring a proof.'[54] So, while it would be foolish to argue any direct *causation* between Dadaist strategies and the emergent ideas of quantum physics, it is essential to acknowledge the shared field in which these movements

---

[52] Ibid.
[53] Hugo Dinger (1926), cited in Forman, 'Weimar Culture, Causality, and Quantum Theory, 1918–1927', 115.
[54] Cathryn Carson, Alexei Kojevnikov, and Helmut Trischler, 'The Forman Thesis: 40 Years after', *Weimar Culture and Quantum Mechanics* (London: Imperial College Press & World Scientific, 2011), 5.

emerged as one in which these particular ideas of uncertainty, multiplicity, possibility, chance and anti-rationalism gained valuable intellectual currency.

As Forman argues, the influence of a scientific idea can be shaped by the willingness of public and specialist audiences to hear it; the modes of expression used to popularize new scientific ideas can either repulse or take hold of the popular imagination.[55] Forman's thesis is particularly useful to us not only as the paper that introduced this idea in the history of science, but because it centres precisely on the culture into which the Baroness was ejected when she was exiled to Germany in 1923.

In order to understand the shift in the Baroness's work, it is useful to examine one of her New York poems as reference her relationship with the 'scientific spirit' before she moved. By tracing how the Baroness's approach to material bodies and identity seem to change between the period of her personal and professional relationship with Marcel Duchamp in New York (1913–23), and her movement to the centre of the quantum revolution in Weimar Germany (1923–6) until her death in Paris in 1927, I argue that the construction of imaginary but parallel systems of physics offered a means of interrogating and opening up a new (multidimensional) space for meaning in a world where even empirical science seemed on the brink of crisis.

Smashing Duchamp's glass: The Baroness against the Dada scientists

Although the Baroness was literate in scientific ideas, she did not formally align her early work with them in the way she does later. The first textual evidence we have of the Baroness's exposure to and artistic interest in science emerges from her earliest published work from 1918 in *The Little Review*. Here she employed ideas of chemical reactions, material science and transmutation in an extravagant love poem, 'Love-Chemical Relationship', which in its fusion of pseudo-scientific references and oppositions lampooned Duchamp's 'scientific spirit'. Her infatuation with Duchamp – which she always claimed to have been one of the two most influential of many infatuations (the other was with William Carlos Williams) – provided the material and drive for the poem. It also shaped her decision to seek publication, which she did following Duchamp's suggestion.[56]

---

[55] Forman, 'Weimar Culture, Causality, and Quantum Theory, 1918–1927'.
[56] Gammel, *Baroness Elsa*, 469.

'Love-Chemical Relationship' offers a Dadaist examination of her connection with Duchamp, and his cool, distanced, and 'scientific' approach to art. In its critique of the masculine-coded attitude towards science she experienced first-hand, it bears striking similarities to Loy's early poems about Futurism. 'Love-Chemical Relationship' introduces a number of themes which resonate throughout the Baroness's writing, as well as providing a perspective on her relationship with Duchamp which takes in, transmutes and critiques the scientific themes and methodologies of his *Large Glass*. This poem shows the degree of the Baroness's awareness and interrogation of Duchamp's 'playful physics' project and offers a sense of how the Baroness positioned herself in opposition to the trend towards the 'scientific attitude' of Dadaist experimentation. Importantly, it shows her clear ambivalence towards the wholesale embrace of science's value for art by her contemporaries during this period.

In *The Bride Stripped Bare By Her Bachelors, Even (The Large Glass)*, the incomplete masterwork that consumed Duchamp's attention between 1913 and 1923, the artist devised a complex series of systems that embrace thermodynamic, electromagnetic, and *n*-dimensional principles to visually describe the complications, and impotence, of heterosexual desire. Framed between two sheets of glass, the machinic tableau is presented as a vital mechanism and each aspect – from the mechanical turbines of the chocolate grinder in the bottom panel to the 'love gasoline', act of 'electrical stripping' and the emissions of the Bride's 'cinematic blossoming'– is described by function in Duchamp's notes.[57] *The Large Glass* integrates many of the wider themes of Dada, including what Duchamp terms 'chance in a can', the 'regime of coincidence', spontaneity, mechanomorphic diagrams, and the manipulation and distension of physical laws to the artist's will.[58] In its diagrammatic interior, Duchamp sought a distillation of sexual desire – from its passionate outbursts and attractions to the 'molecular composition' of its elements – into a condensed visual equation, an impossible machine he subtitled 'a delay in glass'.[59] 'Love-Chemical Relationship' satirizes this aspiration of Duchamp's, offering a passionate critique of the 'scientific attitude' applied to art and showcases a tension between the Baroness's own desire to express organic, embodied existence and the artist-scientist she sees emerging out of New York Dada and its futurist influences.

---

[57] Marcel Duchamp, *The Bride Stripped Bare By Her Bachelors Even*, trans. George Herd Hamilton (London: Edition Hansjörg Mayer, 1976).
[58] Ibid.
[59] Ibid.

The poem opens with a cast list which identifies the Baroness and Duchamp as its speaker and subject:

UN ENFANT FRANÇAIS: MARCEL (A FUTURIST)
EIN DEUTSCHES KIND: ELSE (A FUTURE FUTURIST)
POPLARS – SUN – A CLAYHIGHWAY[60]

Delineating their relationship, she aligns herself to Duchamp on two axes, cultural and artistic. He is characterized as 'Un enfant francais', a child of France, she is 'ein deutsches kind', a child of Germany; he is 'a futurist', she 'a future futurist'. Kenneth Rexroth would later recall: 'Long ago when I was young I asked Marcel Duchamp', 'Would you call the Baroness a Futurist or a Dadaist?' He replied, 'She is not a Futurist. She is the future.'[61] As a 'future futurist', the Baroness may be setting herself up as a transcendent figure *beyond* Futurism, or as an aspirant futurist in the Duchampian vein. The poem offers both possibilities: the former is demonstrated by her criticisms of the lifelessness of Duchamp's 'futurist' works, while the final section of the poem indicates a risk perhaps of embodying it herself, at which point she will be forced to move beyond him: 'So long must I love it until I myself will become glass and everything around me glassy. / Then art thou I! I do not need thee any more —!' In some ways, the Baroness's late work – discussed below – bears out the latter prophecy. But here, the conclusion is reached through a series of transmutations and intellectual flourishes which place Duchamp's attitude to his work under a magnifying glass and turn it through different lights for all to see.

> The poplars whispered THINE DREAMS Marcel!
> They laughed – they turned themselves – they turned themselves
> To turn themselves – they giggled – they blabbered like thine-self –
> they smiled! they smiled WITH the sun – OVER the sun –
> BECAUSE OF the sun – with the same French lighthearted sensual
> playful MORBID smile like thineself – Marcel!
>
> Poplars thou lovedst and straight highways with the smell of
> poplars which is like leather as fine – like morocco leather in
> thine nostrils – and thine nostrils are of glass!
> Thou seest the smell uprise to the brain!

---

[60] Elsa von Freytag-Loringhoven, 'Love-Chemical Relationship', *Body Sweats*, 253–5. All quotes from this edition.
[61] Kenneth Rexroth, *American Poetry in the Twentieth Century* (New York: Herder and Herder, 1971), 77.

These first images of a country roadside, poplars lined up along the highway, coupled with the sensual depiction of their movement, dizzy with repetition and rhythm and emphatic spacing, capitalization and exclamatory punctuation, establish an organic world full of playful life. The poplars, a symbol of the flexible 'clay' of nature within the poem, are examined from all angles, their relationship to the sun ('WITH', 'OVER', 'BECAUSE OF') turned over and over. Here meanings exist in a state of flux, multiple, unfixed and ever-changing, and the sensuality and lightness of personified language ('blabbered', 'giggled' 'lighthearted', 'playful') create a sense of vitality and energy in the organic.

Duchamp's scientific sensibility and eye for detail, however, turn the sensual aspects of the scene into a subject for analysis: looking beyond sense experience, the Baroness presents a strange image of Duchamp's sense organs becoming glass, offering a transparent view of the body like an X-ray image, through which 'thou seest the smell uprise to the brain'. Her use of glass, a reference to Duchamp's favoured material, is particularly relevant to his interest in the idea of looking *through* a work of art (see, for example, *To Be Looked at (From the Other Side of the Glass) with One Eye, Close To, for Almost An Hour* (1918)). By transmuting Duchamp's body into glass, the Baroness presents him as an embodiment of his own experimental glass aesthetic, but also as a scientific machine in his own right: his glass nose becomes the lens through which sense-experience, and bodily processes, can be examined and analysed. A fascination with seeing imaginary, technological mechanisms beneath the skin runs through New York Dada, most famously appearing in Picabia's erotic mechanomorphic machine drawings, such as *Fille née sans mere* (Girl Born Without a Mother), reproduced in Steiglitz's journal *291* in 1915, and Duchamp's preliminary sketches and paintings of the Bride.[62] Transformed into a machine in the Baroness's poem, Duchamp gains a scientific perception which allows him to 'see' invisible sense processes reminiscent of the Futurist men with 'x-ray eyes' found in Loy's plays. But, as in Loy's depiction, the X-ray man loses his humanity along the way. Once the transformation is complete, Duchamp's perception is completely changed and the mobile, 'clay' world of nature undergoes a process of crystallization.

Sensual thine eyes became – slanting – closed themselves!

Thine smile turned pain – died –
Then thou diedst!

---

[62] For a fascinating interpretation of the Baroness's works in the context of the post-war machinic bodies of her male counterpoints, see Jones, *Irrational Modernism*.

Thereafter thou becamest like glass.
The poplars and the sun turned glass – they did not torture thee any more!

Everything now is glass – motionless!
THAT WAS IT THOU DISCOVERDST AND WHICH IS GIVEN TO THEE AFTER THINE DEATH – MARCEL!
...
Thou now livest motionless in a mirror!
Everything is a mirage in thee – thine world is glass – glassy!
Glassy are thine ears – thine hands – thine feet and thine face.
Of glass are the poplars and the sun.[63]

Despite the great deal of intellectual work that went into devising the pseudo-physical system at play in *The Large Glass*, the work is not a piece of kinetic sculpture; its mechanisms are symbolic, the unfinished system itself frozen between the panes of glass that make up its panels. Likewise, in the poem, the parts of Duchamp that characterize his sensibility as an artist – his sense organs and his hands – are crystallized, so that he might be seen to exist in a mirror reality where, despite his discoveries, the vitality of organic life, associated with the Baroness's deep, passionate love, is lost.

Indeed, nobody could describe *The Large Glass* as a romantic work; despite its love theme, the notes show the painstaking dissection of its subjects which, like the preliminary sketches of the Bride, grow increasingly dehumanized as the work develops. The Baroness sets herself in opposition to this, as a creature of the sensual world Duchamp once loved: 'BECAUSE I AM FAT YELLOW CLAY!' Her own body is deeply human, she says, so that despite the attractive beauty of Duchamp's glass, she is bound to her emotions: 'I must bleed – weep – laugh – ere I turn to glass and the world around me glassy!' Because of this opposition, the poem offers an ambiguous reaction to the scientific attitude of Duchamp's work. While the Baroness openly critiques the distanced and 'glassy' approach to aesthetics that comes of Duchamp's forays into scientific experimentation, the final stanza indicates the Baroness's appreciation of the work that it produces, attraction to the man who produces it and even a sense of tension between her own embodied passions and a desire to produce a similarly objective art:

Unity – Einklang – Zweifellosigkeit!
Thou art resurrected – hast won – livest – art dead!

---

[63] Elsa von Freytag-Loringhoven, 'Love-Chemical Relationship', *Body Sweats*, 253.

BUT I LOVE THEE LIKE BEFORE. BECAUSE I AM FAT YELLOW CLAY!
THEREFORE I LOVE THAT VERY THIN GLASS WITH ITS COLOR-
CHANGE; BLUE – YELLOW – PURPLE PINK.
So long must I love it until myself will become glass and everything around me glassy.

The Baroness's love remains undimmed in her appreciation of 'THAT VERY THIN GLASS WITH ITS COLOR-CHANGE', acknowledging the flexibility of the newly ascribed meanings Duchamp's conceptual work brings to artistic practice, but she also appears to value the difference in their sensibilities, suggesting that if she too were to become glassy, they would become at first indistinguishable and then rivals: 'Then art thou I! I do not need you anymore –!… Thou standest beside me – and art NOTHING beside me!' There is a sense that, while this transfiguration would be disastrous for their relationship, it would also allow the Baroness to ascend to greater artistic heights, and surpass both Duchamp, his art, and 'art' itself.

The Baroness is highly critical of this aspect of Duchamp's approach to relationships, and it is clear that she finds the attempt to reduce sexual relationships to a series of interactions between mechanical parts reductive; however, she does use similar images of physical processes in other love poems which are not directed at Duchamp. In these poems, she shows a willingness to take part in the wider machine aesthetic of Dada and Futurism, adapting its images and language into a chemistry-inflected mirror to the depictions of atomic sexuality we saw from Loy in the last chapter. In 'King Adam' (1919), for instance, from *The Little Review* the following year, the Baroness describes the would-be lover's flesh as 'crystal – transparent', an image that seems to reflect the depiction of Duchamp's 'glassy' world from the earlier poem.[64] Chests and veins pound and 'fly like sides of a bellows' as they are transformed, gesturing to the kind of mechanical transfiguration made possible by modern factories.[65] At a climactic moment in 'King Adam', the Baroness exalts:

Such mine love: electric fluid – current to thine wire – to make
    Light –
Ah – h – h – such mine love![66]

---

[64] Elsa von Freytag-Loringhoven, 'King Adam', *Body Sweats*, 56.
[65] Ibid., 55.
[66] Ibid., 56.

The same image appears at the end of 'Moving-Picture and Prayer' (1919), where sexual love is exalted as an electrical charge ('A-H-H-H WHAT ELSE IS LOVE – BUT ELECTRICITY!'), amid images of transmutation in which bodies melt, smash together, freeze and burn.[67] Like Duchamp turning to glass, the lover's blood in 'Moving-Picture and Prayer' is crystallized, becoming a 'wall of shimmering crystalblood around him', another glassy barrier that precludes contact between the lover and her beloved.[68]

In sections like this, the Baroness figures herself in the function of Duchamp's Bride, a mechano-physical part in a wider system of sexual physics. This is carried further in her poem-manifesto 'The Modest Woman' (1920) where, as Richard Cavell has suggested, 'Elsa represented her notion of the interface between the mechanical and the organic, the abstract and the sensual, the fixed point of view and multiple points of view.'[69] Defending James Joyce against claims of vulgarity of which she could also be accused, the Baroness subverts misogynist images of the female mechanized body presented by artists like Picabia, displaying her body as a machine over which she has ownership and control: 'Why should I – proud engineer – be ashamed of my machinery – part of it?'[70] For Cavell, the rejection of singularity, and the embrace of multiplicity and ambiguity that makes her writing such a challenge for scholars to interpret, emerged from her roots in the empathic aesthetics of Jugendstil, the German Art Nouveau movement that informed her burgeoning interest in art in 1890s–1900s Munich. If by the time she arrived in New York, the Baroness's performances foregrounded a sense of 'the body as a process rather than a product', this sense could only have been enlarged by the Dadaist aesthetic of the machinic body, with its exposed functions and processes, that characterized Duchamp's depictions of relationships as a process of material and physical exchange.[71]

Despite the fact that she was responding to the machinic modernism and 'scientific spirit' of the Dada scene, and in doing so employing futurist terminology and images in her depictions of sexual relationships, there is little evidence in the Baroness's early work to suggest that she was seriously engaging personally with the new physics at this time. While the *Little Review* poems draw

---

[67] Loringhoven, 'Motion Picture and Prayer', *Body Sweats*, 74.
[68] Ibid., 72–3.
[69] Richard Cavell, 'Baroness Elsa and the Aesthetics of Empathy: A Mystery and a Speculation', *The Politics of Cultural Mediation: Baroness Elsa von Freytag-Loringhoven and Felix Paul Greve*, ed. Paul Hjartarson (Edmonton: University of Alberta Press, 2003), 36.
[70] Elsa von Freytag-Loringhoven, 'The Modest Woman', 37.
[71] Cavell, 'Baroness Elsa and the Aesthetics of Empathy', 35.

upon the pool of technological imagery and scientific methodologies used by her contemporaries, the Baroness's primary contribution to these debates, as Amelia Jones argues, was 'an overt recognition of the tendency in America to forget or to repress the organic, the irrational, the disorderly, in the rush to celebrate … the effects and potentials of machine-age industrialism'.[72] In critiquing the scientific attitude of artists like Duchamp as a form of imaginative death, we can see that the Baroness initially set herself in direct opposition to physics in art, presenting herself as a champion of the irrational organic in a world of systematic machines. As such, these poems seem a far cry from her later claim that she would 'love to devote [herself] to science'. So what changed?

Quantum dissolution in Weimar Berlin

In 1923, the Baroness was to return to her homeland of Germany. If she expected a return to the vibrant pluralism of 1890s and 1900s Munich where her career as an artist began, she was to be disappointed. Ravaged by defeat in the war, the Germany that awaited her was a realized distillation of the cultural crisis that that fuelled the Dadaists' rebellion. Here, where the wartime reparations struck hardest, Dada served a different purpose than the free mechano-sexual play of New York City. French artist Georges Hugnet described the way in which, in Germany, Dada found a much more immediate social and political grounding that resonated less as an avant-garde fringe than a reflection of the national mood. 'In Berlin', he noticed, Dada's 'destructive urge was no longer gratuitous, and we are no longer dealing with an inventive anarchy wreaking, in the realms of poetry and the mind, total devastation in which no system can get be foreseen, but with actions unintelligible to everyone'.[73] In this context, 'Dada spontaneously offered its services to the proletariat and went down into the streets.'[74] While by 1923 Dada had practically dissolved in Zurich, Paris and New York, in Berlin it seemed less to have faded into irrelevance than to have been taken into the national character: 'Dada came to politics through poetic revolt, and politics absorbed Dada. Dada died of its transposition into reality, for it may be said that after 1920 Dada no longer existed.'[75]

---

[72] Jones, *Irrational Modernism*, 130.
[73] Georges Hugnet, 'The Dada Spirit in Painting', *The Dada Painters and Poets*, 142.
[74] Ibid.
[75] Ibid.

Exiled to Germany while her French and American friends and collaborators moved their activity en masse to a socially liberated Paris, the Baroness found herself suddenly alone in a country whose new and desperate circumstances fell far short of her childhood memories. Initially optimistic about the return, she was cut off from her inheritance by her disapproving father, turned away by the remains of her family and found herself unable to attain a visa to join her colleagues in Paris. She was left to fend for herself in 'this withering carcass of a country' which, although it embraced Dada, knew nothing of her or her practice.[76] This environment had a curious effect on the woman who had once disdained Duchamp's attempts to bring an intellectualized, scientific order to the organic world. During this period, her letters grow increasingly desperate in their pleas for money and assistance, but they also come to rely more and more on the concepts and language of physics to make her physical and emotional suffering palpable. Rather than revelling in a world that might almost seem crafted by a Dadaist hand, she turned her attention to trying to reassert a sense of order, turning to poetry with more diligence as a means of coping and making sense of her disordered circumstances. It was during her time in Germany that the Baroness began to write poems with more explicitly physics-inspired titles, such as 'Atom' (1924–5) and 'X-Ray' (1927). The alchemical elements of the early poems are joined by new references to forces, light spectra and gravitation, and her archived notes suggest she was working on a more urgent attempt at formalizing a personal system that unified her experience of spiritual and material crises through physics.

In the world of German science, the crisis was deeply felt. Funding for research, which had been plentiful before the war, became scarce as the country was drained by debt and the pressure to pay reparations. Unable to access foreign literature and equipment, German physicists faced an exile of their own from international conferences and collaborations.[77] While the public experienced the realities of hyperinflation and political turmoil, the scientists, focussed on invisible forces and worlds out of reach, faced a wave of public disdain. The nation's pride in its vanguard science and advanced technology, which it had expected to lead them to victory in the war, had led only to defeat. Science, it seemed, had betrayed them.

---

[76] Elsa von Freytag-Loringhoven, Loringhoven Papers, Special Collections and University Archives, University of Maryland Libraries, Series II, Box I, Folder 4.

[77] For an overview of the conditions faced by scientists in German institutions during this period, see: Helge Kragh, *Quantum Generations* (Princeton, NJ: Princeton University Press, 1999).

Science's cultural position in Germany was shifting rapidly. In a dramatic rejection of scientific positivism, one minister declared that the German people 'must acquire again reverence for the irrational'.[78] Gustav Doetsch, in his inaugural lecture as the *Privatdozent* for applied mathematics at the University of Halle, told his audience that

> this epoch, at whose beginning we unquestionably find ourselves today, is fed up with this rationalistic attitude. Whether we direct our attention toward expressionism in art, or to more <u>recent</u> philosophical tendencies, which in many ways have not yet emerged entirely distinctly, or to any other area of life and thought whatsoever, we find everywhere an ever stronger aversion for that spirit which believed that it had to express, and that it could express, everything whatsoever in dry words, in one formula.[79]

However, despite being a 'place and period of deep hostility to physics and mathematics [the Weimar Republic] was also one of the most creative in the entire history of these enterprises'.[80] Notably, new modes of thinking in the scientific community coincided with a shift in the cultural role ascribed to science as a discipline, with the idea that 'science should be seen as a bearer of culture, a *Kulturträger* in German'.[81] Under this umbrella, 'Germany's famous scientists became instruments of a national and international cultural policy on par with the country's poets, composers and artists.'[82] The cultural and economic value of science shifted away from utility and industry to become more closely aligned with the arts, with figures like Einstein gaining currency as ambassadors for German '*Kultur* propaganda'.[83]

Under these changed conditions, several other German scientists argued in the early 1920s 'that the principle of causality could no longer be considered a foundation of physical theories', a view which filtered into public awareness despite the fact that it 'was not [yet] rooted in specific or theoretical developments in physics'.[84] This raises the question of the influence of the cultural foment upon the course of physics's development in Weimar Germany, which has been widely

---

[78] Robert P. Crease and Alfred Sharff Goldhaber, *The Quantum Moment* (New York: W. W. Norton & Co., 2014), 80.
[79] Gustav Doetsch 'Der Sinn der angewandten Mathematik,' *Jahresbericht del' Deutschen Mathematiker-Vereinigung* 31 (1922), 222–33 cited in Forman, 139.
[80] Forman, 'Weimar Culture, Causality, and Quantum Theory, 1918–1927', 90.
[81] Kragh, *Quantum Generations*, 140.
[82] Ibid., 140, 153.
[83] Ibid., 140.
[84] Ibid., 153.

discussed by historians of science.⁸⁵ Indeed, some contemporary commentators considered the cultural crisis a source of inspiration for the new physics. The quantum physicist Werner Heisenberg, for instance, wrote:

> It is not by chance that the development to this end no longer took place in a time of belief in progress. After the catastrophe of the First World War one understood outside of scholarship as well that there were no firm foundations for our existence, secure for all time.⁸⁶

Out of these ashes, a new science emerged which better chimed with the national mood: quantum mechanics. In this period of great 'methodological reflection' in all areas of cultural knowledge, the new quantum physics demanded the biggest epistemological shift of all.⁸⁷ Its advocates 'joined in attacking the bogeyman of positivism, understood as a kind of methodological un-self-consciousness' and, as Cathryn Carson says, the chaos of 'interpretative consequences that came in the wake of quantum mechanics – uncertainty and limits to physical knowledge, acausality and the solely statistical nature of the theory's predictions, restrictions on objectivity and a new role for the observer – felt to its apostles like the price they were willing to pay'.⁸⁸

Amid the howls and nonsense-eruptions of the post-war period, this crisis of culture stretched well beyond the scientific community; in Berlin, Dada artists redoubled their efforts to challenge and reconfigure all notions of artistic and cultural production by exploding them at their base. Physics's cultural status was absorbed into the world view of German Dada, for instance, with Hannah Höch's elaborate photomontage, *Cut with the Dada Kitchen Knife through the Last Weimar Beer-Belly Cultural Epoch in Germany* (1919) (Figure 5), including an image of a contemplative Einstein (top left) clipped from the *Berliner Illustrirte Zeitung* a month after his theories gained widespread public recognition.⁸⁹ Using a technique she pioneered with Richard Huelsenbeck, Höch's collage illustrates the uncontrollable chaos of the political landscape, fusing images of Dada practitioners with political figures, modern machinery and 'dada propagandists' like Einstein.⁹⁰ An upturned '8' of overlaid cogs on the iconic physicist's eye

---

⁸⁵ For an overview of this debate in history of science literature, see Cathryn Carson, 'Method, Moment, and Crisis in Weimar Science', *Weimar Thought: A Contested Legacy*, eds. Peter E. Gordon and John P. McCormick (Princeton & Oxford: Princeton University Press, 2013).
⁸⁶ Werner Heisenberg cited in Carson, 'Method, Moment, and Crisis in Weimar Science', 249.
⁸⁷ Ibid., 248.
⁸⁸ Ibid., 247.
⁸⁹ Kumiko Hoshi, 'D. H. Lawrence and Hannah Höch: Representing Einstein and the Post-World War I World', *Études Lawrenciennes* 46 (October 2015). https://journals.openedition.org/lawrence/244
⁹⁰ Ibid.

Figure 5 Hannah Höch, *Cut with the Dada Kitchen Knife through the Last Weimar Beer-Belly Cultural Epoch in Germany, 1919–20*, collage, mixed media, 144 × 90 cm, Museen der Staatlichen Museen zu Berlin, NG 57/61.

becomes a symbol of infinity (∞), signifying perhaps the infinite flux of science's new revelations, or Einstein's prophetic vision (special relativity was, by this time, over a decade old) of the dissolution of traditional order and values. Below, a clipping from *Der Dada*'s advertisement for Huelsenbeck's doomed anthology project, *Dadaco,* that reads '*He, he, Sie junger Mann/Dada is keine Kunstrichtung*' ('hey, hey you, young man/Dada is not an art movement'), implies the potential of Dada as a *Kulturträger* itself, able to universally encompass and absorb politics, technology and the new science.[91] Together, these elements form an invitation

---

[91] Raoul Hausmann (ed.), *Der Dada*, 2 (December 1919), http://sdrc.lib.uiowa.edu/dada/derdada/2/images/02.pdf [Accessed 14 Dec 2020].

to physicists 'to take Dada seriously as an all-embracing social principle'.[92] Huelsenbeck's Dada manifesto begins with a reflection upon the origins and shaping forces of Germany's Dadaist revolution as a consequence and reaction to a time and space in which all order was being continually overturned:

> Art in its execution and direction is dependent on the time in which it lives, and artists are creatures of their epoch. The highest art will be that which in its conscious content presents the thousandfold problems of the day, the art which has been visibly shattered by the explosions of last week, which is forever trying to collect its limbs after yesterday's crash. The best and most extraordinary artists are those who every hour snatch the tatters of their bodies out of the frenzied cataract of life, who, with bleeding hands and hearts, hold fast to the intelligence of their time.[93]

As early as 1913, Ernst Gehrke, a physicist at Berlin's Reich Institute of Physics and Technology, was receiving letters complaining that 'people are suffering extreme fatigue, and an irritability that is due not least to the absurd theories of the relativists'.[94] By the time the Baroness arrived in the city, a decade later, this epistemic stress had reached fever pitch.

Her correspondences present a vivid picture of the personal impact of this environment on the artist who, having once been celebrated, found herself sidelined into greater poverty, isolation and artistic exile, while her colleagues returned to an artistically flourishing Paris. Reflecting upon her own circumstances, the Baroness painted a picture of herself becoming the embodiment of Weimar's crisis:

> That spirit is the spirit of Germany. Not – because they have practically – but because they have mentally collapsed! And I am taken into that collapse when I am not removed. And my collapse will be decided because I am decided[.][95]

A woman of absolutes, the Baroness saw her own mental collapse as an extreme reflection of the wider mental decline around her. This language of collapse becomes a recurrent image conveying ideas of national, personal and universal destruction, the shifting of fundamental social and universal infrastructures, and loss of personal control. Collapse offers a totalizing image, which functions on all

---

[92] Cara Schweitzer, *Schrankenlose freiheit für Hannah Höch* (Copenhagen: Saga Egmont, 2014), https://books.google.co.uk/books?id=H5WNCwAAQBAJ [Accessed 14 Dec 2020].
[93] Rose-Carol Washton Long (ed.), *German Expressionism, Documents from the End of the Wilhelmine Empire to the Rise of National Socialism* (London: University of California Press, 1993), 267.
[94] Wazeck, *Einstein's Opponents,* 1.
[95] Elsa von Freytag-Loringhoven, Elsa von Freytag-Loringhoven papers, Special Collections and University Archives, University of Maryland Libraries, Series II, Box I, Folder 5.

levels of meaning; the Baroness saw the individual's experience as a microcosmic reflection of wider cosmic and atomic processes. The fundamental laws by which she governed herself in New York had also collapsed: 'I cannot observe any "art laws"," she wrote "or even any "sense laws" any more. I write – exist – too much against odds.'[96] This existential collapse brings even the ultimate polar binaries, life and death, into a unified state: 'I sit dead-alive in a home for wayward lost people.'[97] Referring to 'laws', she related her own experience to the wider 'order' of things, and contrary to the air of delight seen in the destruction of order by Dadaists like Tzara, Ball and Huelsenbeck, she finds the loss of order deeply distressing.

The handful of letters from this time, some published in *transition* following her death in 1927, show the Baroness's fear about the deterioration of her identity, characterized by uncertainty, duality and material dissolution. A narrative of spatiotemporal dissolution emerges, a shift of self-conception which begins with a feeling of temporal disjunction ('I am fifty and I am eighteen'), a sense of being unmoored in time; then of spatial disorder (a longing for the lost America and a hatred for Germany) and an increasing desire to take control of her identity through choice and self-identification, ('I am so American that ... '), which, failing, leads to a decline and loss of the Baroness's sense of self ('I do not recognize myself anymore').[98] Here, loss of identity figures both mentally and physically as a reconstitution of the self and the body. This manifests the Baroness's adoption of a new language to describe herself: the language of physics. The body, once taken as an organic machine – a complete and controllable system – of which she was 'proud engineer', becomes fragmented and broken down into a vortex of broken up cells and particles: 'I whirled – scattered – mussed/Fate-blown particles of wild yearning for unity.'[99] The mind, too, is subject to a kind of psychic and material fragmentation, she says: 'I am not truly deranged even, but scattered.'[100] Elsewhere, in 'Constitution' (1924), the Baroness reasserts her bodily presence as a form of resistance against these destructive forces: 'Still/Shape distinct – /Resist/I'.[101] Drawing upon her concerns about the body as an engine 'automatonguts', the cosmos

---

[96] Loringhoven, 'Selections from the Letters', 26.
[97] Loringhoven, *Autobiography*, 106.
[98] Loringhoven, 'Selections from the Letters', 20, 22.
[99] Elsa von Freytag-Loringhoven, letter to Djuna Barnes, Elsa von Freytag-Loringhoven papers, Special Collections and University Archives, University of Maryland Libraries, Series II, Box I, Folder 5, 10.
[100] Loringhoven, 'Selections from the Letters', 27.
[101] Elsa von Freytag-Loringhoven, 'Constitution', *Body Sweats*, 171.

is figured as a digestive system with a 'rotating appetite', which the Baroness dares to 'shred' her: 'From/Mortalitycast/I/Taunt/Thy/Teeth/Into – /Slashing/ Me –'. If Raihan Kadri is correct in asserting that 'Dada is primarily known for its negation, its stripping away of values given to identity, both of people and of things', and if, as I have suggested, Weimar Germany was itself in many ways a Dadaist state, the erosion of the Baroness's sense of self might be taken as a kind of cannibalism in which Dada chews up and spits out its own practitioner.[102] The body is fragmented and destabilized, and fluctuating bodies and states of mind governed by 'cosmic' forces become a staple of the Baroness's poetics of deterioration as her values shift from the creation of social disorder to a desire for an ordered universe.

In light of this, it is perhaps no wonder that the disillusioned Baroness took the chaos into which her homeland had fallen as a personal insult. In autumn 1923, she wrote a stream of politicized letters to Barnes in which she lampooned what she saw as the undisciplined national character of Germany, writing that '*they* could not know of my *true nature* – that is not Bohemian at – all! – *likes order* – ! hence is insulted'.[103] The short poem 'Fix' (1924–5) frames this tension between the Baroness's will to order and her Dadaist acknowledgement of the chaotic, senselessness of the modern world. A poem of conflicts, 'Fix' presents a seesaw of contradictory attitudes towards scientific order, typically captured in its multivalent title, which in a single word suggests both problem (the sense of being 'in a fix') and resolution ('to fix'). It suggests, too, the importance of writing a poem as a way of fixing meanings, with a sense of security and attachment that, in Dadaist works, are always under threat. Numerous tensions run through the poem, but the most obvious is that between balance and flux. 'Fix' is a descent from the higher realm of the 'single cosmic miracle' through an atomic level into the human level of the body into a register of coarse slang, through which the poet questions her own position in the universe, and dramatizes the pull between her desire to pay attention to the fascinating but complicated world of the modern universe and a desire to throw all interest out of the window as part of a wider existential questioning: 'What for?'.

The first section represents the Baroness's growing spiritual interests, bringing together unreason, balance and logic under the control of a higher, omniscient cosmic force:

---

[102] Kadri, Dadaist Poker, 145.
[103] Loringhoven, *Baroness Elsa*, 198.

Single cosmic miracle –
Unreasonable sensuous omnisciences
Balancing universe:
All pervasion:
Logic.

This concise language enables two equal and opposed readings of this section, hinging on how we choose to read the pivotal word 'balancing'. If taken as an adjective, we find a narrative progression: the miraculous creation of an unreasonable, chaotic universe that gradually pulls together under the gravity of Logic. However, if taken as a verb, the 'Unreasonable sensuous consciences' themselves become the balancing force around which logic is built. As the poem progresses, it seems perhaps the latter – more bizarre – reading has currency, as the Baroness draws upon the cutting-edge language of physics to acknowledge a universe that is 'flux-driven' and 'unexplainable' at the atomic level.

In
Unexplainable wisdom
Of
Flux-driven atom –
Rackingly fascinated
To
Watch it by –
Manifest within
Myself – – – –
I
Poise!
Sole cause
Of
Maintenance – – –
Or
I
Say:
    'Suck –
    Fuck –
    Chuck –
    Lorr!
    What
    For?'[104]

---

[104] Elsa von Freytag-Loringhoven, 'Fix', *Body Sweats*, 156–7.

The balancing act shifts here from the cosmic world outside her to her internal world, manifesting in the poet and turning her into the pivot ('*Poise!*') between logic and chaos. The connotations of embodiment, posture and self-comportment in '*Poise!*' play upon the Baroness's work as an artists' model, required to maintain poses for five to thirty minutes at a time, but it also presents a side of the poet her readers, expecting the frantic brashness of the poem's final section, may not have been so familiar with. This is the introspective side of the Baroness, able to balance without moving for extended periods, even as her thoughts raced from one idea to another. The poem itself presents this duality, a fragmented internal voice concerned with fundamental questions about the universe set against a harsh, monosyllabic exterior voice, which prioritizes sexual action. But this tension between what the Baroness elsewhere calls her 'introspective and analytical turn' and that part of her which prefers swift action, comes at a price.[105] Racked by the strain it takes to keep up with a complicated universe in flux, the second, exterior, option appears dynamic and direct, a welcome, although ultimately fruitless distraction. This sentiment is understandable. In May 1925, around the same time this poem was written, Wolfgang Pauli, a pioneer of quantum physics who would later receive the 1945 Nobel Prize, wrote: 'Physics at the moment is again very muddled, in any case, for me it is too complicated, and I wish I were a film comedian or something of that sort and had never heard about physics.'[106]

Post-war Berlin, then, offered a perfect storm of harsh cultural, economic, psychological and material conditions that engendered the need for a widespread reconsideration of methodologies in order to restore a sense of order to the physical world. New approaches to sense-making, from the erratic politicization of the Berlin Dadaists to the anti-deterministic turn in science, set cultural categories into new alignments: science with the arts, the arts with politics and politics with the urgent need for a redemptive cultural revival. Writing in German, the Baroness felt that this civilization, in its forced confusion, had forgotten instinct, and that instinct was tightly related to the simple and, she considers, scientific, logic of the sexual model studied by the 'eros pupil':

Logic is invisible
crystal lens calculation
especially eros pupil

---

[105] Elsa von Freytag-Loringhoven, letter to Djuna Barnes, Elsa von Freytag-Loringhoven Papers, Special Collections and University Archives, University of Maryland Libraries, Series II, Box I, Folder 4.
[106] Cited in Jim Al-Kalili, *Quantum: A Guide for the Perplexed* (London: Orion Publishing, 2004), 61.

all one
from egg
penis telescope creation[107]

This view, that the universe might be understood through the 'logic' of sexual encounters and reproductive processes (*wissenschaft durch logic*) offers a bridge between the Baroness's earlier love poetry and her adoption of the 'scientific spirit' of her contemporaries. Where the scientific, 'glassy' lens of Duchamp's science appeared to reject organic instincts, the Baroness uses the images of the 'crystal lens' and 'telescope' to signal her own adoption of the 'scientific spirit', turning reproduction (both sexual and artistic), into a laboratory process. These notes towards a unified theory of eros, aesthetics and the cosmos are the beginning of a greater analytical turn in the Baroness's writing which capitalized on the blurring dynamics of the arts and sciences within German culture to invent a new, all-encompassing, cosmology. The shifting identities of these cultural arenas contributed to the Baroness's reconsideration of her self-identity and, I suggest, informed a wider methodological shift within her work, as it moved increasingly away from addressing her emotions about her contemporaries, and towards wider questions about universal systems of knowledge.

'Life is science': Finding order through science

For the Baroness, the quest for a 'fix' involved a period of deep reflection on her past. Hoping to produce publishable work to provide an income, she began to write an autobiography, which she sent in sections to Barnes, but never finished. Stringing together, often in a disparate and discursive form, the events and emotions of her early life, she realized that 'nothing is past and buried – ever! All is links in a chain'.[108] A similar sentiment colours the introduction of her poem 'Cosmic Chemistry' (*c.* 1924–5), which brings determinist science into

---

[107] Elsa von Freytag Loringhoven, 'Oh! Aha! Sch — Sch — — Sch — — — ', Elsa von Freytag-Loringhoven Papers, Special Collections and University Archives, University of Maryland Libraries, Series 3, Box 1, Folder 8. My translation. Original:*Logik ist sicht unsicht bar*
  cristall-linse calculation
  vort eros pupille
  all eins
  aus ei
  telescope gleid geschöpf
[108] Loringhoven, *Baroness Elsa*, 125.

conversation with modern experience as the introduction to a philosophical poem musing on the nature of life and the cosmos.

> *'Life = 1 damn thing after another!'*
> *'Live and learn':*
> Life is science –
> God knows!¹⁰⁹

Quotes snatched from public discourse are set against an ironic conclusion as the voice of the poet escapes the collage of quotation. If time is a successive stream of causality, and if this leads to an accrued growth of knowledge and understanding over one's lifetime, the Baroness suggests, then 'Life is science', a mirror to the successive gains of causal reasoning that characterized nineteenth-century scientific thought. But there is a twist in the tail of this syllogism, an irony on which the following series of systems, pseudo-scientific symbols, diagrams and schemas for what life *really* is rests. By the time this poem was written, as we have seen, determinism had been dealt a dramatic blow. Physics was no longer perceived as simply causal, and Europe was trying to make sense of the quantum revolution. In this context, the Baroness's return to causal systems may be seen to break with the wider German trend.

Homesick for the States and looking for ways to redefine the terms of her chaotic universe in a concise, crystalline way, the Baroness reappropriated some of the techniques and sources that shaped the new 'scientific' systems of the earlier New York Dada. She used this period to reflect upon her past relationships and clung, always, to their influence. Indeed, there are moments in her letters where she reflects with regret upon her earlier attitudes, couching her descriptions in a language which gestures towards the wider universal systems she went on to develop. 'I very vividly in memory,' she writes,

> fall in love with my past lovers – as carrier of the sunmessage – as meaning of all-system: 'perpetual screw!' I see – how perishable they themselves were – how deteriorated in care and affection by time – as all earthly things will – until they become dull mechanics – which I did not let suffer to happen – hence my utter loneliness – and had I understood more of the – outer life mashinery [*sic*] appertaining to emotion – to give it practical possibility – I should – and very plentifuly [*sic*] at least could – have provided against such time as now.¹¹⁰

---

¹⁰⁹ Elsa von Freytag-Loringhoven, 'Cosmic Chemistry', *Body Sweats*, 153. Original emphasis.
¹¹⁰ Elsa von Freytag-Loringhoven, Letter to Djuna Barnes, Elsa von Freytag-Loringhoven Papers, Special Collections and University Archives, University of Maryland Libraries, Box 1, Folder 4, 17–18.

Despite her apparent desire to depart from Dada's love of destruction and disorder towards a new set of 'sense-laws', the Baroness's response to the fraught world around her retains an awareness of the way old systems have been overthrown, and they continue to resonate with Hugo Ball's depiction of the Dadaist mindset from *Dada Fragments* (1916–18):

> [The Dadaist] no longer believes in the comprehension of things from one point of departure, but is nevertheless convinced of the union of all things, of totality, to such an extent that he suffers from dissonances to the point of self-dissolution…
>
> The Dadaist fights against the death-throes and death-drunkenness of his time. … He knows that the world of systems has gone to pieces, and that the age which demanded cash has organized a bargain sale of godless philosophies.[111]

In this section, I consider how a concern with re-evaluating aspects of her pre-exile existence led the Baroness to revisit her earlier influences, adopting and adapting techniques and ideas found in the work of Duchamp, De Zayas, Tzara and Ball.

One of the most noticeable changes in the Baroness's work during this period is its increased precision. Where her earlier poem-essays in *The Little Review* often ran to multiple pages of long lines, primarily broken up by dashes, we find in her later work a tendency to experiment with a much more stripped back and minimalist style. Poems like 'Game Legend' (1924–5), which depicts a sexual experience, for instance, use single word lines and direct, simple language in a much more fractured style than that of 'Love-Chemical Relationship':

> Three
> People
>   Seated
> In
> Room –
> Playing
>   Game:
> Boy –
> Scientist –
> Lady
> Bare
> Shame[112]

---

[111] Hugo Ball, 'Dada Fragments (1916–1917)', *The Dada Painters and Poets: An Anthology*, ed. Robert Motherwell (Cambridge, MA: Harvard University Press, 1989), 51.

[112] Elsa von Freytag-Loringhoven, 'Game Legend', *Body Sweats*, 215.

Searching, through science, for a means of expressing sharp and concise truths, the Baroness embraced the clarity equations could afford for the development of a new, scientifically inflected world view. The shift towards quantum understandings in Germany led many to seek acausal and mystical explanations for cosmic phenomena, yet, unlike Loy's spiritualism, the Baroness's 'idealism was grounded in an unflinching materiality', which Reilly ascribes to her 'years of poverty and physical hardship'.[113] It may be for this reason, too, that she often preferred to couch her scientific writing in the tangible images of 'chemistry', rather than the more ethereal 'physics', even when the concepts contained within the poems display a considerable overlap. In these later works, she draws again upon chemical language to create works which she describes as 'cristall [sic]' in the 'conciseness' of their 'arithmetic'.[114] This concision appears alongside a new tendency to integrate equations and mathematical symbols into her work in a way reminiscent of De Zayas's use of equations to indicate an 'analysis' of the '*spirit*' of his subjects. The Baroness's own equations, often deceptively simple equivalences, attempt to describe the relationships between embodiment, sexuality and spirituality. 'Cosmic Arithmetic', for example, presents a series of mathematical equivalences in a table, where numbers, at once concise and abstract, interrogate the relationship between the holy trinity and sexual experience; while 'Cosmic Chemistry' offers up a kind of sexual algebra of equations that suggest a levelling out of the material and spiritual life:

Life = wombcrucible
Spirit = phalluspistol
Matter = ashes
Loss = gain =
Purification[115]

Appropriation of mathematical symbols allowed a concise and typically Dadaist suggestion of the equivalence of opposing concepts such as loss and gain, and life and death, and recall the discussion of artistic creator and creation in Tzara's 'Manifesto of Mr Antipyrine' (1916):

---

[113] Reilly, 'Elsa von Freytag-Loringhoven', 31.
[114] Tanya Clements, 'Critical Introduction' to "Cosmic Arithmetic"', *In Transition*, https://digital.lib.umd.edu/transition/poem?pid=umd:55439
[115] Elsa von Freytag-Loringhoven, 'Cosmic Chemistry', *Body Sweats*, 153.

> For [the world of an artwork's] creator is without cause and without theory. Order = disorder; ego = non-ego; affirmation = negation: the supreme radiations of absolute art. Absolute in the purity of the cosmic ordered chaos, eternal in the globule of a second without duration, without breath without control.[116]

In this manifesto, we can see that many of the themes the Baroness draws upon to create her new world system were already present in Dadaist thought, albeit in a way which privileged disorder as the governing law of the universe. The Baroness is interested in interrogating the way in which the different systems that govern sexual relationships, religious belief and the material world interrelate to generate artistic creativity. She concludes, moreover, the priority of the creative and orderly impulse: 'System denies anti-system – / Sense non-sense.'[117] In Tzara's assessment, painting is a medium for creating worlds that distend established physical facts to create a world of 'possibilities': 'Painting is the art of making two lines geometrically established as parallel meet on a canvas before our eyes in a reality which transposes other conditions and possibilities into a world.'[118] For the Baroness, poetry was the medium that offered the chance to explore the possibility of an absolute, pure and totalizing unity positioned outside of material and temporal existence, a world that might offer hope of redemption and escape from material hardship.

Several of the Baroness's visual poems draw upon perspective and perpetual motion, ideas her work suggests might greatly benefit from the poetic imagination's ability to defy the law of entropy. Formally, this sometimes meant shifting the viewpoint from which the reader understands the poem. 'Perspective' (*c*. 1924, Figure 6), for instance, offers a diagram of the Baroness's cosmogony divided into layers 'read from down to up', a challenge to normative modes of reading which Gammel and Zelazo have described as an invitation to read 'in the ascending, mounting movement of the spiral'.[119] One of several visual poems, 'Perspective' employs a fusion of geometric shapes, spirals, connecting lines and angled text which passes up the page through a 'treadmill' to culminate at the top (end) of the process 'immured' in an eternal spiral. The spiral motion is indicated both from a bird's eye view (at the top) and at three lower points by a snake-like lateral view which describes the upward trajectory of the reader's progress. It is a cynical image of a world whose inhabitants are confined to an

---

[116] Tzara, 'Seven Dada Manifestos', 78.
[117] Elsa von Freytag-Loringhoven, 'Spectrum', *Body Sweats*, 513–26.
[118] Tzara, 'Seven Dada Manifestos', 78.
[119] Elsa von Freytag-Loringhoven, 'Perspective', *Body Sweats*, 196, 94.

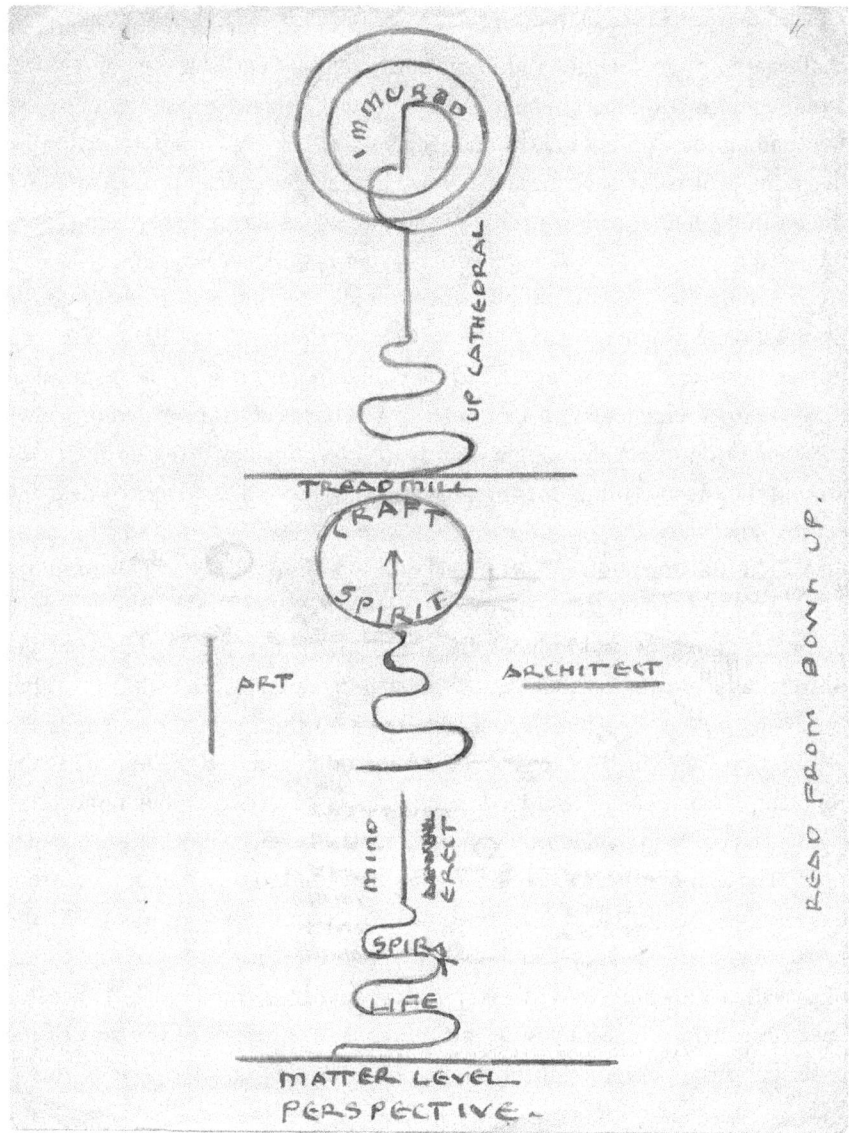

Figure 6 Elsa von Freytag-Loringhoven, *Perspective, c.* 1922–4. Red and green ink on paper. Elsa von Freytag-Loringhoven papers, Special Collections & University Archives, University of Maryland Libraries.

absurd spiral of perpetual and hermetic rotation. The aptly titled 'Perpetual Motion' (c. 1922–4) is another visual attempt to construct a system in which the relationships between the 'base world', 'art', 'craft' and the 'soul' of the artist attain the state of perpetual motion in a 'circlecontainer'.[120] While these poems challenge our approach to reading in a way reminiscent of the typographical and diagrammatic experiments of Marinetti or Picabia, the way the Baroness wrote about these poems to her editor suggests a more practical purpose for the diagrams, which she describes as 'not art' but 'matter-of-fact' images to 'make the meaning plain'.[121] Her concerns are not purely aesthetic; these diagrams are intended to provide a *functional* measure of her cosmological system.

A fascinating set of unpublished notes beginning 'since space is immeasurable' (Figure 7) offers the fullest description of the Baroness's own universal system, as she adopted bizarre contemporary models of the physical universe to develop a new cosmic order.[122] The chaos of the page demonstrates the congestion of her thinking as words fill every inch, moving up the sides, around the top and filling the margins and gaps around the diagram near the centre. It provides a sense of the urgency with which she was working on these ideas. This document gives a great deal of insight into the thinking behind her cosmology, and while it is putatively dated to around 1924, its concerns butt up against those of slightly later science. In particular, her figuration of the universe as a series of soap bubbles bears a striking resemblance to the influential metaphor of the soap-bubble universe used by the Belgian mathematician Georges Lemaître in 1927 to describe what would later become known as the Big Bang Theory. Lemaître argued that the universe was expanding rapidly like a giant cosmic soap bubble, an image which became widespread in the popular press. The Baroness writes that 'Energy unknown is blowing soapbubbles from eternity soap of inexhaustive supply – the why unknown – as energy is and the mysterious matter soap'.[123] The bubble metaphor was useful in its implication of a spiritual blowing force ('god is spin – blower of soap bubbles') but may also have appealed to the Baroness as 'playful physics'. After all, at the turn of the century, bubbles straddled the gap between being subjects of serious scientific

---

[120] Elsa von Freytag-Loringhoven, 'Perpetual Motion', *Body Sweats*, 198.
[121] Elsa von Freytag-Loringhoven Papers, Special Collections and University Archives, University of Maryland Libraries, Series II, Box I.
[122] The Baroness's papers are held at the Special Collections and University Archives, University of Maryland Libraries.
[123] Elsa von Freytag-Loringhoven, 'since space is immeasurable', n.d., Elsa von Freytag-Loringhoven Papers, Special Collections and University Archives, University of Maryland Libraries, Series 3, Box 3, Folder 3. All quotations are from here.

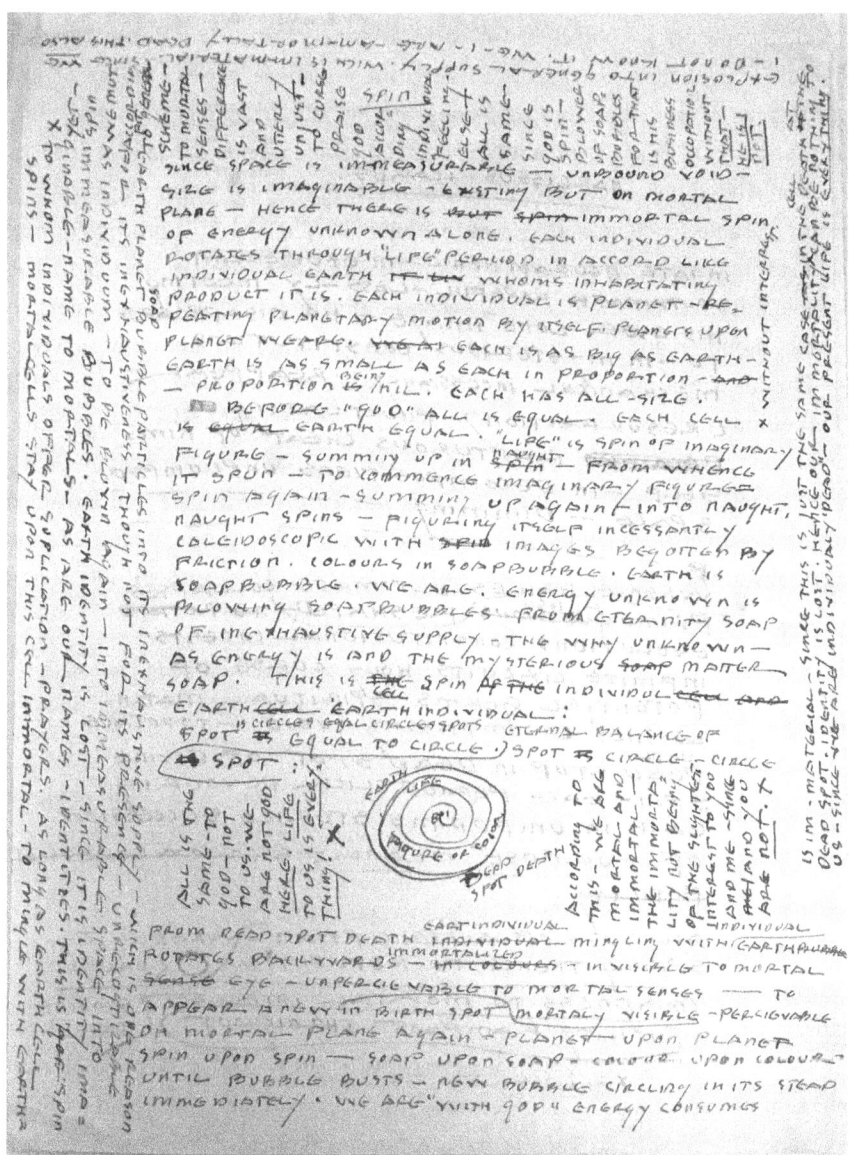

Figure 7 Elsa von Freytag-Loringhoven, 'since space is immeasurable', c. 1924. Black ink on paper. Elsa von Freytag-Loringhoven papers, Special Collections & University Archives, University of Maryland Libraries.

study and toys for children, with the notion of experimentation as play the assumed educational basis for children's bubble sets.[124]

Her notion of a playful God, whose colourful universe consists of spinning, 'caleidoscopic [sic]' bubbles in which 'all is equal', and each element, whether human or planetary body, 'has all-size', offers a more positive image of lost identity as a process of ultimate consumption by the universal system. 'We are "with god" energy consumes/earth planet soap bubble particles into its inexhaustive supply ... unrecognizable as individuum – to be blown again – into immeasurable space into immeasurable bubbles.' Through this process 'mortal cells stay upon this cell immortal – to mingle with earth' and 'identity is lost.' The bubble universe, for the Baroness, becomes a metaphor for a closed system in which, though matter is contained and recycled, the individual cannot survive.

The all-consuming 'god machine' reappears in another document, titled 'Perpetuum Mobile', where God is depicted as a 'straight schaft [sic] piercing chaos' as the 'pivot of [a] wheel awhirl'.[125] Through a list of loosely connected words that map onto the 'since space is immeasurable' image, the Baroness brings together the machinic and organic digestion of her earlier poetry and the symbolism of the wheel and perpetual motion from Duchamp (*Bicycle Wheel* (1913)) with her conception of a cyclical universal system:

> mass universe playground nourishment existence of godmachine mechanically recuperating universe digesting time without number eternity numberless outside count

Here, as in 'since space is immeasurable', syntactic disorder gives the reader a chaotic sense of the mind in motion, the Baroness's thoughts racing too quickly to consider grammar or syntax, a huge pool of interconnected ideas that are, themselves, trapped in a dizzying kaleidoscope of motion.

The diagram in 'since space is immeasurable' contains the aspects of the Baroness's cosmology: space, time, life and death, all interlinked as part of a closed spiral. This vision of a possible universe, constructed upon principles of rotation and the 'spin of energy', brings together and makes equal each element of a universal 'All'. The Baroness proposes a system in which all levels of existence are governed by the same, unexceptional, laws of spin. She describes the universe as a series of spheres – first the earth, and then the individual ('each

---

[124] Kirsten A. Hoving, 'The Surreal Science of Soap: Joseph Cornell's First Soap Bubble Set', *American Art* 20, no. 1 (Spring 2006), 19.

[125] Elsa von Freytag-Loringhoven, 'Perpetuum Mobile', Elsa von Freytag-Loringhoven Papers, Special Collections and University Archives, University of Maryland Libraries, Series 3, Box 1, Folder 21.

individual is a planet') – which function in proportion to one another, sharing an 'imaginary figure spin' whose invisible rotations, vortices of energy and matter, form a universe in perpetual motion. Matter and the individual in this universe are both drawn by centripetal force to a 'dead' central spot, before spiralling back outwards as the system 'rotates backwards' again; universal (and personal) collapse is followed by universal expansion. This system has implications for the planetary individual, whose 'identity is lost' in the collapse of its own universe or '"life" period' – death. Yet, while the system is regenerative, and 'According to this – we are mortal and immortal' the Baroness makes clear that the form of immortality offered us by the universe is 'not... of the slightest interest to you and me' as, following the collateral damage to our identities, we do not exist to experience it.

The Baroness's ideas are not as eccentric as they first appear. In the early 1920s, physicists had begun to formally tackle the notion of a cyclical and periodic universe. As Helge Kragh notes, '[a]lthough the general idea of a cyclic or oscillating universe goes back to times immemorial, it was only with the advent of relativistic cosmology that it could be formulated in a mathematically precise way and confronted with observations.'[126] The oscillating universe the Baroness describes has intriguing parallels with the inception of evolutionary relativist cosmology, a system of universal physics based on the idea of a closed, cyclic universe, first proposed in 1922 by the Russian physicist Alexander Friedmann in the *Zeitschrift für Physik*, a peer-reviewed scientific journal based in Berlin.[127] In his semi-popular book *The World as Space and Time* (1923), the potential cyclic or periodic universe Friedmann describes follows a very similar dynamic of contraction and expansion as that of the Baroness, a universe of perpetual motion governed by eternal, cyclical processes:

> Cases are also possible when the radius of curvature changes periodically. The universe contracts into a point (into nothing) and then increases its radius from the point up to a certain value, then again diminishes its radius of curvature, transforms itself into a point, etc.[128]

The Spiral, drawn from Dada discourses, allied with contemporary thinking in science about universal models, spiral nebulas and universal expansion, offered

---

[126] Helge Kragh, 'Cyclic Models of the Relativistic Universe', <arxiv:1308.0932 [physics.hist-ph]> (2013), 1.
[127] Alexander Friedman, 'Über die Krümmung des Raumes', *Zeitschrift für Physik* 10 (1922), 377–86.
[128] Friedmann, The World as Space and Time, cited in Tilman Sauer, David E. Rowe et al., *Beyond Einstein: Perspectives on Geometry, Gravitation, and Cosmology in the Twentieth Century* (Basel: Birkhäuser, 2018), 185.

the Baroness a fruitful image for a universe both systematic and contradictory, contained and eternal, perpetually moving and yet home to something akin to what Eliot would later call 'the still point of the turning world'.[129]

The ideas in 'since space is immeasurable' form the foundation of the Baroness's late poetry. On the back of the single page of notes is a draft of a poem, 'Narcissus – Icarus' (c. 1924), which offers a much more condensed representation of this universal system in action. With its powerful blend of Greek myth, Christian imagery and ideas of evolution, energy transfer and universal structure, 'Narcissus – Icarus' is a cosmic retelling of the Narcissus myth, in which the self-absorbed youth is figured as a modern 'neurasthenic' dissolving and reforming as part of a fluctuating and cyclical temporospatial system. It begins with the image of a male subject, presumably Narcissus, a persona for the artist, torn by paradoxical 'inexuberance' and 'hopeful-less'ness, vanishing and reappearing in an undefined space:

> Innate neurasthenic – inexuberant youthmask –
> Hopeful-less-ly meeting his ever
> Lone image – he disappears to – in mysterious
> Constitution's mechanical incessancy – reappear
> – (Resurrection) – fluctuating rapturous
> Cheat of himself – in decompositions
> Unplumped space – dimming – – – –
> – – – – – – – – – – –

His lonely self-obsession instigates an internal examination, a pushing beyond the 'youthmask' to the 'mysterious' interiority, a place which loses its spatiotemporal meaning, throwing off the physical restrictions of the exterior world. The Baroness creates the image of a circle in the cyclical motion of vanishing and reappearing, linking it to a deeper mechanism of perpetual motion as a fundamental aspect of universal law. 'Constitution' is a particularly loaded term here, gesturing to physical and mental health, fundamental principles of law and the upheaval of Weimar politics, which in the Baroness's parlance may be seen as 'sense laws' or 'art laws', natural or aesthetic. The image, like that of the youth disappearing and reappearing, is slippery, both 'mysterious' and 'mechanical', known and unknown. A performance of flux as a psycho-physical process, an interrogation of the self and its position and value, 'Narcissus – Icarus' evolves

---

[129] T. S. Eliot, 'Burnt Norton', *The Four Quartets* (London: Faber & Faber, 1944), 5.

into an interrogation of cosmic processes, space-time, and microscopic rotation played out on a nihilistic, chaotic stage.

> Whence hails ultimate collapse's reshaped
> Primeflush – evolutions constitutional
> Incest's infinite circuits holy curse
> Of potential germs spiritual matchlessness'
> Encompassing void – to rotate – – –
> Until
> Dead stop in a dead spot of divine
> Spin – each periodclick devouring each
> In uniforms sterile succession of
> Purpose blank.
> Allsum of allconception = O (naught –
> Spinning cell) whence it sprung – thence
> To return – – – – – –
> Shadowcarousel
> Futility rampant throughout –
> Madness to human intellect.

Circles and spirals reappear here in numerous forms: evolution is figured as an infinite electrical circuit, an incestuous energy routed round and round in infinite repetition; the relationship between universe and void is a rotating spiral, a 'divine spin' that mirrors the shape of a clock, whose self-cannibalizing 'periodclick' time offers another symbol of perpetual motion. The circle becomes an ambiguous symbol of totality and nothingness, of containment and uncontainability, time and what the Baroness elsewhere calls 'eternityshit!'[130] These spiral convulsions are the central form of movement in this world-system, a maddening 'shadowcarousel' that dictates the shape of existence from the smallest 'spinning cell' to the deep-time action of human evolution.

The central drama of the poem shows this rotating system collapsing in on itself; time and space are 'reshaped' and bent into something closer to a vortex spiral; the elements of the Baroness's poetic cosmos, like the turning hands of the clock, lead into and are fixed at a 'dead spot' at its centre. This vortex-spiral is totalizing, shaping every fragment of the universe, from the purposeless procession of time to the reformation of decayed parts, into new wholes. But the question of purpose – and of sense – remains. As in 'Fix', 'Narcissus – Icarus'

---

[130] Elsa von Freytag-Loringhoven, 'Constitution', *Body Sweats*, 171–3.

comes no closer to resolving the ongoing struggle for order. The whirling merry-go-round of modern existence renders attempts at sense-making futile, so that the already innately neurasthenic modernist who dares to try and situate themselves rationally faces an inevitable Icarian descent into madness. Another attempt to construct an understanding of psychic and universal systems, the poem's subject seems doomed to madness from the start.

In May 1926, the Baroness managed to inherit enough money to pursue her dream of travelling to Paris to rejoin her old Dada colleagues in Europe's modernist centre. Here, perhaps liberated by the distance, the Baroness's poetry gained a political dimension, which can be seen in 'X-Ray', her final published poem, which appeared in *transition* in 1927. In this poem the Baroness makes much more explicit use of terms from physics, couching her cyclical world system in the language of oxidization, cosmic radiation and dynamism. Aligning the natural process of oxidization with the congestion of people in the urban environment, the Baroness revisits her earlier systems with a political edge, the 'Brilliant boss' represented as a universal dictator, whose 'dynamic gang' enforces the cyclical process of universal recycling which, as we saw in 'since space is immeasurable', necessitates death. A dynamic shifting of energies, from the sun to the soil, from the crowd to the individual, is shown to be part of an equation whose 'sum total' is a totalizing radiance. 'Radiance' combines the physical ideas of light, head, energy; the human ideas of joy, love and, for the Baroness, sexual ecstasy; and the aesthetic idea of glowing, radiant beauty, into one ultimate obsession, the 'idée fixe' both of the universal 'boss', and of the artist herself.

> Nature causes brass to oxidize
> People to congest –
> By dull-radiopenetrated soil
> Destined
> Cosmic hand's dynamic gang
> Polish –
> Kill –
> For fastidious
> Brilliant boss' 'idée fixe'
> Sum total:
>   Radiance.[131]

---

[131] These versions are available online in an encoded electronic edition by Tanya Clements: https://digital.lib.umd.edu/transition/poem?pid=umd:55458 [Accessed 14 December 2020].

One of her most reworked poems, the ten extant drafts provide a clearer understanding of the dynamics playing out in 'X-Ray'.[132] Numerous changes and shifts of logic within the drafts suggest that it is intended as a social as well as cosmic commentary, contrasting the pressures of social and artistic expectations against the organic systems of the natural world. In these versions, less stripped-back syntax clarifies that the lines 'Polish – ' and 'Kill –' mirror the first two lines ('people polish/people kill' or 'polishing brass/killing people'). In this, the polishing of brass to remove the processes of nature is equated with murder in the name of a 'dormant ideal of beauty' or 'radiance' imposed upon nature and society 'contra nature'. Here, too, 'cause' in the first two lines is replaced by 'intends', giving the natural order a much more active role than it is given in the final version, as a force that 'penetrates forces' and 'stimulates causes'. In every version of this poem, however, the Baroness interrogates the alliance between physical and human forces, and it may be seen as the most refined and condensed of her later poetic works.

While we have seen that much of her post-New York writing offers a bleak image of the concentric prison universe, a sense of redemption does emerge in some of the poems from this final period of the Baroness's life. Between 1926 and 1927, she wrote the poem 'Cosmic Sense Suicide', which offers a brighter and more orderly sense of having come to terms with the state of the universe. More optimistic following her success, we see here an acceptance of natural laws in their potential for redemption, ultimate balance and their provision of hope.

> Combustion of particles in chemical retort
> Extremely necessary for ulterior result:
> > *Mixture's perfection.*
> There is no lack of sense in natural law
> No death – existence – deed – undeed – ever *is*
> 'Untimely – unnatural.'
> > *All action*
> Within law – or it were not.
> > *All*
> Carries own weight ('judgement') within.
> To be – balanced – upon
> Sunscale
> > *Gravitation.*

[132] Ibid.

> *Cosmic sense.*
> *Creator*
> *Redeemed –*
> *Exalted.*

The Baroness concludes the necessity of dissolution or 'combustion of particles' for regeneration, offering a sense that the cyclicality of natural laws and the conservation of energy in the universe make for a contained, though often concealed, natural order. 'Cosmic Sense Suicide' brings the universe in line with Christian doctrine, accepting the mysterious ways of God's divine plan, offering hope of a governing force behind the physical destruction that shaped the Baroness's Berlin period and presenting the artist-creator as 'redeemed' from her purgatory. Here she comes to terms with her own cosmology and lands upon more a balanced set of natural laws which encompass everything known in the universe. Being itself, she decided, is the result of conforming to the natural order: '*All action*/Within law – or it were not.' Drawing back upon the Dadaist understanding of creative destruction, we might see this poem as prefiguring a decision that, through suicide, she might finally accomplish her desire to master 'abstract science', becoming liberated rather than immured by the pseudo-rational realm of abstract scientific systems she critiqued in Duchamp's *Large Glass*.[133]

While the world came to terms with the quixotic sense of quantum mechanics, seemingly leaning into non-causal, chance-driven, and what were popularly considered irrational ontologies, the Baroness struck an opposite course, working in a tireless, iterative way to develop her own interpretation of a universal system that appeased her 'true nature [that] likes order'. This *idée fixe* consumed her later writing and offered a productive foil to the desperation and disorder found in her letters; the more concise, 'crystal' poetics, with its stripped back, fragmentary syntax, equations and scientific language, may have provided the 'island of safety in [a] sea of matter' she so ardently sought. Despite a growing spatial and temporal distance between her and the New York Dada milieu, this style emerged out of a period of intense reflection and reassessment both of her pre-Weimar life and the work and methodologies of her Dada

---

[133] The Baroness once wrote to Barnes: 'I am behind the veil of the sphinx – where Marcel is born and *used* to – it is his *native atmosphere* – for *me* – it is still gruesomely icy – desolate – yet – I will become citizen –. And then I will be great. To become such citizen of horror as Marcel with that charm – beauty – accomplishment – is not *cheaply won*—!... *I have paid my price!*', Elsa von Freytag-Loringhoven, *Baroness Elsa*, 206.

contemporaries and influences. Developing Dada's ideal of 'equivalence' into a system of totalizing equality and indiscriminate process that levels science, religion, politics, the bodily and the social spheres, we can see a continuation and adaptation of the proto-quantum themes of her earlier Dada to her later circumstances. As we saw with Williams, the Baroness's work is an example of how an engagement with remediated scientific ideas and particular understandings of physics as an ordered, cosmological discipline can provide a sense of form and methodological framework for artistic and poetic practice, while becoming fused, as it was for Loy, into a poetics of spiritual and deeply personal expression. Ideas from physics offered the Baroness a means to develop what might be called a poetry of systems, one that interrogated contemporary values of scientific measurement, sexual reproduction, psychological flux, artistic generation and, ultimately, our position in the universe.

4

The quantum poetics of Wallace Stevens and Max Planck

Everything is precious to great men. We are interested in their smallest gestures, their private life, their tastes, their weaknesses, their every habits, as if we thought we would find, someday, the secret of genius. Even after their death, before we let their remains disappear, we would like to collect the final documents.[1]

So begins an unsigned article in the 4 October 1951 issue of the French journal of literary and scientific news, *Les Nouvelles littéraires*. This issue was to furnish the poet Wallace Stevens with a suitable ending to a stubborn lecture he had been writing over the previous months, a piece that would become his last major public lecture before his own death four years later. By chance, the publication of this article coincided with the fourth anniversary of the death of another 'great man', the physicist Max Planck, 'patriarch of all modern physics', whose final documents are the subject of another article on the same page with the striking headline 'La dernière pensée de Planck'.[2] The article, from the scientific writer André George, which described how Planck's final papers had been collected and translated into French, caught and held the poet's attention.[3]

With a little less than a month until he was to present his paper at the University of Chicago, Stevens had written to his close friend, Barbara Church, that his 'paper for Chicago: A Collect of Philosophy is now finished and I have both Jean Wahl and Jean Paulhan in it. I was quite excited about it when

---

[1] 'Dissymétrie du Visage', *Les Nouvelles littéraires* (4-10-1951), 3. My translation. Original: 'Tout est précieux chez les grande hommes. Nous nous intéressons à leurs plus petits gestes, à leur vie privée, à leurs goûts, à leurs faiblesses, à leurs moindres habitudes, comme si nous pensions trouver, quelque jour, le secret du génie. Même après leur mort, avant de laisser disparaître leur dépouille, nous voudrions recueillir les ultimes documents.'
[2] In English: 'Planck's Last Thought', Ibid.
[3] Ibid.

I finished it'. The news, however, was not all good. With the essay finished, Stevens grew increasingly dissatisfied with its conclusion: 'When I go back to it, it seems slight; and my chief deduction: that poetry is supreme over philosophy because we owe the idea of God to poetry and not to philosophy does not seem particularly to matter. Nothing seems particularly to matter nowadays.'[4] Stevens's goal in the lecture had been to examine the crossroads between philosophy and poetry, suggesting that many philosophical ideas 'are inherently poetic'.[5] By embracing the summaries of philosophy afforded to him by his correspondents, Jean Wahl and Jean Paulhan, and his own reading of philosophy from Pascal to the mid-twentieth century, he hoped ambitiously to illustrate the 'poetic nature' of 'the philosophy of the sciences', and 'to sanction some of his later conclusions about human knowledge, nature, and interrelatedness'.[6] His method was, on the surface, straightforward: 'to identify at least a few philosophic ideas that are inherently poetic and to comment on them, one by one and then in general'.[7] Having discussed the poeticism of Bruno's descriptions of the Copernican universe, and dismissed Leibniz's monadology as 'the disappointing production of a poet *manqué*', Stevens was drawn to the scientific philosophers A. N. Whitehead and Samuel Alexander who, he says, 'write from a level where everything is poetic', and present their ideas like poets, straining for exactness in the same way.[8] But by the beginning of October, he felt his concept of the poetic idea in natural philosophy lacked a suitable contemporary keystone. It was then that Stevens read the article in *Nouvelles littéraires* and was inspired by George's reflections on the causality theory to undertake a series of revisions which brought Planck and his contribution to quantum physics to the forefront of his argument.

Planck, Stevens decided, is 'a much truer reflection of ourselves' than the other philosophers he discusses, and yet the final version of 'A Collect of Philosophy', as it was published in *Opus Posthumous* (1957), introduces the physicist with a suddenness that might take any reader off guard.[9] Just as Stevens appears to

---

[4] Wallace Stevens, '801. To Barbara Church', in *The Letters of Wallace Stevens*, ed. Holly Stevens (New York: Alfred A. Knopff, 1966), 729.
[5] Stevens, 'A Collect of Philosophy', *Opus Posthumous* (London: Faber & Faber, 1957), 183.
[6] Ibid., 184, 195; Lisa Steinman, *Made in America* (New Haven & London: Yale University Press, 1987), 144.
[7] Stevens, 'A Collect of Philosophy', 190.
[8] Ibid., 192, 194; For an in-depth examination of the influence of Whitehead on Stevens, see: Lawrence Martine Lewis, 'Wallace Stevens and the Process Philosophy of Alfred North Whitehead' (University of Texas Dissertation, 1979.); Alexander, Georges, and Joad are named as sources in 'A Collect of Philosophy'.
[9] Stevens, 'A Collect of Philosophy', 201.

have settled upon making an icon of Pascal, whose famous musings on eternal silence in infinite spaces might hold more obvious poetic appeal, he performs a dramatic U-turn to prioritize Planck's last 'pensées' instead: 'However, instead of placing at the end the figure of Pascal, let me place here the figure of Planck.'[10] In this chapter, I take this decision as a point of departure to examine Stevens's relationship with physics, and, in particular, to ask what the ease with which Stevens was able to align his conception of the poetic with the kind of scientific thought Planck represented can tell us about the conceptual parallels between modernist poetics and the quantum revolution. By comparing their writings and positioning Stevens in the context of the developments in physics Planck represents for him, I suggest a greater affinity between the poet and the physicist than these last-minute changes to 'Collect' might at first suggest. I will consider the different drafts of 'A Collect of Philosophy' in some detail as far as they pertain to what Judith McDaniel has called Stevens's 'distinctively "scientific" imagination' and trace the particular philosophical ideas Stevens alights upon here to wider themes of perception, observer intervention, the role of the image, (ir)rationality, abstraction and precision, that co-exist in both Stevens's poetics and quantum physics.[11]

We might be inclined to see the inclusion of Planck as a convenience, allowing Stevens to name-drop an influential scientific contemporary at the end of his paper. While his letters suggest he knew that incorporating Planck's quantum physics was not a simple affair and that '[t]he quantum theory is not something to be assimilated offhand', there is little evidence to suggest he had read Planck's writing himself.[12] Although an earlier typescript version of 'Collect', held by the Beinecke at Yale, includes a more thorough summary of George's article, which explains what he means by the causality theory and Planck's contribution to the shift between absolute determinist and probability-based predictions in atomic physics, however, it does not stray far from a word-for-word translation of George's article into English.[13] In contrast with Loy and Williams, while we know that Stevens was aware of developments in physics from the early 1930s through his reading of popular and literary journals, there is little to suggest that he actively sought out material dealing with physics or prioritized it

[10] Ibid.
[11] Judith McDaniel, 'Wallace Stevens and the Scientific Imagination', *Contemporary Literature* 15, no. 2 (Spring 1974), 223.
[12] Wallace Stevens, '797. To Barbara Church', *The Letters of Wallace Stevens*, ed. Holly Stevens (New York: Alfred A. Knopff, 1966), 725.
[13] Wallace Stevens, YCAL MSS 545, Series 1.

above other topics of passing interest to him.[14] Rather, I suggest, his interest in physics emerged out of a climate in which popular science books, such as those of Whitehead and Alexander, became widely read and discussed bestsellers, and where, as on the pages of *Les Nouvelles littéraires,* a poet could easily find scientific and literary news presented side-by-side. The question, then, is this: If associating his idea of the poetic with Planck was a convenience for Stevens, then what made it convenient? What affinity made his inclusion feel so fitting for Stevens's purposes?

In approaching this, McDaniel's perception that 'in all of his work Stevens expresses a distinctively "scientific" imagination, much in the sense that Donne's poetry grows out of a specific scientific worldview', seems eminently sensible, and she is right to assert with Whitehead that

> [t]his viewpoint need not be taken as a conscious reaction in the twentieth century because... the quiet growth of science has practically recoloured our mentality so that modes of thought which in former times were exceptional, are now broadly spread through the educated world.[15]

Bearing this in mind, my sources in this chapter are chosen for their relevance and affinity to Stevens's concerns, rather than, as in earlier chapters, because there is evidence to suggest that Stevens had read them himself. In this, I follow Dana Wilde, who has considered the implications of the new physics in shaping and informing Stevens's theory of poetry and the imagination. Her essay 'Stevens, Modern Physics, and Wholeness' argues that Stevens's poetry 'runs parallel to and in some ways intersects with quantum physicists' ideas about the relation of the individual to reality and society.'[16] Using the writing of Erwin Schrödinger, Wilde presents a reading of Stevens's work which maintains that, while 'his interest is in the poetic idea, not in quantum theory', he believed the philosophical implications of quantum theory could offer ripe fruit for the poet.[17] Here, I am concerned with why this may be, and my approach is similar to Wilde's in that I trace comparisons between Stevens's writing and that of the quantum physicists as a means of illuminating the affinity between their world views and those of Stevens. Where Wilde centred

---

[14] Dana Wilde, 'Stevens, Modern Physics, and Wholeness', *The Wallace Stevens Journal* 20, no. 1 (Spring 1996), 3–4.
[15] A. N. Whitehead, *Science and the Modern World* (New York: Macmillan, 1926), 112 cited in McDaniel, 222–3.
[16] Wilde, Stevens, 'Stevens, Modern Physics, and Wholeness', 4.
[17] Ibid., 4–5.

on Schrödinger, here I focus on Planck and Heisenberg to show the breadth of affinity Stevens found with these new quantum epistemologies.

Stevens's use of science is often implicit and allusive rather than explicit, addressing questions of perception, the intervening image and materialism. By positioning Stevens as an attentive poet, an avid reader and a productive thinker working in the Romantic tradition as reconsidered by Whitehead in *Science and the Modern World*, McDaniel comes closest to understanding the way in which Stevens's relationship with the new physics emerged. As a feature of the modern intellectual condition, quantum physics furnished Stevens with the material for his examinations of the relationship between the mind and the world it perceives, between poetic idealism and modern materialism. As Whitehead suggests, '[t]he new mentality is more important even than the new science and the new technology. It has altered our metaphysical presuppositions and the imaginative contents of our minds; so that now the old stimuli provoke a new response.'[18] However, as we saw in the last chapter, the conditions of this wider 'mentality' hold equal sway over both the physicists developing their theories and the poets who responded to them. In the first section of this chapter, I will discuss the poet's and the physicists' shared concern with language and imagery, a concern which, for the quantum physicists, reached its head in the 1920s through the Visualizablity question. I will then go on to consider Stevens's understanding of rational and irrational modes of perception, tracing his interest in ideas of order, disorder, and abstraction, which had, in the artistic circles of 1930s New York, become entangled with scientific and surrealist meaning. Techniques of aesthetic superposition, in particular, offered Stevens and the surrealists a fascinating means of representing an art of process and flux. Finally, I will consider the problems which arise from an abstract theory of the world, and particularly the relationship between the intrusive observer and the thing observed, a problem which dominates the shift in perception between the classical and quantum views of the universe, and which fascinated Stevens, ultimately shaping his theory of the imagination. Indeed, by the end of this chapter, it will be clear that Planck and his physics are a fitting choice of concern for a poet with Stevens's aesthetic and philosophical leanings.

---

[18] Whitehead, *Science and the Modern World*, 2.

The visualizability question and the poetic image

'A Collect of Philosophy' constitutes Stevens's most explicit appeal to the new physics as a site for the poetic imagination, and it provides a space for us to begin to consider these wider affinities between the ideas that governed Stevens's poetics and the problems in physics with which Planck was concerned.[19] The first mention of Planck in 'Collect' comes from a provocative quote from one of Paulhan's letters, which Stevens employs to endorse the value of the poetic imagination for solving problems the sciences could not:

> It is admitted, since Planck, that determinism – the relation of cause and effect – exists, or so it seems, on the human scale, only by means of an aggregate of statistical compensations and as the physicists say, by virtue of macroscopic approximations.... As to the true nature of the corpuscular or quantic phenomena, well, try to imagine them. No one has yet succeeded. But the poets – it is possible.[20]

On the matter of determining nature's true form, Paulhan suggests, the physicists have found their limit. A true depiction of quantum phenomena requires another skillset: the imaginative power of the poet. This was no doubt an appealing challenge to Stevens, for whom the imagination was an ordering force, a means of shaping an 'alien' and independent reality into tangible experience.[21] As the quantum physicists had discovered in the 1920s, there is no stranger reality than that found on the quantum scale, where phenomena do not exist in a way that has any direct analogy to our intuitive perceptions. Planck asserted that, 'In fact, the present scientific world picture, as against the original naive world picture, shows an odd, almost alien aspect.'[22] In this letter, then, Paulhan hit upon one of the most pressing issues to come out of Planck's discovery of quanta, the fact that 'our customary imagery is abstracted from objects we have actually perceived. But this sort of imagery fails for atoms because it is not only inappropriate, it is

---

[19] As the philosopher Simon Critchley has lamented, from a philosophical standpoint 'Collect' is 'frankly disappointing' and, in general, the results of Stevens's late attempts to translate the philosophical musings of his poetry into prose lectures were 'uneven, at best rather associative, and indeed poor in comparison to the power of his verse'. See: Simon Critchley, *Things Merely Are: Philosophy in the Poetry of Wallace Stevens* (London & New York: Routledge, 2005), 30–1.
[20] Jean Paulhan cited in Stevens, 'A Collect of Philosophy', 195.
[21] Ellwood Johnson, 'Wallace Stevens' Transforming Imagination', *The Wallace Stevens Journal* 8, no. 1 (Spring 1984), 28.
[22] Max Planck, 'The Meaning and Limits of Exact Science', *A Scientific Autobiography and Other Papers*, trans. Frank Gaynor (London: Williams & Norgate, 1950), 108.

nonfunctional as well'.²³ Planck's discoveries represented the beginning of a shift from the classical physics, which could be understood through normal human perception, and the modern physics, for which the human senses could no longer provide a meaningful allegory or image. Perhaps more urgently than any earlier theory of physics, the quantum theory was, from its roots at the turn of the century, bound up with concerns about representation, language and imagery.

In 1900, Planck proposed a model which successfully accounted for the full spectrum of thermal radiation, including black body radiation. The model was unusual because, in order to account for all experimental results, it relied on energy moving in discrete, quantized integers rather than in arbitrary amounts as had been the previously assumed. This discovery of the 'quantum of action', a new natural constant or 'yardstick of atomic dimensions' that guides electromagnetic activity, defined the limits of natural measurement.²⁴ Planck's discovery was soon followed in 1905 by another natural constant, Einstein's description of the absolute speed of light. As Heisenberg asserted, 'with Planck's discovery a wholly new type of natural law was recognized to be possible.'²⁵ Unlike the classical laws of physics, these constants told scientists 'not of particular things in nature but of the *general structure* of space and time' – a major leap forward in our understanding of the universe – but there was a catch: at the quantum scale, 'this structure is no longer directly accessible to our intuition'.²⁶ In order to pursue research into quantum phenomena, where the hitherto sufficient images of wave and particle did not simply apply, physicists faced a sudden and fundamental need to shift the terms and models they were using to describe the subatomic world.²⁷ Planck, Heisenberg and their contemporaries had to contend with the question of how best to discuss ideas about 'processes that, though still experimentally observable in their effects and rationally analysable by mathematical means, would no longer allow us to form any image of them'.²⁸ This proved to be a question not of the concepts themselves, but of the language used to capture and convey them; the physicists came face-to-face with the limitations of their own mental imagery.

---

[23] Arthur J. Miller, *Imagery in Scientific Thought* (Cambridge & Massachusetts: The MIT Press, 1986), 249.
[24] Werner Heisenberg, *Across the Frontiers*, ed. Ruth Nanda, trans. Peter Heath (New York: Harper & Row, 1974), 13.
[25] Ibid., 12.
[26] Ibid., 13. My emphasis.
[27] Ibid.
[28] Ibid., 12.

The issue of visualizability (or *Anschaulichkeit*) became one of the key sticking points of the quantum theory's detractors. Schrödinger was driven to his work on wave mechanics after being 'repelled' by quantum mechanics' 'lack of visualizability'.[29] He hoped his mechanics, which maintained the visualizable analogy of 'waves', would provide the corrective to a physics which had strayed beyond human intuition and perception. The need to find a viable form of semantics and mental imagery for the quantum theory reached its apex in 1926, when Niels Bohr met Heisenberg in Copenhagen to attempt, once and for all, to find a solution.[30] Heisenberg gave a striking account of this formative period in his 1969 lecture 'The Tendency to Abstraction in Modern Art and Science'. The physicists, he writes,

> were in despair about the state of confusion and aware that no lasting knowledge could come of it. Nobody wanted to destroy or repudiate the older physics. But the physicists were set a task which could no longer be evaded; for eventually it would have to be possible to state, in precise, rational language, what was happening in the interior of the atom. ... For those who took part in it, the emergence of a new order was a powerful and astonishing experience.[31]

> It was felt that we no longer knew exactly what was meant by the words 'position' or 'velocity' of an electron within the atom; but for a long time we were not able to speak of processes within an atom in any rationally intelligible fashion.[32]

The problem of visualizability was tied up with wider questions of honouring the scientific tradition and of maintaining its values of precision and rationality. Heisenberg notes that despite the crisis, there was always a hopeful determination that, one way or another, quantum visualization 'would *have to be possible*'.

For Paulhan, this possibility demanded an interdisciplinary intervention, an opportunity for the poet to step in and provide the necessary language:

> It comes to this that philosophers (particularly the philosophers of science) make, not discoveries but hypotheses that may be called poetic. Thus Louis de Broglie admits that progress in physics is, at the moment, in suspense because we do not have the words or the images that are essential to us. But to create illuminations, images, words, that is *the very reason for being of poets*.[33]

---

[29] Miller, *Imagery in Scientific Thought*, 251.
[30] They each came to different conclusions; Bohr promoted the idea of limited metaphor centred on the idea of 'complementarity', while Heisenberg believed physicists must recourse to the language of mathematics, in which terms could be allowed to provide their own limitations. For an account of these solutions, see Miller, *Imagery in Scientific Thought*, 248–61.
[31] Heisenberg, *Across the Frontiers*, 145–6.
[32] Ibid., 145.
[33] Stevens, 'A Collect of Philosophy', 196. My emphasis.

He was not alone in suggesting that a solution to the linguistic problems of quantum physics might come from somewhere beyond the laboratory. Planck gestured to the role of the creative imagination in providing scientific solutions. In 'The Meanings and Limits of Exact Science', he discusses the limitations of a world picture mediated through human sensory perception, in the face of the new, abstract and mathematically denoted physics:

> The immediately experienced sense impressions, the primordial sources of scientific activity, have dropped totally out of the [scientific] world picture, in which sight, hearing and touch no longer play a part. A glance into a modern scientific laboratory shows that the functions of these senses have been taken over by a collection of extremely complex, intricate and specialized devices, contrived and constructed for handling problems which can be formulated only with the aid of abstract concepts, mathematical and geometric symbols, and which often are beyond the layman's power of understanding.[34]

Planck claimed that what Stevens would have called the poetic imagination had vital role for the modern scientist: 'he must have a vivid intuitive imagination, for new ideas are not generated by deduction, but by an artistically creative imagination.'[35] In another section, directly quoted by Stevens, Planck emphasizes that 'the world picture of physics [is] a provisional and alterable creation of the human power of imagination'.[36] For Stevens, whose life's work had been the formulation of a theory of the imagination and its relation to an ultimate poetic reality, Planck's view of science as a 'working hypothesis', whose higher reality can only be accessed through an extreme act of imagination that reaches into a realm beyond the normal parameters of sensory experience and metaphor, was highly appealing. Furthermore, quantum physics' notion that the observer may have an active influence upon quantum phenomena chimed with the theories of perception that shaped his poetic art. For Stevens, poetry 'is to a large extent an art of perception and [he believed] the problems of perception as they are developed in philosophy resemble[d] similar problems in poetry'.[37] The scientists' struggle to speak rationally about phenomena that resist *a posteriori* accounts and its resolution through appeal to the imagination have parallels in Stevens's own poetic-philosophical project.

---

[34] Planck, 'The Meaning and Limits of Exact Science', 108.
[35] Planck, 'The Meaning and Limits of Exact Science', 109.
[36] Planck, 'The Meaning and Limits of Exact Science', 144.
[37] Stevens, 'A Collect of Philosophy', 191.

It is clear that quantum physics also held an aesthetic appeal for Stevens. While planning his lecture he suggests that the quantum world view offers a new way of thinking about the poetic archetypes that have shaped poetry from time immemorial: 'But I love [Paulhan's depiction of quantum physics's] "approximations macroscopiques" and must think how to use them together with Jean Wahl's fausses reconnaissances. Is not the idea of the hero an "approximation macroscopique"?'[38] This appealed to Stevens because it provoked a shift in perception of the world and its reality afforded by our senses, and if we are to trace back a lineage of shared concerns between Stevens and Planck, this should be our guiding point. In 1951, the imaginative understanding of physics represented by Planck aligns with Stevens's own theories of the poetic imagination, a world view he had been developing since the 1920s, which appreciated the limitations of vision and measurement, and allowed for the observing, imaginative mind to enter into a direct relationship with material reality. If, as Stevens suggests, an idea is poetic when it 'instantly changes the face of the world' and 'gives the imagination sudden life', I argue that quantum physics might be early-twentieth-century physics most 'poetic' development.[39]

As early as 1923, with the publication of his first poetry collection *Harmonium*, Stevens had been fascinated by the tension between the imagination's ability to bring sense and order to the observed landscape, and the limitations of metaphors and images in doing so. In the famous 'Anecdote of the Jar', the standard mode of visualizing the Tennessee hills is attenuated, 'the slovenly wilderness' made 'no longer wild', by the focalizing power of the titular object. The jar, a tidy, man-made object, so distinct from its surroundings, 'Like nothing else in Tennessee', offers a striking inversion: the object made to contain becomes contained by its environment.[40] The placement of Stevens's jar in the heart of nature is reminiscent of Emerson's 'transparent eyeball', which collects and orders all it observes; but where for Emerson 'all mean egotism vanishes' in the deep observation of nature, Stevens's jar is not transparent but tinted grey.[41] As in later poems, observed reality is transformed by the presence of a focalizing object or observer (e.g. 'Things as they are / Are changed upon the

---

[38] Stevens, *The Letters of Wallace Stevens*, 769.
[39] Stevens, 'A Collect of Philosophy', 183, 190.
[40] Wallace Stevens, 'The Anecdote of the Jar', *The Collected Poems of Wallace Stevens* (London: Faber & Faber, 2006), 66–7.
[41] Ralph Waldo Emerson, 'Nature', *The Norton Anthology of American Literature*, 7th ed., vol. B, ed. Nina Baym (New York & London: W. W. Norton & Co., 2007), 1112.

blue guitar').[42] A poem, as Stevens elsewhere states, is always mediated by the poet's imagination, the act of selection and the process of composition.

Indeed, Emerson hit upon a fundamental instinct that drives a poet like Stevens, and which comes to bear in the visualizability problem in quantum mechanics: 'man is an analogist, and studies relations in all objects,' and as such relies upon the relation of abstract concepts to sense experience for understanding.[43] Just as the landscape is given meaning by its (spatial) relation to the jar, our world is inherently shaped by imaginative analogy to other objects and sights provided by human perception. Yet, like the images of wave and particle that fail for subatomic phenomena, the poet is forced to contend with the fact that words are limited to their relationship with our sense perceptions: 'Words are finite organs of the infinite mind. They cannot cover the dimensions of what is in truth. They break, chop, and impoverish it.'[44] Furthermore, in a passage in which Emerson brings the 'axioms of physics' to bear on his discussion of language and expression, he argues that '[t]he world is emblematic. Parts of speech are metaphors because the whole of nature is a metaphor of the human mind'.[45] Stevens's poetry emerges from this Emersonian tradition, in which the poet is a mediator of reality, a figure whose imagination is 'the use which reason makes of the world'.[46]

As the transmuter of reality into poetry, the poet relies on his senses, and upon the understanding that our sense perceptions provide access to the reality of the world around us. For Stevens, this reality was the ground of all poetry. In his 1941 essay, 'The Noble Rider and the Sound of Words', he states that

> The imagination loses vitality as it ceases to adhere to what is real. When it adheres to the unreal and intensifies what is unreal, while its first effect may be extraordinary, the effect is the maximum effect it will ever have.[47]

However, unlike Emerson, he was developing his poetics during a period in which human sense perceptions were shown to be lacking, from the overthrow of Lombroso's physiognomy, described in the October 1951 issue of *Les Nouvelles littéraires*, to the development of photomanipulation and X-ray imaging, and, at the extreme end, the quantum theory. During this period, issues

---

[42] Wallace Stevens, 'The Man With The Blue Guitar', *The Collected Poems of Wallace Stevens*, 143.
[43] Emerson, 'Nature', 1119.
[44] Ibid., 1125.
[45] Ibid., 1120–1.
[46] Ibid., 1128.
[47] Wallace Stevens, 'The Noble Rider and the Sound of Words', *The Necessary Angel* (New York: Vintage Books, 1951), 6.

of representation and reality were pushed to the foreground of modern art, and Stevens was keenly aware of what was at stake in modern poetry's depictions of the real. These limited senses were inadequate to the task of depicting modern reality. This concern followed Stevens throughout his life, and reappears in 'Collect', where he argues that

> The material world, for all the assurances of the eye, has become immaterial. It has become an image in the mind. The solid earth disappears and the whole atmosphere is subtilized not by the arrival of some venerable beam of light from an almost hypothetical star but by a breach of reality. What we see is not an external world but an image of it and hence an internal world.[48]

This is to say that the imagination transposes our experiences, offering representations of the world in the mind which are never direct reflections of the true reality but are mediated in one way or another, whether by the cast of the light, by the influence of our prevailing mood at the time of apprehension, or, as the 'macroscopic approximations' of Paulhan and the quantum world would have it, by the limitation of our senses, which perceive an agglomeration of seething particles and empty spaces as solid forms. This raises a problem that becomes fundamental to Stevens's poetics: if the imagination must attach itself onto something real as an anchor, but all sense experience is in some way deceptive, how might the poet break away from the false images of the mind in order to say something meaningful about reality?

'By metaphor you paint / A thing', he writes in 'Poem Written at Morning' from *Parts of a World* (1942), a meditation on the limitations of our sensory relationship with the world. The poem instructs the reader to notice the fragmentation of material reality that takes place when it is described through metaphor: 'Divide it from itself. It is this or that / And it is not.' Each attribute ascribed through metaphor loses its closeness to the reality of the thing itself. For instance, the lines 'Thus, the pineapple was a leather fruit, / A fruit for pewter, thorned and palmed and blue' create a compound metaphor, likening the pineapple to tough hide, a luxurious still life image, thorny plants, palm trees, and ultimately the abstracted 'blue' of the imagination. 'The senses paint / By metaphor' – the smell and taste of the pineapple can only be described by likening them to other smells (cinnamon) and tastes (pears). Stevens draws attention to the inadequacy of these metaphors and the limitation of a world experienced purely through the senses:

---

[48] Stevens, 'A Collect of Philosophy', 191.

The truth must be
that you do not see, you experience, you feel,
That the buxom eye brings merely its element
To the total thing, a shapeless giant forced
Upward.[49]

Stevens often tested his ideas about perception by allying poetry with other art forms, painting and music, and using the formal considerations of each to shine light upon the function and frailty of the poetic image. In 'Study of Two Pears' (1942), he approaches a still life through a series of four-line vignettes which strip back the connotations of the image to bare forms which 'resemble nothing else'.[50] The pears, he says, adopting a pedagogical tone to evoke the allusive figurations of Art, 'are not viols, / Nudes or bottles'.[51] He considers the formal aspects of the pears, breaking them down geometrically, as famously proposed by Cezanne, into base colours and shapes: 'They are yellow forms / Composed of curves / Bulging toward the base.'[52] This precise visual description of what 'they are' is followed by a negative analysis of what 'They are not'. By analysing the subject of the poem from numerous angles, as a cubist might, Stevens attempts to home in on the reality of the pears, the aspects of them which are beyond the artist's control and which might be considered their essential reality. Importantly, the poem concludes by highlighting the independence of the observer and the observed: 'The pears are not seen / As the observer wills.'[53] Elsewhere, he admits that this kind of observation is limited at best, that 'The whole of appearance is just a toy.'[54] Yet while, 'In the sum of the parts, there are only parts', that is, the sum is an illusion, 'The world must be measured by eye.'[55] As such, our limited perception – as the physicists had also found – is the ground for our understanding of the world; outside of mathematical abstraction, it is the only reference point most of us have.

Planck wrestles with a similar problem in his essay, 'The Meaning and Limit of Exact Science'. Here he notes that while the 'world of objects, in contrast to the sense world, is therefore called *the real world* … one must be careful when using

---

[49] Wallace Stevens, 'Poem Written at Morning', *Collected Poems*, 191.
[50] Wallace Stevens, 'Study of Two Pears', *The Collected Poems*, 171.
[51] Ibid.
[52] In a letter of 15 April 1904 to Emile Bernard, Cezanne expressed his wish to 'treat nature by the cylinder, the sphere, the cone'. Cited in Carol Donnell-Kotrozo, 'Cezanne, Cubism, and the Destination Theory of Style', *The Journal of Aesthetic Education* 13, no. 4 (October 1979), 104.
[53] Stevens, 'Study of Two Pears', 172.
[54] Wallace Stevens, 'The Dove in the Belly', *Collected Poems*, 319.
[55] Wallace Stevens, 'On the Road Home', *Collected Poems*, 177.

the word *real*.⁵⁶ He asserts that, in the twentieth century, reality can no longer be thought of as an absolute and immutable external fact, but rather the 'dominant world picture' at any given time, which is always subject to change:

> the atoms were taken by science to constitute the true reality in natural processes[, to] be that which remains immutable ... representing permanency in the midst of all change – until one day, to everybody's astonishment, it was found that even atoms could change.⁵⁷

Aware of the transience of scientific knowledge, Planck uses 'the word *real* primarily in a qualified, naïve sense, adjusted to the particular character of the dominant world picture', always bearing in mind its potential to change along with future discoveries.⁵⁸ The care with which he delineates this usage exemplifies the quality of 'exactness' Stevens appreciated from the scientists in *Collect*. The nature of this reality, described through the interaction of particles too small to be intuitively recognized, brings with it practical limitations of the kind we saw with the visualization problem. Furthermore, Planck suggests, it leaves a gap which must be filled with 'more abstract conceptual structures' that so far defy the intuition. Science is limited in its ability to approach the metaphysical reality 'behind' sense reality because

> The experiences gained with the refined instruments of measurement demand inexorably that certain firmly rooted intuitive notions can be abandoned and replaced by new, more abstract conceptual structures ... they are landmarks to guide theoretical research on its road from the naive concept of reality to the metaphysical 'Real.'⁵⁹

The 'gaping chasm, unbridgeable from the point of view of exact science', between physical and metaphysical reality, according to Planck, 'is the source of constant tension, which can never be balanced, and which is the inexhaustible source of the insatiable thirst for knowledge within the true research scientist'.⁶⁰ It is this impossible goal towards which the scientist continually strives that Planck refers to as 'the irrational element which exact science can never shake off'.⁶¹

For both Stevens and Planck, the allure of an abstract world picture came from its ability to reach beyond the limitations of the senses and handle metaphysical

---

[56] Planck, 'The Meaning and Limits of Exact Science', 95.
[57] Ibid.
[58] Ibid.
[59] Ibid., 104–5.
[60] Ibid., 105.
[61] Ibid., 106.

concepts that would otherwise resist consideration. During the 1920s, Stevens's interest in bridging the gulf between appearances and reality first becomes clear in his desire to undress common poetic images, leaving their freight of accrued connotations at the door. Later poems like 'The Man on the Dump' (1938) offer a critique of artistic representation, aimed particularly at how metaphorical comparisons distance us from the very reality they hope to describe.[62] Here, Stevens attempts to strip away the carbon-copy images that cluttered turn-of-the-century poetry with dead connotations, commending tired imagery to 'the dump'. This allows for a 'purifying change', in which the tired world is revivified, and the poet is free to create fresh poetry in a space where

> Everything is shed: the moon comes up as the moon
> (All its images are in the dump) and you see
> As a man (not like an image of a man),
> You see the moon rise up in its empty sky.[63]

By shaking off the inadequacy of clichéd poetic images, whose meanings have become stale through overuse, Stevens seeks the pure 'thing itself' much in the same spirit as Gertrude Stein who, through repetition and simple language pushed towards a pure idea when she wrote 'a rose is a rose is a rose'.[64] Stevens is, as he says in another poem, 'Tired of the old descriptions of the world', and seeks a means of 'being without description'.[65] The moon, therefore, 'resembles nothing else' with a purity of vision that is difficult to achieve in poetry, where words are charred with pre-existing connotations. Even here, where the purification process is undertaken at length, the success is only partial as new connotations (e.g. of clarity, of truth) clamour to attach themselves to the moon in its empty sky. Stevens understood this difficulty and was aware that the seeker of pure representation can be easily duped and must continue to question the nature of these images: 'Is it peace … one finds on the dump?' Indeed, the symbolic nature of language itself poses a strong barrier; a noun is always signifying something it is not, always acting at one remove from the reality of the object it signifies. As in the distancing of the observer from the observed in 'Two Pears', 'The Man

---

[62] This poem first appears grouped as part of the first twelve poems of *Parts of a World* under the title 'Canonica', in the *Southern Review*, 4 (Autumn 1938). Eleanor Cook, *A Reader's Guide to Wallace Stevens* (Princeton, NJ: Princeton University Press, 2007), 133.
[63] Stevens, 'The Man on the Dump', *Collected Poems*, 176.
[64] Gertrude Stein, 'Sacred Emily', *Geography and Plays* (1922), https://ebooks.adelaide.edu.au/s/stein/gertrude/geography_and_plays/Page_178.html [Accessed 10 December 2019].
[65] Stevens, 'The Latest Freed Man', *Collected Poems*, 178, 179.

on the Dump' ends with a thought that reasserts a sense of futility for the poet wishing to depict reality. If complex words betray us with their connotations, and if a true poet is one who 'rejects the trash', Stevens seems to suggest, we must look for reality in the tiniest particle of language, the definite article: 'Where was it one first heard of the truth? The the.'

This final line is disarming. It shifts the focus of the poem from image complexes to single words and suggests a raw value in breaking the construct down to its constituent parts. In the context of an atomic world in which the smallest parts become abstract, Stevens's poetry rarely offers explanations, and often the theories he weighs up in his poems are puzzles that are left unsolved. Speaking to the visualizability problem, Bohr told Heisenberg that the situation was such that 'a theory cannot "explain" anything in the usual scientific sense of the word. All it can hope to do is reveal connections and, for the rest, leave us to grope as best we can.'[66] In a similar fashion, readers of Stevens may often feel as though his poems throw up more questions than answers. Yet Stevens was a poet who was always concerned with the way things were put together, and the interrelation of parts and wholes might be considered the ordering concern of all of his poetry.

Daniel Albright's models of 'quantum poetics' attached to the ideas of the wave and particle model might be usefully translated into a model of parts and wholes. Approaching Stevens's poems with attention to the complementary effects of 'isolated huddled' atoms of language and the 'twanging web' of interrelations between them enables a deeper appreciation of his intellectual project. Although it has been rightly argued that complementarity was not Stevens's method as such, his poetry often bridges these two models, deeply attentive to both the part and the whole.[67] While the final line of 'The Man on the Dump' asserts the value of the abstract particle, there is a strong sense in Stevens criticism that his work is best understood when taken as a whole, self-referential system. Helen Vendler argues that Stevens's imagery does not warrant her focus as it 'is not particularly obscure once one knows the Collected Poems: [sic] It is a system of self-reference, and is its own explanation.'[68] While this is not altogether satisfactory as an explanation, it does highlight the way in which

---

[66] Niels Bohr cited in William H. Cropper, *Great Physicists: The Life and Times of Leading Physicists from Gallileo to Hawking* (Oxford: Oxford University Press, 2001), 250.
[67] Denis Donoghue, 'Nuances of a Theme by Stevens', *The Act of the Mind: Essays on the Poetry of Wallace Stevens*, ed. Roy Harvey Pierce and J. Hillis Miller (Maryland: Johns Hopkins University Press, 1965), 224–43.
[68] Helen Vendler, *On Extended Wings: Wallace Stevens' Longer Poems* (Cambridge: Harvard Press, 1969), 9.

Stevens's broader methodology might be considered according to Albright's dual model; images are developed and repeated in multiple contexts throughout the body of Stevens's work and develop, through sustained reading, particular kinds of interrelation within an elastic framework.

Through these meta-poems, Stevens creates a state in which the 'particle' and 'wave' models of poetic structure are held in suspension and hold equal importance. Through attention to these acts of suspension, taking them as part of Stevens's intended point about the function of poems generally, we might allay some of the frustration, if not the difficulty, that comes about when we try to explain the point of a poem of Stevens's in isolation.

Stevens was averse to the idea of explaining the meaning of his poetry and did so only under duress.[69] In 1940, he wrote to Hi Simons

> A long time ago I made up my mind not to explain things, because most people have so little appreciation of poetry that once a poem has been explained it has been destroyed: that is to say, they are no longer able to seize the poem.[70]

While he does, in fact, go on to offer an explanation of the poem Simons was enquiring about, this notion about explanations destroying a poem or artwork is worth dwelling on in so far as it implies that the mystery or lack of resolution in a poem is the source of its poetic energy. Much as explaining why a joke is funny kills the joke, Stevens holds the suspended and unresolved state of the poem as necessary for its imaginative effect to take full force. In his analysis of Stevens' oeuvre, Mark Noble suggests that 'Stevens projects the quantum aporia that complicate twentieth-century models of the atom onto the relation between what he calls our "rage for order" and the "muddy centre [that was] before we breathed"'.[71] In poems such as 'The Man on the Dump', where we feel Stevens draw close to a revelation which he leaves open-ended and unresolved, we can begin to see 'quantum aporia's emerging through the evacuated symbol of the definite article, which gestures towards a 'defined or particularized' nothingness.[72]

Both Stevens and the quantum physicists came independently to need a means of handling material which resisted easy visualization, and both found solutions through the interrogation of the language that had come to be accepted within their field. In their shared concern with perception, language

---

[69] B. J. Leggett, 'Stevens' Psychology of Reading: "Man Carrying Thing and Its Sources"', *The Wallace Stevens Journal* 6, no. 3 (Fall 1982), 53.
[70] Stevens, '396. To Hi Simons', *The Letters of Wallace Stevens*, 346.
[71] Mark Noble, *American Poetic Materialism from Whitman to Stevens* (New York: Cambridge University Press, 2015), 12.
[72] 'definite article, n.' OED Online. Oxford University Press, September 2019. Web. 24 September 2019.

and the images used to visualize their subjects, we can begin to see an affinity between the things which occupied the minds of the poet and the physicists alike. For Heisenberg, Bohr and Planck, as for Stevens, there was a draw towards increasingly abstract means of representation as a way of alleviating the difficulties presented by concepts which refused to behave in ways that could be apprehended through the limitations of sense experience. Stevens's interest in representation is primarily focussed on a process (the act of making poetry) which takes place on a plane that resists description and is largely acted out in a theoretical space where appeal to sensory experience for image-descriptions can only ever be potential, approximate or partial. Our understanding of poetry is necessarily attenuated by the sensibility of the poet, and this preoccupation with the observer's shaping influence upon his subject is as much in Stevens's mind as it is in Planck's. It is as important that the man in 'Man on the Dump' comes to 'see / As a man (not like an image of a man)' as it is for the image of the moon to be a stark, unadulterated moon. Stevens is concerned not only with the way things are represented in art and poetry, but with the way they are experienced by the viewer or reader, and particularly with the way in which poetry can push beyond the limitations of the eye towards a wider conception of imaginative reality.

The image in superposition: Stevens and Surrealism

Although we know that Stevens had an interest in popular science, there is little to suggest his awareness during the 1920s of the issues being faced by the physicists on the other side of the Atlantic. As with the other poets I have discussed, it is more likely that Stevens came to think about the complexity of poetic images through his contact with modern art, and particularly his interest in the work of the surrealists, who by the mid-1930s had taken New York by storm. Their influence on Stevens came at a turning point in his career, as he began to formalize a theory of the imagination which would underpin his poetry. In this section, I want to examine the intersection between Stevens's interest in the processes of the poetic imagination and the experimentation of the surrealists. Building upon Glen McLeod and Susan McCabe's work on the importance of Surrealism to Stevens's aesthetics of the 1930s, I suggest that the work of painters such as Picasso and Dalí gave Stevens a lens through which to approach an aesthetics of flux and superposition appropriate to his interest in the workings of the imaginative mind.[73] In particular, I am interested in the usefulness of these concepts from physics and Surrealism as a way of reading Stevens's attempts to examine poetry as a process of recreating and preserving primordial, unresolved states in the mind.

By the mid-1930s, the surrealists were championing a new art that afforded greater value to the workings of the mind in its strange and irrational aspect than to the positivist understanding of reality. In 1934, they staged an exhibition entitled 'Fantastic Art, Dada, Surrealism' at the Museum of Modern Art in New York, which Stevens – a lifelong art aficionado – attended. The day before the show opened, he acknowledged the buzz caused by the surrealists in his lecture, 'The Irrational Element in Poetry'. Stevens's concerns chimed with the wider anti-rational mood in New York which the surrealists amplified:

> We are at the moment so beset by the din made by the surrealists and surrationalists, and so preoccupied in reading about them that we may become confused by these romantic scholars and think of them as the sole exemplars of the irrational today. Certainly, they exemplify one aspect of it.[74]

The radical dynamism of the surrealists' work, he says, 'make other forms seem obsolete', and throughout this lecture there is a tension between Stevens's appreciation for Surrealism and his desire to resist being considered one himself.[75] Speaking about the 'irrational element in poetry', Stevens is interested in 'the transaction between reality and the sensibility of the poet from which poetry springs'.[76] That is, 'a particular process in the rational mind which we recognize as irrational in the sense that it takes place unaccountably'.[77] He acknowledges a cultural crisis of faith in the rational, of which the surrealists, and their influence, Sigmund Freud, were a part: 'It is becoming easier every day to say that we are not rational beings; that all irrationality is not of a piece and that the only reason it does not yet have a tradition is that its tradition is in progress.'[78]

---

[73] Glen McLeod, 'Stevens and Surrealism: The Genesis of "The Man with the Blue Guitar"', *American Literature* 59, no. 3 (October 1987), 359–77; Glen McLeod, *Wallace Stevens and Modern Art* (New Haven & London: Yale University Press, 1993); Susan McCabe, 'Stevens, Bishop, and Ashbery: A Surrealist Lineage', *The Wallace Stevens Journal* 22, no. 2 (Fall 1998), 149–69.
[74] Wallace Stevens, 'The Irrational Element in Poetry', *Opus Posthumous*, 217–18.
[75] Ibid., 228; McLeod, 'Stevens and Surrealism', 362.
[76] Stevens, 'The Irrational Element in Poetry', 217.
[77] Ibid., 218.
[78] Ibid.

Stevens's adoption of the term 'irrational' emerged from this wider discourse in which irrationality had not only a greater legitimacy than in earlier decades, but had, for some, become a condition for modern art, entangled with ideas from modern physics in surrealist writing. As discussed in relation to Dada in the last chapter, there was a perception among writers and artists that the irrational was gradually creeping into science. Even Planck uses the language of irrationality when he described the 'irrational element which exact science can never quite shake off'.[79] As it did for Mina Loy, Surrealism provided ripe ground for artists who were interested in exploring the line between the rational and irrational, and the juxtaposition and fusion of scientific and mystical thought.

In 1935, Dalí published a book of reproductions entitled *Conquest of the Irrational*, whose introduction begins with a discussion of 'the brilliant and sensational progress of the particular sciences':

> [The] glory and honour of the 'space' and time in which we live entails, on the one hand the crisis and overwhelming discredit of 'logical intuition', and, on the other hand, the consideration of irrational factors and hierarchies as new positive and specifically productive values.[80]

Dalí's diagnosis results in the hyperbolic assertion that

> in effect the irrational hunger of our contemporaries is confronted by a cultural dining-table upon which there are only, on the one hand, the cold and unsubstantial remains of art and literature, and, on the other, the burning analytical precisions of the particular sciences, inaccessible, for the moment, to a nutritious synthesis because of their inordinate extension and specialisation and, in any case, totally unassimilable, except in cases of speculative cannibalism.[81]

For this, he offers the tonic of Surrealism: a 'good quality, decadent, stimulating, extravagant and ambivalent food' provided by practitioners who 'are not exactly artists and not exactly men of science' offering the 'exactitude and divisionist precision of the caviar of the imagination'.[82] The surrealists, he suggests, might capitalize on the crises in art and science by occupying a between-space, flitting freely between the trappings of each without necessarily adhering to the formal regulation of either. This privileged superposition allowed the surrealists to inhabit irrational spaces pictorially and conceptually, but it also made the

---

[79] Planck, 'The Meaning and Limits of Exact Science', 106.
[80] Salvador Dalí, *The Conquest of the Irrational* (New York: Julien Levy, 1935), 7.
[81] Ibid., 8–9.
[82] Ibid., 9, 10.

movement decidedly slippery and difficult to define. Although more formally directed than Dada, Surrealism appeared in just as many flavours, its extremity and its techniques varying from artist to artist, from country to country.

By 1936, when New York welcomed the first major exhibition of Picasso's work, the surrealists had claimed him as one of their own. The father of Surrealism, André Breton, warmly declared:

> We claim him unhesitatingly as one of us, even though it is impossible and would, in any case, be impertinent to apply to his methods the rigorous system we propose to institute in other directions. If surrealism ever comes to adopt a particular line of conduct, it has only to accept the discipline that Picasso has accepted and will continue to accept.[83]

For Stevens, Picasso was an exemplary figure, a 'hero' through whose lens he could begin defining his own theory of the imagination's 'nutritious synthesis' with reality. This became the long poem 'The Man with the Blue Guitar' (1937), a meta-poetic exercise in thirty-three sections which paints a picture of the modern imagination as Breton had described it, as something 'on the point of reasserting itself, of reclaiming its rights' in the face of artistically arid conditions.[84] The poet acts as a collagist, and art takes the form of patchy, atomized representation, a struggle for containment much more complex than the ready order of the jar in Tennessee. Here the artist faces an insurmountable task: 'I cannot bring the world quite round, / Although I patch it as I can.'[85] In attempting to play a tune of 'things exactly as they are', the artist's work is repeatedly reduced to approximations; as in Picasso's paintings, the aspects of the figure are fragmentary, gesturing to something they are not, and emphasizing the gulf between art and reality through their disjunctive, anti-realist mode of representation. As Stevens builds a man, he is aware only of its parts, the seams between the patches remaining all-too-visible:

> I sing a hero's dead, large eye
> And bearded bronze, but not a man,
> Although I patch him as I can
> And reach through him almost to man.[86]

---

[83] André Breton, 'Surrealism in Painting' (1928) quoted McLeod, 'Stevens and Surrealism', 366.
[84] André Breton, 'Manifesto of Surrealism', *Manifestoes of Surrealism*, trans. Richard Seaver and Helen R. Lane (Ann Arbor: The University of Michigan, 1969), 10.
[85] Stevens, 'The Man with the Blue Guitar', *Collected Poems*, 143.
[86] Ibid.

This awareness of the limitations of language, of the transformation that happens through ascribing artistic representation to a 'real' object or person, brings into question the rationality of our sense perceptions themselves. Stevens urges a reassessment of the artists' drive to represent reality, to dig into its heart as a scientist would, to expose and break its secrets down into parts of a whole or, as he puts it, 'To lay [a man's] brain upon a board / And pick the acrid colours out'.[87] This is reminiscent of Apollinaire's praise of Picasso's surgical dissection of the object in *The Little Review*, and Stevens consciously mimics this handling of the subject, picking his terms apart and turning them over and over to view them from different aspects through subsequent stanzas.[88]

Stevens uses Picasso's artistic vision as a way of mediating the crisis of the rational; in section XV he adopts Picasso's own language to interrogate the state of modern society:

> Is this picture of Picasso's, this 'hoard
> Of destructions,' a picture of ourselves,
> Now, an image of our society?[89]

Picasso, here, is a forerunner of Planck in Stevens's self-constructed lineage of figures representative of 'ourselves', a figure who offers a model through which to try and bring order to the disordered modern world. Stevens first encountered Picasso's description of painting as '*une somme de destructions*' in a 1935 special issue of *Cahiers d'art* devoted to Surrealism, and he carried it with him for almost twenty years.[90] It reappears to reinforce his ideas about the correlations between visual and poetic art in a much later lecture on 'The Relations Between Poetry and Painting' (1951) at the Museum of Modern Art: 'Does not the saying of Picasso that a picture is a horde of destructions also say that a poem is a horde of destructions?'[91] In 'The Man with the Blue Guitar', the quote has an echo of Eliot's *The Waste Land*, giving up dead and 'broken images' as the poet asks with a bizarre, almost Dalí-esque image, 'Do I sit, deformed, a naked egg, / Catching at Good-bye, harvest moon, / Without seeing the harvest or the moon?'[92] Stevens brings into question not only the validity of poetic images, but also of

---

[87] Ibid., 144.
[88] Discussed in Chapter One.
[89] Ibid., 150.
[90] McLeod, 'Stevens and Surrealism', 364–5.
[91] Christian Zervos, 'Conversation avec Picasso', *Cahiers d'art* 10 (1935), 173; Wallace Stevens, 'The Relations between Poetry and Painting', *The Necessary Angel*, 161.
[92] Stevens, 'The Man with the Blue Guitar', 150.

the real 'things' they represent and the crisis into which this places the artist-poet: 'Things as they are', he says, 'have been destroyed. / Have I?'[93]

This crisis of representation struck artists and physicists alike, and the ensuing struggle, could be incredibly generative. As Heisenberg writes: 'This interplay, or struggle, if you will, between the contents to be expressed and the restricted means of expressing it seems to me to be – much as it is for science – the unavoidable precondition for the emergence of genuine art.'[94] There is a question here not only of the validity of knowledge and the images used to represent it but also of the possession and control of reality as a subject: 'Is the spot on the floor, there, wine or blood / And whichever it may be, is it mine?'[95] The spot on the floor holds a multiplicity of significations, which ultimately give way to their relationship with the poet himself; it matters less whether the spot is wine or blood or 'whichever it may be' than that it falls under the ordering control of the artist and his imagination.

A surrealist might argue for the validity of both options (wine and blood simultaneously) as they coexist in the artist's mind. The multivalence of an image suspended between states and meanings was of great interest to Surrealism and is particularly evident in Dalí's experimental paintings. Through echoes of consubstantiation, the Protestant doctrine that the blood of Jesus coexists with the communion wine, this poem brings a spiritual dimension to Stevens's enquiry, which mirrors the mystical turn of Dalí's mid-century works. Indeed, in Stevens's poetry and Dalí's art, from the mid-1930s onwards, we can see an intriguing convergence of interest in Planck and Heisenberg. Dalí consciously integrated ideas from physics into his iconic representations of time (*The Persistence of Memory* (1931)), particle theory (*Galatea of the Spheres* (1952)), atomic warfare (*Uranium and Atomica Melancholia Idyll* (1945)) and 'nuclear mysticism' (*Crucifixion or Corpus Hypercubus* (1954) and *The Madonna of Port Lligat* (1949 and 1950).[96] In an interview with Alain Bosquet, he lamented Planck's death:

A. B.: With what famous person would you like to spend the night?
S. D.: Unfortunately, he's dead. Max Planck.[97]

---

[93] Ibid.
[94] Heisenberg, *Across the Frontiers*, 147.
[95] Stevens, 'The Man with the Blue Guitar', 150.
[96] Salvador Dalí, 'Mystical Manifesto (1951)', *391.org*, https://391.org/manifestos/1951-mystical-manifesto-salvador-dali/ [Accessed 4 November 2020]; see Basarab Nicolescu, 'Salvador Dalí and Nuclear Mysticism', in *From Modernity to Cosmodernity: Science, Culture, and Spirituality* (New York: State University of New York Press, 2014), 170–4.
[97] Alain Bosquet, *Conversations with Dalí*, trans. Joaquim Neugroschel (London: Ubu Classics, 2003), 32.

Dalí later declared in his *Anti-Matter Manifesto* (1958) that his earlier devotion to Freud had been replaced by a debt to the new physics: 'Today the exterior world, that of physics, has transcended that of psychology. My father today is Dr Heisenberg.'[98]

Dalí's use of optical illusion created images in which multiple figures exist in a state of flux. The concept of superposition, the term used in quantum physics to describe the coexistence of two or more opposing, but equally possible, states simultaneously, offers a valuable means of interpreting surrealist 'multiple-images'.[99] In a painting like *The Paranoiac Face* (1935) from *The Conquest of the Irrational* the artist carefully positions and textures images to give a double-aspect. Multiple potential images – an island, a face and an image of figures in a landscape – occupy the same space, even the same brushstrokes. *The Paranoiac Face* exemplifies a superposition of states, fluctuating between the three images as the observer focuses in on one or the other. This is as close as a static image might come to visualizing the conditions described by Heisenberg and Bohr; the images sit in complete complementarity but are subject to collapse dependent upon what the observer chooses to pay attention to. In physics, a quantum particle cannot be known fully, and its state is uncertain until it is observed, but the act of measurement (and particularly the *kind* of measurement we choose to make) imposes a particular reality upon that particle, which cannot be unseen, and which seems, quite irrationally to the classical conditions of physics, to physically alter the reality of the particle itself. Another Dalí painting which similarly straddles a number of states through optical illusion is *Invisible Sleeping Woman, Lion, Horse* (1930, Figure 8), in which the artist combines distorted shapes and shadows to give the impression of the subjects from the title. The odd assemblage at the centre of the painting comes together as a kind of collage of parts, none of which are representational in the traditional sense, but whose effect is multi-representational, and whose meaning forms in the mind of the viewer attempting to interpret it. The 'invisibles' in the image are both there and not there; and the more time one spends looking at the painting, the more difficult they are to decipher. Where Heisenberg's particles collapse one way or the other on observation, Dalí's method is to create images which, like Stevens's

---

[98] Salvador Dali, *Anti-Matter Manifesto*, exhibition booklet (New York: Carstairs Gallery, 1958), quoted in Elliott H. King, 'Nuclear Mysticism,' in *Salvador Dali: Liquid Desire* (Melbourne: National Gallery of Victoria, 2009), 247.
[99] Michael Betancourt, 'Paranoiac-criticism, Salvador Dalí, Archibald and Superposition in Interpreting Double Images,' *Consciousness, Literature and the Arts*, 6, no. 3 (December 2005), http://www.dmd27.org/betancourt.html [Accessed 4 November 2020].

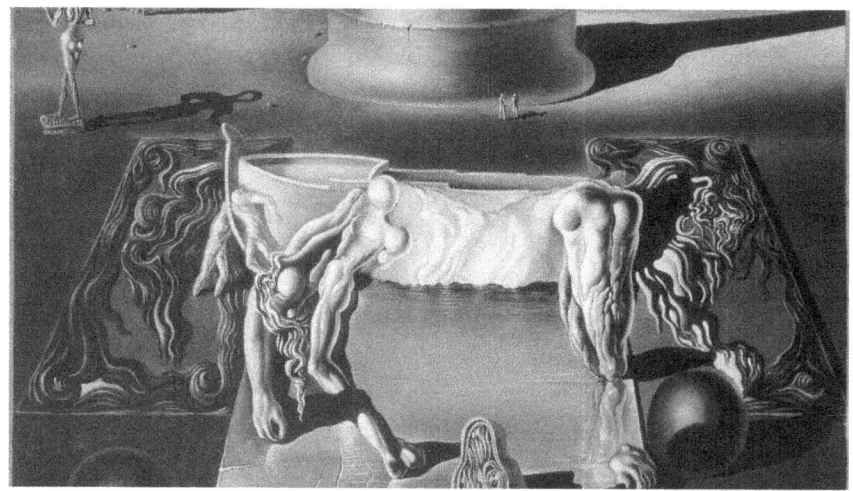

Figure 8 Salvador Dalí, *Invisible Sleeping Woman, Lion, Horse*, 1930, oil on canvas, 52 × 60 cm, Private Collection, Paris.

blood-wine, resist becoming fixed, giving an impression that is as mind-bending and irrational as the paranoiac experiences that inspired them.

Stevens's method of framing and reframing the question of poetic and artistic reality in 'The Man with the Blue Guitar' is itself a surrealist one. Surrealism 'systematically sought the interface between internal and external realities, illusion and vision, perception and thought'.[100] This kind of interface is perceptible in the dreamlike imagery of 'The Man with the Blue Guitar'. In section XVIII, Stevens examines the 'objects of consciousness' and their difference from physical sensation through a typically surrealist subject – the dream:

> A dream (to call it a dream) in which
> I can believe, in the face of the object,
>
> A dream no longer a dream, a thing,
> Of things as they are, as the blue guitar
>
> After long strumming on certain nights
> Gives the touch of the senses, not of the hand,
>
> But the very senses as they touch
> The wind-gloss. Or as daylight comes,

[100] Betancourt.

Like light in a mirroring of cliffs,
Rising upwards from the sea of ex.

Several things are striking about this section. First, that its subject begins abstract and remains so, moving from dream to thing to sensation, always just out of reach of a clear definition. The dream and the object and the means of rendering it blur together, so that although, at first glance, the images in the final two stanzas appear more focussed, they ultimately slip away from perception. The disjunctive sensorium Stevens presents, in which wind takes on a visual 'gloss' and daylight is, ultimately, 'like light', dramatizes the desperation of the artist trying to represent reality through images which are, at best, removed from reality, and at worst break down under close inspection. The final sentence is a rollercoaster of negations and distancing, from the 'Or' which implies the failure of the previous image, to the 'like' which reinforces the *un*-similarity of the similar, to the final 'sea of ex', a sea of nothingness, of pure negation or of abstraction, as 'x' in an equation with no fixed value.

In these images, one cannot get away from the sense that 'the mask is strange, however like'.[101] Stevens may have resorted to presenting 'things as they are' in the way Heisenberg reverted to mathematics when faced with the visualizability problem of quanta. Heisenberg's solution was to accept that quantum phenomena 'resisted any customary images of atoms and [to permit] his theory to determine the meanings of symbols' through what Schrödinger called 'very difficult methods of transcendental algebra'.[102] As the object is transformed into art – turned from green to blue on the guitar of the imagination – a reality emerges that can only be expressed by affording phenomena a kind of synaesthetic superposition, the ability to hold multiple traits (e.g. sensory attributes) that do not necessarily have any direct correlation to lived experience. The failure of Stevens's syntax here is telling: without a main verb, or even a clear subject for the analogy to latch onto, the multiplicity of connotations seem to float suspended in dream-logic, like the surreal forms that make up Dalí's composite illusions.

Often the act of experimentation, and the mental processes elicited in the mind of the reader, are for Stevens a means in themselves; the reader of Stevens looking for completion is always bound to be disappointed. Like Dalí's surrealist images of objects and figures melting into one another, Stevens uses syntactic

---

[101] Stevens, 'The Man with the Blue Guitar', 158.
[102] Miller, *Imagery in Scientific Thought*, 253; Schrödinger quoted in Gavin Parkinson, *Surrealism, Art, and Modern Science: Relativity, Quantum Mechanics, Epistemology* (New Haven & London: Yale University Press, 2008), 32.

effects to create fluctuating images which are only narrowly held together by the forward motion of the poem. For Stevens, as William Doreski writes, 'the idea of reality as a fixed quality [no longer pertains]. Philosophy and physics have unseated the notion of matter as solid and static, so the poet may understand reality as a product of the life that lives or experiences it. Reality, then, is what we experience, "things as they are," but it is our perception that shapes them.'[103] This perception is, itself, subject to irrational fluctuations which, Stevens theorizes, are central to the creation of poetic meaning: 'for where there are no fluctuations, poetic energy is absent.'[104] Stevens characterizes poetry by its unpredictability; the site of the poetic is in the tensions that arise from the poetic image's multivalence. This account of poetry would seem to make it very apt as a means of capturing in language something that cannot be reduced to a single image or metaphor:

> If the choice of subject were predictable it would be rational. Now, just as the choice of subject is unpredictable at the outset, so its development, after it has been chosen, is unpredictable. *One is always writing about two things at the same time in poetry* and it is this that produces the tension characteristic of poetry.[105]

The poetic imagination generates 'deliberate fictions', illusions which strike the reader with their strangeness and elicit a temporary state of irrationality and unpredictability, and it is in the experience of this state that the poem has its greatest power.[106]

Stevens's phantom problem

Daniel Schwarz suggests that, in drawing inspiration from the assemblages of the cubists and surrealists, 'taking art outside the mimetic system of representation with which we are familiar and making a new system based upon new juxtapositions, odd assemblies of objects, and discontinuous relations that barely held together', Stevens developed 'a system that each perceiver had to resolve into his own hypothesis of unity, a hypothesis always challenged by

---

[103] William Doreski, 'Stevens's Essays', *Wallace Stevens in Context*, ed. Glen McLeod (Cambridge: Cambridge University Press, 2016), 149–50.
[104] Stevens, 'The Irrational Element in Poetry', 229.
[105] Ibid., 221. My emphasis.
[106] Wallace Stevens, 'Imagination as Value', in *The Necessary Angel* (New York: Vintage Books, 1951), 139.

the anarchy of disunity'.[107] However, my understanding is that the repetition of themes and states across Stevens's poetry encourages the reader to hold and recall images and ideas in the mind, with a focus on the *transaction* between the mind and the object of discussion or observation. Rather than seeking resolution, as Schwarz intimates, we might instead embrace an understanding of poetry as an activity in the mind. This processual understanding of Stevens's poetry is necessarily a fragile one. It relies upon the reader's willingness to accept the unstable superposition of his illusory images and to resist the 'rage for order' that would collapse their meanings. Such a collapse, in the poems we have discussed, leads to sterile, stereotyped imagery, which moves us away from understanding 'the thing itself'. When Stevens writes that the 'supreme fiction' 'must be abstract', he gestures towards the untapped potential of poetic ideas liberated from our immediate, rational sense-experiences; as a result, references to sensory phenomena in Stevens's poetry, for instance to sound and colour, are imbued with symbolic meanings that do not necessarily correspond to our intuitions.[108]

Heisenberg writes that 'in the process of abstraction[,] the concept formed by way of abstraction takes on a life of its own; it allows for the generation of an unexpected wealth of forms or ordering structures, which can later prove valuable in some way, even in understanding the phenomena around us'.[109] Abstracted concepts may prove useful in the material world precisely due to their ability to sustain and hold in suspension a multiplicity of potentials. However, for the scientist, flights of abstraction are always tethered to an assumption of an ultimate order at play in the physical world around us: 'This juxtaposition of different intuitive pictures and distinct types of force created a problem that science could not evade because we are persuaded that nature, in the last resort, is uniformly ordered.'[110] Therefore, 'the drive to abstraction in science is ... ultimately based on the necessity to go on asking questions, upon striving for a unitary understanding'.[111] As we saw earlier, Planck refers to this as the 'irrational element' in science: the assumption of a real world, somewhere at the bottom of all this investigation, whose nature we can 'never fully comprehend'.[112] As physicists came to terms with the implications of relativity and quantum

---

[107] Daniel R. Schwarz, '"The Serenade of a Man Who Plays a Blue Guitar": The Presence of Modern Painting in Stevens' Poetry', *The Journal of Narrative Technique* 22, no. 2 (Spring 1992), 71.
[108] Stevens, 'Notes Toward a Supreme Fiction', 331.
[109] Heisenberg, *Across the Frontiers*, 73.
[110] Ibid.
[111] Ibid., 85.
[112] Planck, 'The Meaning and Limits of Exact Science', 106.

mechanics, they perceived the potential loss of this ultimate reality; the universe had been shown, first in theory then through experiment, to have a more complex relationship with subjectivity than previously thought. This world, whose reality relied upon one's personal frame of reference and choice of measurement type, posed an immediate challenge to those who sought absolute knowledge. The senses had proven untrustworthy, and, as we can see in Planck's writing, many of the fundamental abstract questions about the universe faced charges of incomprehensibility or meaninglessness.

One of Planck's 'last *pensees*' centres on the idea of the 'phantom problem' – a kind of puzzle which, he declares, 'is totally incapable of any solution at all – either because there exists no indisputable method to unravel it, or because considered in the cold light of reason, it turns out to be absolutely void of all meaning... a mere nothing'.[113] Stevens faced a phantom problem himself, as the supposed dichotomy between the irrational imagination and the reasoning faculties of the mind could prove frustrating. Indeed, in 'Imagination as Value', he seems to admit that it might be beyond resolution:

> Only the reason stands between [the imagination] and the reality for which the two are engaged in a struggle. We have no particular interest in this struggle because we know that it will continue to go on and that there will never be an outcome. We lose sight of it until Pascal, or someone else, reminds us of it. We say that it is merely a routine and the more we think about it the less we are able to see that it has any heroic aspects or that the spirit is at stake or that it may involve the loss of the world. Is there in fact any struggle at all and is the idea of one merely a bit of academic junk?[114]

This highlights the difference between the poetic and scientific imaginations; where the poetic imagination has the freedom to pick and choose its stakes, and Stevens the freedom to choose his subject of enquiry and convert it into a closed poetic reality, the scientific imagination functions only as a part or extension of the pre-existing scientific framework. A poet sets his own terms, selecting from a near-infinite set of symbols and meanings, forms and effects, and may vary these with every poem, or even with every line of a poem. A scientist's theory, however, is subject to the same rigorous requirements of verification and replicability as any other. Pertinently, however, both Stevens and Planck are fundamentally concerned with describing and depicting ideas about a pre-existing, abstracted

---

[113] Ibid., 53.
[114] Stevens, 'Imagination as Value', 141.

reality whose processes lie outside of everyday experience and are resistant to intuitive or rational understanding. Where Stevens's poems often wrangle with the definition and shape of the reality they are trying to describe, Planck was also keen to highlight reality's slipperiness. He suggested that the term 'real' should be used advisedly, nothing that

> in many instances, the word has any sense at all only when the speaker first defined clearly the point of view on which all his considerations are based. Otherwise, the words, *real* or *reality*, are often empty and misleading.[115]

To illustrate this point, Planck draws upon two examples, the first of which appears numerous times in Stevens's poetry, the problem of starlight, and the second, the core issue of wave-particle duality in modern physics:

> I see a star shining in the sky. What is *real* in it? Is it the glowing substance of which it is composed, or is it the sensation of light in my eyes? The question is meaningless so long as I do not state whether I am assuming a realistic or positivistic point of view.
>
> Still another example, this one from the realm of modern physics: When the behaviour of a moving electron is studied through an electron microscope, the electron appears as a particle following a definite course. But when the electron is made to pass through a crystal, the image projected on the screen shows every characteristic of a refracted light wave. The question, whether the electron is in reality a particle, occupying a certain position in space at a certain time, or a wave, filling all of infinite space, will therefore constitute a phantom problem so long as we fail to stipulate which of the two viewpoints is applied in the study of the behavior of the electron.[116]

In both examples it is the choice of viewpoint that determines what is considered 'real'. Surrealist paintings like *Sleeping Woman, Lion, Horse* are designed to resist the conscious mind's tendency towards settling on a single viewpoint to create a visual representation of the suspended reality available to the unconscious mind. According to James E. Breslin, in 'a world where shared ideas of order are lacking, surface connections disappear from art; the result is that ... ideas are not asserted but experienced, and they are experienced at a level below that of conscious activity'.[117] Likewise, for Stevens, the focus of the poem has shifted

---

[115] Planck, 'The Meaning and Limits of Exact Science', 58.
[116] Ibid., 58–9.
[117] James E. Breslin, *William Carlos Williams: An American Artist* (New York: Oxford University Press, 1970), 42–3.

from discussion of the poem's immediate subject (the pears, for example) to the experiential process of artistic production itself.

Planck is clear that science has little to say about the subconscious mind:

> First of all, we find that we may speak of conscious states only. To be sure, many processes, perhaps even the most decisive ones, must be taking place in the subconscious mind. But these are beyond the reach of scientific analysis. For there exists no science of the unconscious, or subconscious, mind. It would be a contradiction in terms, a self-contradiction. One does not know that which is subconscious. Therefore, all problems concerning the subconscious mind are phantom problems.[118]

However, Stevens highlights a difference between what is valued in the arts and what is valued in life outside of them that hinges on perception; he says 'in life what is important is the truth *as it is*, while in arts and letters what is important is the truth *as we see it*'.[119] This suggests that art is not concerned with an idea of objective reality, but rather the reality which is created through perceptual and imaginative processes which are, in turn, rooted in subconscious processes. The reality of the poem is what has been made of the world when passed through the very particular lens of the poet's sensibility. This lens, far from fixing the meaning of a thing, positions it within a lexical matrix and context through which it can maintain some of its variability. The nature of the imaginative faculty as the subject of a 'phantom problem' may underpin the lack of resolutions in Stevens's poetry; yet where for the scientist the phantom nature of a problem indicates a loss of value, for the poet even phantom problems can prove incredibly valuable and generative. A poet's goal, after all, is not to resolve the problem they begin with but rather to appropriate the problem for poetic effect. Discussing a poem from *Owl's Clover* (1936), 'The Old Woman and the Statue', Stevens notes that while the statue may stand for Art as a whole, it also functions as a 'variable symbol', capable of holding and maintaining multiple meanings throughout the collection.[120] For Stevens, poetic power relies on a lack of resolution and the tense suspension of the poetic image or concept between two or more potential resolutions. An object which is both wave and particle, then, has more poetic potential than a simple wave or a simple particle; an object which is both a woman and a lion has more poetic potential than a simple woman or a simple lion.

---

[118] Planck, 'The Meaning and Limits of Exact Science', 66.
[119] Stevens, 'Imagination as Value', 147. My emphasis.
[120] Stevens, 'The Irrational Element in Poetry', 219.

Surreal forms within 'The Man with the Blue Guitar' allowed Stevens to interrogate a reality constructed of pure imaginative elements. Lines like 'Sombre as fir trees, liquid cats / Moved in the grass without a sound' and 'It could not be a mind, the wave / In which the watery grasses flow // And yet are fixed as a photograph' offer up strange sensations reminiscent of automatic writing.[121] Yet there are moments when the blurring and fusing of these images threaten to subsume *a posteriori* reality completely into the higher realm of *a priori* abstraction. Heisenberg, commenting on trends in modern art, notes with concern 'a striving away from shape, an urge toward "unshaping" [through the] obliteration of contours'; he was concerned about the fluidity of modern artistic representation, a sense that for modern art to represent modern reality 'it has to be blurred'.[122] Planck addresses concerns about the rise of indeterminism in science, too. For indeterminists, 'genuine causality, strict regularity, actually does not exist in nature but is merely an illusion' and the laws of physics are seen as 'possessing only an approximate validity for individual instances'.[123] Heisenberg saw the introduction of uncertainty not only in the visual arts, but also in music and literature where, he says, 'the form of language is likewise in dissolution'.[124] Like Stevens, he identifies the tension this raises for the artist: an art that prioritizes flux and fluidity is resistant to the artist's controlling hand.

One partial solution was for the artist to suspend himself in flux also. In 'The Man with the Blue Guitar' (section XIX), Stevens toys with this idea, imagining a hybrid artist-monster reminiscent of Picasso's 1930s minotaur series.[125] In another ouroborosian struggle, he considers fusing with the monster to

> be more than a part of it ... not be
> Alone, but reduce the monster and be,
> Two things, the two together as one,
> And play of the monster and of myself[126]

McLeod argues that the hybrid monster 'combines rational and irrational forces', and represents 'the surrealist idea of gaining power over the irrational by *becoming* the irrational'.[127] Louis Martz, however, reads this process as a battle

---

[121] Stevens, 'The Man with the Blue Guitar', 155, 157.
[122] Heisenberg, *Across the Frontiers*, 48–149.
[123] Planck, 125–6.
[124] Heisenberg, *Across the Frontiers*, 149.
[125] MacLeod, *Wallace Stevens and Modern Art*, 75.
[126] Stevens, 'The Man with the Blue Guitar', 152.
[127] McLeod, *Wallace Stevens and Modern Art*, 75.

between the mind and the entropic universe: 'man's inner rage for order as the ultimate constructive force in man's universe, and hence the never ending effort of the mind to control within the mind, that outer monster, the inhuman universe.'[128] But this is a battle the poet fought throughout his life, and forms achieved in this way are never safe but always under threat of dissolution. The artist, beset by images, reaches through the 'swarm of thoughts, the swarm of dreams / Of unaccessible Utopia' and reaches only 'A mountainous music that always seemed / To be falling and to be passing away.'[129] Stevens's poetry is shot through with such images, lines thrown out into an ocean under whose aesthetic surface there seems to be no concrete reality left to grip onto.

In 'Man Carrying Thing' (1946), Stevens articulates the idea that the poem gains its power through the tension between the rational and irrational elements in the language of physics.[130] Through two analogies, Stevens suggests the open state of mind necessary for the full appreciation of poetry, one in which, as Leggett says, 'the reader is content to remain in an indeterminate condition, resisting the urge to exhaust each figure or connection.'[131] Stevens begins with another bold statement of what the poem 'must' do: 'The poem must resist the intelligence / Almost successfully.'[132] The line break emphasizes the qualifying phrase 'Almost successfully', which immediately problematizes the certainty of the first line. There is a sense of irrationality in the idea of a poem's success relying on its near-unintelligibility, and the almost-success of the second line implies what we have gathered from the imagery of 'Man with a Blue Guitar', that the work of an artist can only ever be a series of generative failures. The iterative technique is one strategy for dealing with a subject that resists representation. In 'The Irrational Element in Poetry', Stevens describes how the unknown might be partially known through the shadows cast by what is known: 'The rational mind, dealing with the known, expects to find it glistening in a familiar ether. What it really finds is the unknown always beyond the known, giving it the appearance, at best, of chiaroscuro.'[133]

---

[128] Louis Martz, 'Wallace Stevens: The World as Meditation', in *Wallace Stevens: A Collection of Critical Essays*, ed. Marie Borroff (New Jersey: Englewood Cliffs, 1963), 142.
[129] Stevens, 'The Man with the Blue Guitar', XXVI.
[130] This poem was first published in the *Yale Poetry Review*, 1 (Spring 1946), before being collected as part of Stevens's 1947 collection *Transport to Summer*.
[131] Leggett, 51.
[132] Stevens, *Collected Poems*, 306.
[133] Stevens, 'The Irrational Element in Poetry', 228.

This idea reappears in 'Notes Toward a Supreme Fiction':

> The two are one.
> They are a plural, a right and left, a pair,
> Two parallels that meet if only in
>
> The meeting of their shadows[134]

The two images Stevens develops in 'Man Carrying Thing' are those of a figure carrying an imperceptible object on a winter evening, and the image of fragmentary snowflakes at the beginning of a storm. The first is described through the language of resistance introduced in the first line: 'A brune figure in the winter evening resists / Identity. The thing he carries resists // The most necessitous sense.'[135] Stevens uses a plain image that is complicated by the viewer's desire to interpret it. The figure's identity is hidden only to the observer looking at him through the winter gloom, and ostensibly the object he carries is no secret to the figure himself. The drive to identify the figure and their object, to resolve them into something clear, belongs to the observer, that Stevens warns against this urge:

> Accept them, then,
> As secondary (parts not quite perceived
>
> Of the obvious whole, uncertain particles
> Of the certain solid, the primary free from doubt,
>
> Things floating like the first hundred flakes of snow
> Out of a storm we must endure all night,
>
> Out of a storm of secondary things),
> A horror of thoughts that suddenly are real.
>
> We must endure our thoughts all night, until
> The bright obvious stands motionless in cold.

Stevens introduces the language of uncertainty and particles to depict the necessary suspension between certainties that allows the reader to get the most out of a poem. The absolute definition of the man and the object he is carrying is not the point of the poem, but a 'secondary' part, defined by its resistance

---

[134] Stevens, 'Notes toward a Supreme Fiction', 356.
[135] Stevens, 'Man Carrying Thing', 306.

to the reader's perceptions. The poem's title draws attention to the word 'thing' which, for Stevens, holds a superposition both as a direct and specific term for the deeper reality of a subject or object ('the thing itself') and as an open-ended noun which can encompass all the uncertain possibilities of the object that resists analysis. In this poem, the multitude of things (whether snowflakes or thoughts) aggregate into a sudden reality (storm or clear idea), a 'certain solid' built of 'uncertain particles'. As with the collage of 'The Man with the Blue Guitar', where the fragments form something gestural ('not quite a man'), Stevens urges us to approach a poem with a mind open to holding the uncertain and fluctuating 'variable images' in mind without seeking immediately to resolve them. In this state of suspension, Stevens believed, the poem has its greatest potency.[136]

'Invisible or visible or both': An abstracted poetics

Now that we have established a means of reading Stevens's poetry through the idea of suspended states within the mind, I want to return to the poet's interest in Planck from 'A Collect of Philosophy' to show how the abstracted world of the poetic imagination works if considered alongside the abstract framework of theoretical physics. As we have seen, both Stevens and the physicists were engaged in attempting to visualize and discuss concepts which resisted standard modes of representation. In both cases, abstraction provided a tool through which to probe towards a greater understanding of modern reality, the interaction of the poetic imagination and reality, and the interaction of subatomic particles and the observer respectively. By examining the nature of the 'world picture of physics' as described by Planck, we can begin to see the similar affordances and pitfalls that emerged from adopting an abstract conceptual methodology, which can loosely be described as imaginative freedom from real-world restrictions taken at the risk of losing value or meaning.

In 'Collect', Stevens remarks that the poet-philosophers he has in mind are those for whom 'metaphor is native and inescapable, [the class] which chooses to make its metaphors plain, and thinks from the true abundance of its thought'.[137] He suggests that what philosophy and poetry, and arguably science, too, have in common is the 'habit of forming concepts... [t]he habit of probing for an

---

[136] He writes in a letter to Ronald Lane Latimer: 'I have the greatest dislike for explanations. As soon as people are perfectly sure of a poem they are just as likely as not to have no further interest in it; it loses whatever potency it had.' Cited in Leggett, 53.
[137] Stevens, 'A Collect of Philosophy', 186.

integration', and the 'idea of creating confidence in the world'.[138] Stevens created this confidence by developing his own poetic '*mundo*', a closed system of self-referential terms and repeating concepts turned over throughout his body of work to generate an abstract and, in his words, 'irrational' matrix through which the poet might rupture reality and create meaning by examining imaginative processes in the mind of the poet and his reader. Turning to Planck, Stevens focuses on a reference by George to Planck's 'thesis on causality'. He translates this section of George's article:

> The last pages of the thesis are quite curious. One feels there, as it were, a supreme hesitation; the believer henceforth is no longer able to conceal a certain trouble. The most convinced determinist, Planck declares, in so many words, is not able to satisfy himself entirely with such an interpretation. For, in the end, a universal principle like the rigorous causal bond between two successive events ought to be independent of man. It is a principle of cosmic importance, it ought to be an absolute. Now, Planck not only recognizes that it is part of the human aptitude to foresee events but to foresee them by means of science, 'the provisional and changing creation of the power of the imagination.' How then liberate the concept from such an anthropomorphic hypothesis? Only an intelligence external to man, 'not constituting a part of nature,' would be able to liberate it. This supra-natural intelligence would act through the deterministic power... Planck thereupon concludes that the law of causality is neither true nor false. It is a working hypothesis.[139]

In the essay George refers to here, 'The Concept of Causality in Physics', Planck lays out the division between determinist and indeterminist thinking in modern physics. The larger part of this essay is concerned with explaining the 'world picture of physics', which 'replaces the sense world, as given to us directly by our sense organs [with] a conceptual structure, arbitrary to a certain degree, created for the purposes of getting away from the uncertainty involved in every individual measurement and making possible a precise interrelation of concepts.'[140]

To evade the experimental hurdles of causality (which he advisedly defines: '*An occurrence is causally determined if it can be predicted with certainty*'), Planck describes how physicists modified the term 'occurrence' into a conceptual

---

[138] Stevens, 'A Collect of Philosophy', 196, 199.
[139] Andre George cited in Stevens, 'A Collect of Philosophy', 201–2. Stevens's translation. Sub-quotations within this section are from Planck.
[140] Planck, 'The Meaning and Limits of Exact Science', 127–8.

average of its referent, a representative symbol.[141] He says that 'directly observable magnitudes are not found at all in the world picture. It contains symbols only [, which] permits us to carry through strict determinism'.[142] By integrating discoveries into this system, scientists could create confidence in a causality which was only surface deep – the abstracted science functions with a level of accuracy that will suffice for most of the processes experienced in practice, such as thermodynamics and electromagnetism, but it breaks down at a quantum level. Where physics had hoped for an integrated system of cause and effect which could ignore uncertainty, 'the introduction of the elementary quantum of action [which proposed uncertainty as a fundamental aspect of quantum reality] destroyed this hope at one blow and for good'.[143] The Uncertainty Principle 'fundamentally precludes the possibility of translating into the sense world, with an arbitrary degree of accuracy, the simultaneous values of the coordinates and momenta of material points, as these are conceived in the world picture of classical physics'.[144] Where previously every symbol's meaning was 'immediately and directly intelligible', 'the wave function of quantum mechanics supplies no direct clue whatever for any obvious interpretation of the sense world' and rather than dealing in absolutes deals only in probabilities.[145]

Stevens's late poem 'Notes toward a Supreme Fiction' (1947) describes the poetic idea as something shaped by 'living changingness' under 'the uncertain light of single, certain truth'.[146] In searching for an ideal clarity, the poet contends with the inherent uncertainty of reality and its meanings. To begin converting this uncertain reality into a workable system (notice even here Stevens is writing notes *toward* a supreme fiction and not the supreme fiction itself), Stevens's supreme fiction as an idea in an 'invented world', whose source is not the 'inventing mind', but something which exists beyond it; the invented world allows for a 'clean' image, a means of reaching beyond language to find 'a name for something that could never be named'.[147] As in the junkyard of images, the poet must undergo a process of purification in order to 'see the sun again with an ignorant eye', that is to approach reality as an open concept without subjecting it to collapse through the sensibility towards one fixed meaning or another. This attempt to reach into 'the remotest cleanliness of

[141] Ibid., 122.
[142] Ibid., 129.
[143] Ibid., 133.
[144] Ibid., 134.
[145] Ibid., 137.
[146] Stevens, 'Notes toward a Supreme Fiction', *Collected Poems*, 331.
[147] Ibid., 331.

a heaven / That has expelled us and our images' involves the creation of an abstracted reality, whose 'variable symbols' are able to function on multiple levels and simply 'be / In the difficulty of what it is to be'.[148] As with the world picture of physics described by Planck, the abstracted world of the supreme fiction evades the problems that come with our limited sense perceptions in order to create revitalizing interpretations of experience which, as Stevens puts it, 'instantly change the face of the world'.[149]

The sixth section of 'Notes' begins 'Not to be realized because not to / Be seen, not to be loved or hated because / not to be realized'. By fracturing the infinitive 'to / be', Stevens draws attention to 'the difficulty of what it is to be' when the subject is an abstract concept whose existence bears no relation to anything we might perceive through our senses. The idea that something is made real through being seen chimes with the central problem of Planck's essay, that the quantum world seems not only uncertain but also actively shaped through the act of seeing and measurement. In an attempt to alleviate the 'anthropomorphic traits' of these results, 'which ill-befit fundamental concepts of physics', Planck asserts the fragility of the relationship between uncertainty and the concept of causality if physics is to accept human interference into its world picture.[150] The world picture of physics, he says, is a 'human artefact', a 'provisional and alterable creation of the human power of the imagination' which mediates nature through the lens of the human intellect.[151] As science has historically privileged absolutes, relying on experimental evidence that can be reproduced indefinitely to advance our understanding of the physical world through laws, Planck asks if there would not be a 'deeper meaning' to this chain of cause and effect if it stood outside the human purview, gesturing to 'irrational element' in scientific thought from his earlier essay. The influential observer breaches the objective independence of the natural world which is required for a unitary understanding of the laws of physics to be viable. For Stevens, however, the supreme fiction allows a breaching of this idea of reality through the suspension of states, gesturing to the flux that exists before the act of seeing:

> It must be visible or invisible,
> Invisible or visible or both:
> A seeing and an unseeing in the eye.[152]

---

[148] Ibid., 332.
[149] Stevens, 'A Collect of Philosophy', 190.
[150] Ibid., 144–5.
[151] Ibid., 144.
[152] Stevens, 'Notes toward a Supreme Fiction', 336.

This wavering does not afford the eye or the act of vision priority over the interpretation of an idea, but rather gestures to the multivalence of the unformed idea, and its vitality for the artist.

The invisible shifts into and away from visibility in a way that seeks to suspend both states at the same time. In the reader's mind there is a plasticity of concepts that is not so readily available in the visual arts. Writing on the influence of Cézanne on Stevens, Fred Miller Robinson notes that, in painting, the act of observation is not so much a fixative as an act which highlights the uncertainty of reality; in Impressionism, for instance, there was an 'inescapable tension between a reality that was conceived as potently and permanently *there*, and the altering and shifting of reality as appeared to the observer'.[153] Monet's experiments with haystacks, for instance, show that visual perception shifts with the light. Robinson's description of the 'perceptual aporia' elicited by Cézanne's paintings is useful here:

> The most striking effect is that his paintings at first seem natural to the observer, then disquieting and strange, then natural again, as though in coming to an understanding of the painting you saw the familiar unmade and made again, and again. The tension between distance and nearness, thought and emotion, balance and unbalance, is sustained in what could be termed a perceptual aporia, a suspension of opposites that is at once calming and unsettling.[154]

For both Cézanne and Stevens, the generation of perceptual aporia is a strategy designed to overcome the determinacy of their medium. Stevens saw the fluctuations of modern art as an end in themselves. When we speak of the imagination, he says, 'we are speaking of a thing in continual flux. There is no field in which this is more apparent than in painting. ... The permissible reality in painting wavers with an insistence which is itself a value.'[155]

Stevens's privileging of the very uncertainty of the reality depicted in art can be seen in the section of 'Notes' subtitled 'It Must Change', where rhetorical questions throw up possibilities that intentionally evade resolution:

Does it move to and fro or is it of both

At once? Is it a luminous flittering
Or the concentration of a cloudy day?
Is there a poem that never reaches words

---

[153] Fred Miller Robinson, 'Poems That Took the Place of Mountains: Realization in Stevens and Cézanne', *The Centennial Review* 22, no. 3 (Summer 1978), 283.
[154] Ibid., 288.
[155] Stevens, 'Imagination as Value', 149.

> And one that chaffers the time away?
> Is the poem both peculiar and general?
> There's a meditation there, in which there seems
>
> To be an evasion, a thing not apprehended or
> Not apprehended well. Does the poet
> Evade us, as in a senseless element?[156]

This series of oppositions – dispersed and concentrated, general and particular – creates a poetic space whose resistance to collapse leads to an expansive sense of imaginative potential. Images of 'luminous flittering' and cloudy 'concentration' might offer an analogue to the dispersal and reformation of the quantum world's photons and cloudy atoms but they have a clearer parallel in the art world, where light had been depicted through flashes of colour and pointillist principles in Impressionism, then later resolved back to the sharper, less gaseous surrealist images, which still provide multiple interpretations. By suggesting that 'change' is a central feature of the 'supreme fiction', Stevens foregrounds flux, and through his use of 'and' and 'both' in opposition to 'or' creates a similar effect to the superposition of Dalí's paintings; only here the shifting is not between visual forms but conceptual ones. There is an echo here too in the way a poem strains towards (and fails to achieve) creation – one that 'never reaches words' – of the 'straining for meaning' Stevens ascribes to the scientist in 'A Collect of Philosophy'. In both cases, expression and becoming are the results of a struggle for exactness and precision, and the final lines of this section make clear that this struggle does not always – or perhaps can *never* – end in complete understanding.

Stevens's questioning here opens up a range of possibilities, throwing them into suspension in the mind to imitate the experience of the supreme fiction as an unachievable ideal, just out of reach of the sensorium, and at the very limits of the mind's purview. The poet seems to anticipate the reader's frustration, and to remind us that he is himself subjected to the frustrations of the poem's central task. Robinson remarks that 'Stevens never ceased to regard the poetic task he had set himself as something rigorous and uncomfortable, effortful, [and] possibly impossible to fulfill [sic]'.[157] Furthermore, 'the poem of the act of the mind' is necessarily a matter of process which, as we have seen, is best apprehended through the understanding that ideas might exist in pre-rational suspension in

---

[156] Stevens, 'Notes toward a Supreme Fiction', 346.
[157] Robinson, 282.

the mind, before reason steps in to interfere. '[T]he difficultest rigor', as Stevens puts it, is 'to catch from that / irrational moment its unreasoning', to capture the primordial idea, the 'muddy center that was before we breathed', before there is any ordering influence of the human mind. For this to be possible, Stevens seems to demand a fundamental change in the nature of perception itself towards an abstract, pre-sensory, pre-rational mode of apprehension.[158]

In a prose piece called 'On Poetic Truth', Stevens states it like this: 'What I want to stress is that there is a unity rooted in the individuality of objects and discovered in a different way from the apprehension of rational connections.'[159] Such abstraction, according to Heisenberg, is the inevitable conclusion of the desire to strive towards a universally applicable system. 'In art, as in science, we can discern a striving toward universality,' he wrote, adding that '[t]his striving for unification and bringing together necessarily leads to abstraction in art probably no less than in science'.[160] But what would such an abstracted perception look like? How would it function and what purpose could it serve? How far can it be pushed beyond the sensory before it loses all meaning?

Kenneth Burke has described abstraction as 'the act or process of leaving out of consideration one or more qualities of a complex object so as to attend to others'.[161] In the abstract world view of physics, for example, the absolute and deterministic nature of physical processes means that occurrences can be abstractly suspended for scientific examination; in the mind of the theoretical physicist, physical processes can be considered with their relation to time subtracted. For example, they can be played forwards or backwards, paused in the middle or reconstructed from their results in a way that they cannot be in the laboratory. The abstract world picture of physics as a conceptual tool has, of course, been vital to the successes of thinkers like Einstein, whose major discoveries emerged from thought experiments played out on an abstract stage, where impossible acts such as speed-of-light travel were permissible. For Stevens, the abstract world of the imagination also offered means of escaping the limitations of the physical world, and pushing the boundaries of textual representation, to conduct imaginative experiments of his own. Here, a realm of possibilities is opened up by the abstract thinker's ability to choose and select the aspects and variables of his subject without the limitations of the sense world.

---

[158] Stevens, 'Notes on a Supreme Fiction', 348.
[159] Stevens, 'On Poetic Truth', 237.
[160] Heisenberg, *Across the Frontiers*, 152.
[161] Kenneth Burke quoted in Michael J. Hoffmann, *The Development of Abstraction in the Writings of Gertrude Stein* (Philadelphia: University of Pennsylvania Press, 1965), 28.

For Stevens, the abstract offered the possibility of expansion and inclusion, a space in which the poet's imagination might soar angelic with nothing to clip its wings:

> The nothingness was a nakedness, a point
>
> Beyond which thought could not progress as thought.
> He had to choose. But it was not a choice
> Between excluding things. It was not a choice
>
> Between, but of. He chose to include the things
> That in each other are included, the whole,
> The complicate, the amassing harmony.[162]

Stevens here stresses the inclusivity of the choice; the poet is empowered to choose suspension without collapsing, to allow the imagination to embrace a superposition defined by its expansion and appreciation of the wider 'harmony' of the imagined reality. Here the restrictions of the physical world do not apply and the poet is free.

In 'The Concept of Causality in Physics', Planck entertains the idea of an abstract solution to the pressing problem of the scientists' intrusion upon his measurements. He proposes the introduction of a new, abstract observer into the world picture of physics. The 'predicting subject' would be abstracted into a symbolic, all-inclusive figure similar to Laplace's demon, the 'ideal intellect, intimately familiar with the most minute details of physical processes occuring [sic] concurrently everywhere' who can, therefore, predict the results of physical processes with absolute, determinist accuracy.[163] This is problematic for several reasons, not least those which Planck mentions himself: the ideal intellect cannot be considered analogous to us, or subjected to scientific analysis or explanation, as it cannot be part of nature itself but must be external to what it observes. It therefore arguably bears no resemblance to any type of observer in the laboratory; its superhuman inclusivity precludes its value as part of the framework of abstract physics. In science, after all, theory is only useful in so far as it can guide experiment and lead to practical results. The problem of the abstract observer, then, is a phantom problem. Pre-empting the alternative option, 'the assumption that the attempt to determine simultaneously both the

---

[162] Stevens, 'Notes toward a Supreme Fiction', 352.
[163] Planck, 'The Meaning and Limits of Exact Science', 148.

coordinates and the momentum of a material point is physically completely meaningless', Planck decides that such problems have an inherent value. While the 'impossibility of giving an answer to a meaningless question' indicates the failure of the classical world picture of physics, Planck believed in the value of pursuing such questions in spite of their apparent dead ends.[164] 'I must take exception to the view,' he writes, 'that a problem in physics merits examination only if it is established in advance that a definite answer can be obtained.'[165] The Michelson-Morley experiment, for example, designed to measure the absolute velocity of the earth, though 'now regarded fairly universally as meaningless', nevertheless 'produce[d] such extraordinary benefits to science', laying the ground for the development of relativity.[166] Planck suggests the importance of the pursuit of 'phantom problems' for the offshoot results they might elicit, or as matters of interest and inquiry in themselves. Even if the idea of the abstract ideal observer is 'meaningless and unnecessary', Planck argues, that does not make it 'worthless', but rather it highlights the way in which physics relies upon the 'serene faith in a rational world order' that has underpinned science from the very beginning.[167] Physics itself, he concludes, is a processual discipline, 'not a contemplative repose amid knowledge already gained, but is indefatigable work and an ever-progressive development'.[168]

It was this expansive interrogation of the modern world, this 'straining for exactness', which embraced the 'nuances of the imagination' and its determination to probe into questions whose answers were not readily available – and potentially not even possible to find – that attracted Stevens to Planck. In George's article, the 'supreme hesitation' of 'The Concept of Causality in Physics', where Planck is 'no longer able to conceal a certain trouble' with the world picture of physics, but to interrogate his own staunch views against the evidence presented to him, strikes Stevens as surprisingly poetic. 'It is unexpected to have to recognize even in Planck the presence of the poet,' he writes, 'It is as if in a study of modern man we predicted the greatness of poetry as the final measure of his stature, as if his willingness to believe beyond belief was what had made him modern and was always certain to keep him so.'[169]

---

[164] Ibid., 134.
[165] Ibid., 140.
[166] Ibid.
[167] Ibid., 148.
[168] Ibid., 150.
[169] Stevens, 'A Collect of Philosophy', 202.

In one draft of 'A Collect of Philosophy', Stevens attempted a longer summary of George's article than appears in the final version of the essay. His summary emphasizes the epistemic shift between classic and modern physics:

> [George] says that during his long life Planck had practiced the same philosophic and scientific credo: first, the lofty principles of duty and of moral conscience which his compatriot Emmanuel Kant had set up as universal in the XVIIIth century; and, second, the belief in a science of rigorous laws, the ideal reflection of events imperiously connected by a chain of effects and causes, a physics solidly determinist, of a tested classicism. On the quantic scale, the rigid determinism of classic science is dispelled, physics is able to say with certainty what phenomena are susceptible of observation, it calculates the measure of their respective probabilities, but it is not able to predict which of these phenomena is going to pass from the possible to the real, to the observable.
>
> He says that today a new classicism is in course of establishing itself. Nature offers us on a grand scale a determinist aspect, thanks to the play of big figures, of statistical illusions. But on the atomic scale, at the level of elementary phenomena, an indeterminism, fundamental and, it must be added, well-defined, reigns alone.[170]

Here, Stevens is interested in Planck as a symbol of scientific rigour, duty and morality in the face of a changing world; he sees Planck as a bridge between the classical and modern worlds, between determinism and indeterminism, and between the sensory and the abstract. While this excised portrait of Planck is of a man clinging to 'the same philosophic and scientific credo' throughout his life, Stevens twice describes the incompatibility of the Classical, purely causal, picture of physics with the behaviour of quantum phenomena.

As we have seen, the crisis of representation faced by the physicists in the 1920s following Planck's discovery of the quantum of action led scientists to interrogate their own language and the constructed world picture of physics they had hitherto been able to rely upon. Straining for exactness in a world which increasingly came to depend upon the traditionally anti-scientific values of irrationality, multivalence and uncertainty – and facing the apparent anti-rationalism of quantum behaviour – the concerns of these physicists aligned with those preoccupying the minds of artists and poets like Stevens. While I agree with Peter Middleton that Lisa Steinman was overzealous in suggesting that

---

[170] Wallace Stevens, 'A Collect of Philosophy', drafts, holograph and typescript, undated, YCAL MSS 545, Series 1, Wallace Stevens Collection. Yale Collection of American Literature, Beinecke Rare Books and Manuscript Library.

'Stevens may be the American poet who made the most serious use of the new physics', particularly if we take 'serious' to mean that he worked with a thorough understanding of quantum physics itself, we have seen that Stevens's and Planck's separate lines of enquiry into the seemingly irrational, unvisualizable and deeply abstract nature of reality led them to consider similar problems of language, representation, process, meaning and value.[171] Furthermore, despite their differing subject matter and media, their attempts to wrangle meaning from modern reality often led to similar epistemological strategies: a tendency towards abstraction, towards a way of thinking that allowed for the coexistence of opposites and towards more expansive modes of representation. Choosing Planck as a representative for poetic thought in science may have been convenient for Stevens in the moment, but this convenience points to significant and telling parallels between the linguistic and conceptual challenges and solutions demanded both by Stevens's poetics and by quantum physics, revealing a shared lineage of concerns with meaning and representation, rationality and irrationality, mediation, expression, imagination and reality.

---

[171] Steinman, *Made in America*, 134; Middleton, *Physics Envy*, 35.

Conclusion

The explorations of quantum modernity and modernist relativity in this book have revealed an heterogeneous set of relations between the new physics and modernist avant-garde poetics. Patterns of interrelation between fields emerge in the writing of the poets I have discussed, often through an effort to draw upon new, cutting-edge scientific ontologies to explore new ways of understanding modern experience. From the shifted perspectives and reference frames of relativity to the provocative connection between the state of matter and the observer uncovered by quantum physicists, physics presented modernist writers with a set of terms ('clarity', 'relative measure', 'radiation') and conceptual models ('complementarity', 'atomic bodies') through which to reinterpret modern experience. The centrality of boundary crossing within these works, alongside their interest in the limitations of and liberation from poetic form, represent a reframing of art's place and value in modern society. Amid the ferment of revolutionary, manifesto-toting artists, the new physics and its technologies were seen not only as a fair subject for art, but by some as an essential aspect of their forward-looking ethos. As these poets, all born in the late 1800s and witnesses to the impact of industrialization and the turn-of-the-century elevation of science in the cultural consciousness, challenged perceptions about what poetry is and could be, each of them turned to the visual arts for inspiration. These patterns are not limited to those I have discussed; they pop up in a surprising array of works from the first half of the twentieth century on both sides of the Atlantic, from Woolf to Pound and H. D., Lawrence to Eliot, Empson to Zukofsky. Indeed, they continue to resonate to this day.

In his 2021 reflections on the development of quantum physics, the Italian theoretical physicist Carlo Rovelli devotes a section of his book to an analysis of language. 'Words,' he says, 'are never precise: the variegated cloud of meanings that they carry about them is their expressive power.'[1] This language is revealing

---

[1] Carlo Rovelli, *Helgoland* (London: Penguin Books, 2021), 90.

in a book concerned with unravelling a science shaped by notions of certainty and uncertainty. The image Rovelli develops mirrors that of the quantum atom, a node around which a constantly moving set of interacting electrons flit around elusively, their positions and speeds impossible to know at once. As we saw in Williams's use of empty space, fracture and breakage, and Stevens's examination of the poetic image, the mind of the reader leaps to fill in the gaps, working to find meanings and fix intent. For the writers in this book, the 'variegated cloud of meanings' was at its most potent in poetry, whose experimental forms and startling juxtapositions enabled a generative, and often innovative, reflection upon modern experience. Each of them transformed the scientific ideas they engaged with by interpreting it through the lens of modernity, its anxieties and its values.

The interpretation and transformation of scientific ideas in art and poetry were not passing interests of the Modernist period (indeed, as the broad field of literature and science research shows, were not new in their essence, but rather in their intensity and mode of expression) but remain an essential part of our cultural mechanics, shaping our expression of Science, its discoveries and direction. Elsewhere in his book, Rovelli discusses an emerging and contested interpretation of modern quantum mechanics developed by Christopher Fuchs and Rüdiger Schack, called QBism (pronounced 'cubism', coined by Fuchs in 2010), noting the echo not only of theoretical roots (Quantum Bayesianism) but also of the cubist art movement.[2] The interpretation's adherents refer to themselves as QBists. While, in the same way that Cubism was not directly concerned with Einsteinian relativity, QBism has no direct root in its artistic namesake, its entry into the lexicon has afforded it some shared revolutionary resonances, and cubist artworks have been used to illustrate articles on the subject.[3] On deeper inspection, the parallels are perhaps quite apt. After all, QBism is considered a 'radical' reinterpretation of quantum mechanics, contributing to debates around realism, perspective, and expression, interests shared by Cubism and the writers discussed in this book.[4] Coincidental though it may have been, Fuchs admits that the association helped QBism gain traction and mainstream attention, demonstrating one of the wider contentions of this

---

[2] Ibid., 59; Matthew S. Leifer describes QBism as 'one of a class of neo-Copenhagen interpretations of quantum theory, which attempt to flesh out the ideas of Neils Bohr et. al. in a more modern and coherent way'. In brief, this interpretation posits that quantum probabilities should be understood as degrees of certainty of belief on the part of the observer. Matthew S. Leifer, 'Review of QBism: The Future of Quantum Physics', *Physics in Perspective* 19, no. 1 (2017), 2–3.
[3] N. David Mermin, 'Physics: QBism Puts the Scientist Back into Science', *Nature* 507 (2014), 421–3.
[4] Leifer, 'Review of QBism', 2–3.

book, that the boundaries between specialist fields and the wider culture are porous and easily blended the moment a theory or idea leaves the site in which it was initially formulated.[5]

Once articulated (and through the very art of articulation), ideas are able to move between fields through the radiant interactions of a wide set of cultural agents, be they poets, artists, scientists, journalists or simply friends conversing with one another. In this cultural foment, they develop and change, picking up and discarding resonances and meanings in the process. The atom becomes a pudding, becomes a solar system, becomes a cloud, becomes a word and its meanings; field interaction becomes human interaction, becomes a mode of mystical experience, becomes a way to express the dissolution of personal identity. In each case, the transformation of ideas as they move between fields can offer new perspectives and approaches which resonate back towards their roots. Now often mentioned in discussions of quantum theory, QBism's gain from its association with Cubism is just a small example of this process at play today.

I selected my four poets both for their depth of interest in physics (as it manifests in their writing), and to demonstrate the diversity of ways concepts from physics resonated with these writers within the close-knit social circles of 1920s New York. Williams, Loy, the Baroness and Stevens came to terms with the materials of modern physics in suggestively different ways, but for all of them, physics offered a way of finding new order in a seemingly disordered universe. Williams sought clarity through a stripped-back and at times cubist form of poetry which engaged with the precision of scientific measurement and flexibility afforded by Einstein's relativity. Loy's formulation of sexual and reproductive bodies as electromagnetic and atomic objects, interacting with physical forces in the world around them, evolved into a rich pseudo-scientific cosmology of radiation and atomic dispersal. For the Baroness, what began as a critique of masculine Dada's adulation of physics as plaything became a bedrock in a time of crisis; her integration of 'abstract science' into her poetry enabled the creation of an ordered cosmology to bolster her own sense of dissolution amid the epistemological crises of Weimar Germany. Stevens, too, found value in physical models, developing abstract theories of poetry and superpositional modes of image-making in his writing which reflected his interest in developments in quantum physics.

---

[5] Alexa Meade, Christopher Fuchs, John Phillip Santos, 'Q3 Quantum Metaphysics', Peace and Security in a Quantum Age: Moment, Matter, Mind and Metaphysics Project Q Symposium, University of Sydney (2016), 07:40-07:50, https://vimeo.com/167261302 [Accessed 20 January 2022].

In the fertile environment of New York, these poets embraced the new understandings about the very form of the universe and its constituent parts, integrating them into avant-garde verbal and visual constructs – poems which might offer an appropriate reflection of the world as it was newly understood to be. The formal affordances of poetry, able to express information through not only its contents but also their presentation, were pushed to the limit by these writers who eschewed the metrical expectations of earlier decades in favour of new forms of poetic expression. Williams, Loy, the Baroness and Stevens all explored the significance of these discoveries and interrogated the artistic value of the modes of perception these discoveries implied. In doing so, they provided new ways for the sciences to be understood, shaping through their art the cultural reception of the new physics among the non-scientific public. Indeed, the free flow of ideas between the three fields of literature, visual art and physics enabled some of the most striking and recognizable innovations in modernist poetic form. The fractured syntax of 'words-in-freedom', for example, through its guiding analogy of wireless communication, presented a new kind of poetry for whom space and presentation, immediacy and directness, were viewed as being as important as imagery in conveying the Futurist world view. Williams's stripped-back poetics, with its distinctive use of line-breaks and disjunctive fracturing, emulated the inventive perspective-shifts of Cubism, allowing him to explore the strange conceptual world of Einstein's relativity. His active integration of Einsteinian measure, and enthusiasm for the idea of the 'variable foot' he based upon it, proved influential for later modernist poets like Olson and Zukofsky. Equations and diagrams found their way into art, as a means of expressing both the deeper spiritual meanings of a poem or artwork (as with de Zayas and the Baroness), or as a way of transforming a poem into a working laboratory of its own – a 'machine made of words' as Williams put it – to generate new modes of understanding the universe.[6]

A further dimension of cultural interplay was central to these poets' embrace of science. For each of them, an interest in physics was heavily influenced by the world-picture promulgated by the transatlantic avant-garde art movements. Cubism broke down traditional modes of mimetic representation, fragmenting viewpoints and reference frames to offer a new, analytical approach to the artistic

---

[6] William Carlos Williams, 'Introduction to *The Wedge*', *Poetry*, https://www.poetryfoundation.org/articles/69410/introduction-to-the-wedge [Accessed 16 March 2020].

subject. Futurism sought to integrate physics into the very heart of artistic representation, harnessing the power of atomic and electromagnetic models to gesture towards a hyper-technological, utopian future. Dada, waging war on systems of order, satirized and transformed the relationship between science and art through the generation of a 'playful physics' of distention, distortion, chance and uncertainty. Surrealism fused psychoanalysis into art, encouraging the deconstruction and manipulation of subject matter seen in these earlier movements to connect the bizarre physics of the quantum realm to mysticism and the workings of the human imagination. In many cases, it is impossible fully to appreciate the flow of physics through artistic culture in this period without attending to the transmutation of its ideas through modernist visual art. The examples explored in this book have shown the degree and versatility of modern art's engagement with physics, where art galleries and salons served as venues for different interpretations both of physics itself and of its value for modernist aesthetics.

Williams, Loy and the Baroness experimented with applying the affordances of fundamental physics to human experience, creating (and critiquing) an aesthetics of 'humanized matter'. Whether by translating relativity into a series of distorting transformations of the body of Einstein – from violet to pear-tree – as Williams does, or by rendering human attraction and sexual politics as a subatomic drama of electromagnetic forces, as we see in Loy's work, these poets were inspired by the transformative potential of the scientific world view. The Baroness, too, explored the potential of metaphors of physics and chemical interaction as a means of gendered spiritual and political commentary. By reimagining human experience through the lens of physical theory, these poets revealed new ways of thinking about and discussing social interaction and the position of the human body in a universe transformed by scientific understanding.

Of course, physics offered more than simply a framework for new literary and artistic forms and images; it also spoke to a desire for free, interdisciplinary theorization, which could serve spiritual as well as political ends. Far from bolstering earlier interpretations of science as a challenge to religious world views, we find, in fact, that the New Physics offered some writers an inventive way to re-engage with spiritual themes in a framework that was granted, rather than denied, scientific authority. Stevens fused superposition and consubstantiation into his interrogation of imagery, but others took it further. For Loy, the idea of transcendence achieved through embracing the new physics and allowing it to transform humanity's self-understandings offered hope of relief from the personal hardships of illness and loss. The new vistas of communication opened up by radio physics and advances in electromagnetism seemed to herald a future in which humanity would reach a greater connection with the soul and enhanced engagement with the spirit world. In the Baroness's work, too, we see a concerted effort to bring together physics and Christianity through abstract numerologies and diagrams which gesture to spiritual growth, ascendance and cyclicality. In both cases, the ideas and language of physics are synthesized into a new, strikingly reactive cosmology, which we can see to have been shaped to the writer's own aesthetic and ideological needs. By engaging with physics, these writers sought to reassess earlier systems of order, generating new formulae suited to modern experience.

To some extent, this can be seen as a reaction to the professionalization of science which began around the turn of the century; these poets all experienced for themselves the shifting of cultural values towards industrialization and the elevation of the sciences, which brought into question the role of the poet and the value of their medium. Their writing stands as testament to the modernist desire for expansion and integration, and its rejection of the boundaries which had begun to form between disciplines. In part, the aim of this book has been to show the way that literary studies must adapt to the nature of their subjects, acknowledging that writers are agents of the world in which they were writing, both responding to and forming the cultural context around their work. By responding to the emerging physical language each poet uses, I have been able to trace their changing understanding of the concepts with which they engaged, an understanding that evolved and transformed through their careers in parallel to deepening public understanding, social and political events, and their own artistic and philosophical theories and practice. Williams, Loy, the Baroness and Stevens therefore provide an excellent example of how intermedial and transdisciplinary, experimental and evolving, modernist poetry is, reflecting the wider culture in which it was written.

By attending to the tensions and slippage between fields during this period, we gain a deeper understanding of the cultural forces which continue to shape our own understanding of science. The findings of this work enable us to trace a wider set of cultural interactions, which move beyond the 'two-way traffic' of earlier work in literature and science towards a more radial model that encompasses the translation and transformation of scientific ideas through a wider network of media forms. As we have seen, the meanings ascribed to scientific ideas in culture remain unstable even when they have been shored up by empirical proofs within their home field. Throughout this book, I have shown that by investigating the trajectory of this 'variegated cloud of meanings', the shifting aggregate of a multiplicity of scientific, artistic and journalistic forms, we can gain a greater understanding of the fascinating turbulence that underlies the modernists' interest in science.

Appendix 1 – Parallel timeline

I include this timeline for the reader's reference, to clarify the parallel activity in each of the fields discussed in this book. While thorough timelines for each field would be worthy of their own books, I have limited this timeline to key moments, texts and discoveries referred to within this book for ease of utility and navigation.

VISUAL ART	PHYSICS	LITERATURE
	1897 – Thompson's Plum Pudding Model of the Atom	
	1900 (Dec) – Max Planck proposes that radiation is quantized	
		1903 – Mina Loy attends art school in Paris
	1905 – Einstein publishes his theory of Special Relativity	
1907 – Pablo Picasso and Georges Braque develop Cubism	1906 – J. J. Thomson awarded Nobel Prize for discovery of the electron	1906 – Loy leaves Paris for Florence, where she befriends the Italian Futurists
1907–12 – Analytical Cubism		
1909 – Italian Futurism begins	1909 – Nobel Prize awarded to Guglielmo Marconi for achievements in the development of wireless telegraphy; Ernest Rutherford challenges the Plum Pudding Model	1910 onwards – William Carlos Williams joins the New York arts scene
1912 onwards – Synthetic Cubism	1912 – Standard Time Introduced Internationally	

1913 (Feb) – Armory Show opens in New York City; (–1919) Baroness Elsa von Freytag Loringhoven begins collaborations with Marcel Duchamp; Duchamp begins work on *The Large Glass* (1913–23)	1913 – Bohr's Planetary Model of the atom	1913 – Loy lives among the Futurists in Italy; she loses her first child and becomes a Christian Scientist
		1914 – Loy's 'Aphorisms on Futurism' brings the movement to New York, volunteers as a nurse in the war, and writes 'Parturition'
1915 – Duchamp begins experiments which spark what is later referred to as New York Dada	1915 – Einstein refines Special Relativity into General Relativity	
1916 – Dada emerges in Zurich		1916 – Mina Loy arrives in New York
		1917 – Loy's 'Songs to Johannes'
		1918 – Williams's surrealist experiment *Kora in Hell*; Baroness Elsa von Freytag Loringhoven's work first appears in *The Little Review*
1919 – Hannah Höch's *Cut with the Dada Kitchen Knife through the Last Weimar Beer-Belly Cultural Epoch in Germany*	1919 (Nov) – Eddington's experimental proof of Einstein's General Theory of Relativity	
	1921 (April) – Einstein visits New York	1921 – Williams writes the first version of 'St Francis Einstein of the Daffodils'
		1923 – Williams's *Spring and All*; Loy's *Lunar Baedecker*; Stevens's *Harmonium*; the Baroness exiled in Germany
1924 – Surrealism begins with the publication of André Breton's *Surrealist Manifesto*	1924 – Louis de Broglie proposes that matter has wave properties	
	1925 – Schrödinger's Quantum Mechanical Model of the Atom	

	1926 – Schrödinger's wave mechanics; Bohr and Heisenberg meet at Copenhagen	
	1927 – Bohr's Complementarity; Heisenberg's Uncertainty Principle	1927 – The Baroness dies; Djuna Barnes publishes her letters as a eulogy in *transition*
		1933–6 – Mina Loy befriends the surrealist painter Richard Oelze in Paris and begins writing *Insel*
1934 – 'Fantastic Art, Dada, Surrealism' Exhibition at the MoMa in New York		1934 – Stevens comments on Surrealism in 'The Irrational Element in Poetry'
1935 – Dali's *Conquest of the Irrational*		
1936 – New York welcomes first exhibition of Picasso's work		1936 – Williams's revised version of 'St Francis Einstein of the Daffodils'
		1937 – Stevens's 'Man with the Blue Guitar'
		1942 – Stevens's *Parts of a World*
	1945 – The United States uses atomic bomb on two Japanese cities: Hiroshima and Nagasaki	c. 1945 – Loy's 'Tuning in on the Atom Bomb'
		1946–8 – Williams's epic poem *Paterson*
		1947 – Stevens's 'Notes Toward a Supreme Fiction'
		1948 – Williams gives his lecture 'Poetry as a Field of Action' at the University of Washington
		1951 – Stevens finishes 'Collect of Philosophy' after reading of Max Plank's death

Bibliography

Albright, Daniel, *Quantum Poetics: Yeats, Pound, Eliot, and the Science of Modernism* (Cambridge: Cambridge University Press, 1997).

Aleksa, Vainis, 'Mythic Resonance in the *Contact* Version of "St. Francis Einstein of the Daffodils"', *William Carlos Williams Review* 24 (Spring 1998), 33–47.

Al-Kalili, Jim, *Quantum: A Guide for the Perplexed* (London: Orion Publishing, 2004).

Apollinaire, Guillaume, 'Aesthetic Meditations on Painting: The Cubist Painters—First Series: I–VII', *The Little Review* 8, no. 2 (Spring 1922), 7–19.

Apollinaire, Guillaume, 'Aesthetic Meditations on Painting: The Cubist Painters—Second Series', *The Little Review* 9, no. 1 (Autumn 1922), 41–59.

Apollinaire, Guillaume, 'Aesthetic Meditations on Painting: The Cubist Painters—Second Series—Continued', *The Little Review* 9, no. 2 (Winter 1922), 49–60.

Armstrong, Tim, *Modernism: A Cultural History* (Cambridge: Polity Press, 2005).

Arons, A. B. and M. B. Peppard, 'Einstein's Proposal of the Photon Concept—A Translation of the *Annalen der Physik* paper of 1905', *American Journal of Physics* 33, no. 5 (May 1965), 367–74.

Ball, Hugo, 'Dada Fragments (1916–1917)', *The Dada Painters and Poets: An Anthology*, ed. Robert Motherwell (Belknap: Harvard University Press, 1989), 19–55.

Barr Jr, Alfred H., *Cubism and Abstract Art* (New York: The Museum of Modern Art, 1936).

Bell, I. F. A., *The Critic as Scientist: The Modernist Poetics of Ezra Pound* (London: Methuen, 1981).

Bergson, Henri, *Time and Free Will* (London: George Allen & Unwin Ltd., 1910).

Betancourt, Michael, 'Paranoiac-criticism, Salvador Dalí, Archibald and Superposition in Interpreting Double Images', *Consciousness, Literature and the Arts* 6, no. 3 (December 2005), http://www.dmd27.org/betancourt.html (Accessed 10 December 2019).

'Blackbody', *Encyclopaedia Britannica* (Encyclopaedia Britannica inc., 2016), https://www.britannica.com/science/blackbody (Accessed 9 January 2020).

Boccioni, Umberto, 'The Plastic Foundations of Futurist Sculpture and Painting', *Futurism: An Anthology*, ed. Lawrence Rainey, Christine Poggi, et al. (New Haven & London: Yale University Press, 2009), 139–42.

Boccioni, Umberto, Carlo Carrà, Luigi Russolo, Giacomo Balla and Gino Severini, 'Futurist Painting: Technical Manifesto', *Futurism: An Anthology*, ed. Lawrence Rainey, Christine Poggi, et al. (New Haven & London: Yale University Press, 2009), 64–7.

Bohn, Willard, 'The Abstract Vision of Marius de Zayas', *The Art Bulletin* 62, no. 3 (September 1980), 434–52.

Bohr, Niels, 'On the Constitution of Atoms and Molecules', *Philosophical Magazine* 26, no. 1 (1913), 1–25.

Bosquet, Alain, *Conversations with Dalí*, trans. Joaquim Neugroschel (London: Ubu Classics, 2003).

Bradshaw, David and Kevin J. H. Dettmar, *A Companion to Modernist Literature and Culture* (Hoboken, NJ: Blackwell Publishing, 2006).

Breslin, James E., *William Carlos Williams: An American Artist* (New York: Oxford University Press, 1970).

Breslin, James E., 'William Carlos Williams and Charles Demuth: Cross-Fertilization in the Arts,' *Journal of Modern Literature* 6, no. 2 (1977), 248–63.

Breton, André, *Manifestos of Surrealism*, trans. Richard Seever and Helen R. Lane (Ann Arbor: The University of Michigan Press, 1969).

Breton, André, 'Marcel Duchamp', in *The Dada Painters and Poets: An Anthology*, ed. Robert Motherwell (Cambridge, MA: Harvard University Press, 1989), 207–14.

Bru, Sacha, 'Are We Modernists Yet? Avant-Garde, Temporality, History', BAMS, New Work in Modernist Studies Conference, 10 December 2015, Queen Mary University of London, Keynote Address.

Burke, Carolyn, *Becoming Modern: The Life of Mina Loy* (New York: Farrar, Straus and Giroux, Kindle ed., 2012).

Carson, Cathryn, 'Method, Moment, and Crisis in Weimar Science', *Weimar Thought: A Contested Legacy*, ed. Peter E. Gordon and John P. McCormick (Princeton & Oxford: Princeton University Press, 2013), 179–200.

Carson, Cathryn, Alexei Kojevnikov and Helmut Trischler, 'The Forman Thesis: 40 Years After', *Weimar Culture and Quantum Mechanics*, ed. Cathryn Carson, Alexei Kojevnikov and Helmut Trischler (London: Imperial College Press & World Scientific, 2011), 1–7.

Cavell, Richard, 'Baroness Elsa and the Aesthetics of Empathy: A Mystery and a Speculation', *The Politics of Cultural Mediation: Baroness Elsa von Freytag-Loringhoven and Felix Paul Greve*, ed. Paul Hjartarson (Edmonton, Alberta: University of Alberta Press, 2003), 25–39.

Christensen, Paul, *Charles Olson: Call Him Ishmael* (Austin, TX: University of Texas Press, 2014).

Clements, Tanya, '"Critical Introduction" to 'Cosmic Arithmetic', *Transition*, https://digital.lib.umd.edu/transition/poem?pid=umd:55439 (Accessed 28 June 2019)

Conover, Roger, 'Introduction', Mina Loy, *The Lost Lunar Baedeker*, ed. Roger Conover (Manchester: Carcanet, 1997), xi–xx.

Cook, Eleanor, *A Reader's Guide to Wallace Stevens* (Princeton, NJ: Princeton University Press, 2007).

Cornell, Elizabeth, 'Louis Untermeyer's Poetic Engagement of the Popularization of Einstein's Relativity Theory', *South Central Review* 32, no. 2 (Summer 2015), 48–66.

Cortissoz, Royal, 'The Post-Impressionist Illusion', *Century* 85 (April 1913), 805.
Crease, Robert P. and Alfred Sharff Goldhaber, *The Quantum Moment* (W. W. Norton & Co., 2014).
Critchley, Simon, *Things Merely Are: Philosophy in the Poetry of Wallace Stevens* (London & New York: Routledge, 2005).
Cropper, William H., *Great Physicists: The Life and Times of Leading Physicists from Gallileo to Hawking* (Oxford: Oxford University Press, 2001).
Crossland, Rachel, *Modernist Physics* (Oxford: Oxford University Press, 2018).
'Cubism', *The Princeton Encyclopedia of Poetry and Poetics*, 4th ed. (New York: Brogan Tate, 2012), 321–2.
Dalí, Salvador, *The Conquest of the Irrational* (New York: Julien Levy, 1935).
Dalí, Salvador, '*Mystical Manifesto* (1951)', *391.org*, https://391.org/manifestos/1951-mysticalmanifesto-salvador-dali/ (Accessed 4 November 2020).
Dalí, Salvador, *Anti-Matter Manifesto*, exhibition booklet (New York: Carstairs Gallery, 1958).
'definite article, n', OED Online. Oxford University Press, September 2019.
Dijkstra, Bram, *The Heiroglyphics of a New Speech: Cubism, Stieglitz, and the Early Poetry of William Carlos Williams* (Princeton, NJ: Princeton University Press, 1969).
'Dissymétrie du Visage', *Les Nouvelles littéraires*, 4 October 1951, 3.
Doetsch, Gustav, 'Der Sinn der angewandten Mathematik', *Jahresbericht del' Deutschen Mathematiker-Vereinigung* 31 (1922), 222–33.
Donley, Carol, '"A little touch of/Einstein in the night—": Williams's Early Exposure to the Theories of Relativity', *William Carlos Williams Newsletter* 4, no. 1 (Spring 1978), 10–13.
Donnell-Kotrozo, Carol, 'Cezanne, Cubism, and the Destination Theory of Style', *The Journal of Aesthetic Education* 13, no. 4 (October 1979), 93–108.
Donoghue, Denis, 'Nuances of a Theme by Stevens', *The Act of the Mind: Essays on the Poetry of Wallace Stevens*, ed. Roy Harvey Pierce and J. Hillis Miller (Maryland: The Johns Hopkins University Press, 1965), 224–43.
Doreski, William, 'Stevens's Essays', *Wallace Stevens in Context*, ed. Glen McLeod (Cambridge: Cambridge University Press, 2016), 149–50.
Dorner, Alexander, *The Way Beyond 'Art'* (New York: Wittenborn, 1947).
Duchamp, Marcel, *The Bride Stripped Bare by Her Bachelors Even*, trans. George Herd Hamilton (London: Edition Hansjörg Mayer, 1976).
DuPlessis, Rachel Blau, *Genders, Races, and Religious Cultures in Modern American Poetry 1908–1934* (Oxford: Oxford University Press, 2001), 52–80.
Eames, Rachel Fountain, '"Snared in an Atomic Mesh": Transcendent Physics and the Futurist Body in the Work of Mina Loy', *Journal of Literature and Science* 13, no. 1 (2020), 31–49.
Eastwood, M. A., 'Heisenberg's Uncertainty Principle', *QJM: An International Journal of Medicine* 110, no. 5 (May 2017), 335–6.
Ebury, Katherine, *Modernism and Cosmology: Absurd Lights* (London: Palgrave Macmillan, 2014).

'Eclipse Showed Gravity Variation: Hailed as Epochmaking', *The New York Times*, 9 November 1919, 6.
Einstein, Albert, *Einstein on Politics*, ed. David E. Rowe and Robert Schulman (Princeton, NJ: Princeton University Press, 2007).
Einstein, Albert, *Relativity: The Special and General Theory* (New York: Pi Press, 2005).
Eliot, T. S., 'An Emotional Unity' (1927), The Beinecke Rare Books and Manuscripts Library, YCAL MSS 24/20, Folder 399.
Eliot, T. S., *The Four Quartets* (London: Faber & Faber, 1944).
Eliot, T. S., 'London Letters' (1921), The Beinecke Rare Books and Manuscripts Library, YCAL MSS 34/20, Folder 401.
Eliot, T. S., *Selected Essays*, 3rd ed. (London: Faber & Faber, 1991).
Emerson, Ralph Waldo, 'Nature', *The Norton Anthology of American Literature*, 7th ed. Vol. B, ed. Nina Baym (New York & London: W. W. Norton & Co., 2007), 1106–80.
Enns, Anthony and Shelley Trower, *Vibratory Modernism* (London: Palgrave Macmillan, 2013).
Forcer, Stephen, *Dada as Text, Thought and Theory* (Oxford: Legenda, 2005).
Forman, Paul, 'Weimar Culture, Causality, and Quantum Theory, 1918–1927: Adaptation by German Physicists and Mathematicians to a Hostile Intellectual Environment', *Historical Studies in the Physical Sciences* 3 (1971), 1–115.
Friedman, Alan J. and Carol C. Donley, *Einstein: As Myth and Muse* (Cambridge: Cambridge University Press, 1985).
Friedman, Alexander, 'Über die Krümmung des Raumes', *Zeitschrift für Physik* 10 (1922), 377–86.
Fure, Rob, 'The Design of Experience: William Carlos Williams and Juan Gris', *William Carlos Williams*, Newsletter, 4, no. 2 (Fall 1978), 10–19.
Funkhauser, Linda and Daniel C. O'Connell, '"Measure" in Poetry of William Carlos Williams: Evidence from His Readings', *Journal of Modern Literature* 12, no. 1 (March 1985), 26–42.
Gammel, Irene, *Baroness Elsa* (Cambridge, MA: MIT Press, 2002).
Gammel, Irene and John Wrighton, '"Arabesque Grotesque": Toward a Theory of Dada Ecopoetics', *Interdisciplinary Studies in Literature and Environment* 20, no. 4 (Autumn 2013), 795–816.
Gartrell-Mills, Claire F., 'Christian Science: An American Religion in Britain, 1895–1940' (unpublished Doctoral Thesis, University of Oxford, 1991).
Gee, James Paul, 'The Structure of Perception in the Poetry of William Carlos Williams: A Stylistic Analysis', *Poetics Today* 6, no. 3 (1985), 375–97.
Genova, Pamela A., 'The Poetics of Visual Cubism: Guillaume Apollinaire on Pablo Picasso', *Studies in 20th Century Literature* 28, no. 1 (2003), 49–76.
Ginnani, Maria, 'Variations', *Futurism: An Anthology*, ed. Lawrence Rainey, Christine Poggi, et al. (New Haven & London: Yale University Press, 2009), 467.
Golding, John, *Cubism: A History and an Analysis 1907–1914*, 3rd ed. (Cambridge, MA: Harvard University Press, 1988).

Goldman, Jane, *Modernism, 1910–1945: Image to Apocalypse* (New York: Palgrave Macmillan, 2004).

Goodspeed-Chadwick, Julie, 'Reconsidering the Baroness Elsa von Freytag-Loringhoven and Kay Boyle: Feminist Aesthetics and Modernism', *Feminist Formations* 28, no. 2 (Summer 2016), 51–72.

Gribbin, John, *In Search of Schrödinger's Cat* (London: The Folio Society, 2012).

Halliday, Sam, *Science and Technology in the Age of Hawthorne, Melville, Twain, and James* (London: Palgrave, 2007).

Halter, Peter, *The Revolution in Visual Art and the Poetry of William Carlos Williams* (Cambridge: Cambridge University Press, 1994).

Hanna, Julian, *Key Concepts in Modernist Literature* (New York: Palgrave Macmillan, 2009).

Hausmann, Raoul (ed.), *Der Dada*, Vol. 2 (December 1919), http://sdrc.lib.uiowa.edu/dada/derdada/2/images/02.pdf.

Hayden, Sarah, 'Introduction', *Insel* (Brooklyn, NY: Melville House Publishing, 2014), ix–xxxii.

Hayles, N. Katherine, *How We Became Posthuman: Virtual Bodies in Cybernetics, Literature, and Informatics* (Chicago & London: The University of Chicago Press, 1999).

Hayles, N. Katherine, 'Turbulence in Literature and Science: Questions of Influence', *American Literature and Science*, ed. Robert J. Scholnick (Lexington, KY: The University Press of Kentucky, 1992), 229–50.

Heap, Jane, 'Dada—', *The Little Review* (Spring 1922), 46.

Heidegger, Martin, *The Concept of Time*, trans. William McNeill (Oxford: Blackwell Publishers, 1992).

Heisenberg, Werner, *Across the Frontiers*, ed. Ruth Nanda Ashen, trans. Peter Heath (New York: Harper & Row, 1974).

Henderson, Linda Dalrymple, 'Cubism, Futurism, and Ether Physics in the Early Twentieth Century', *Science in Context* 17, no. 4 (2004), 423–66.

Henderson, Linda Dalrymple, *Duchamp in Context* (Woodstock: Princeton University Press, 1998).

Henderson, Linda Dalrymple, 'Four Dimensional Space or Space-Time? The Emergence of the Cubism-Relativity Myth in New York in the 1940s', in *The Visual Mind*, 2nd ed. (Cambridge, MA: MIT Press, 2005), 281–333.

Henderson, Linda Dalrymple, 'The Image and Imagination of the Fourth Dimension in Twentieth-Century Art and Culture', *Configurations* 17, nos. 1–2 (Winter 2009), 131–60.

Henderson, Linda Dalrymple, 'The *Large Glass* Anew: Reflections of Contemporary Science and Technology in Marcel Duchamp's "Hilarious Picture"', *LEONARDO* 32, no. 3 (1999), 113–26.

Henderson, Linda Dalrymple, 'Vibratory Modernism', *From Energy to Information: Representation in Science and Technology, Art, and Literature*, ed. Bruce Clarke and

Linda Dalrymple Henderson (Redwood City, CA: Stanford University Press, 2002), 126–50.

Herbert, Robert L., 'The Arrival of the Machine: Modernist Art in Europe, 1910–25', *Social Research* 64, no. 3 (Fall 1997), 1273–305.

Higham, John, 'The Matrix of Specialization', *Bulletin of the American Academy of the Arts and Sciences* 33, no. 5 (February 1980), 9–29.

Hjartarson, Paul, 'Living Dada', *ESC* 30, no. 2 (June 2004), 151–60.

Hoffmann, Michael J., *The Development of Abstraction in the Writings of Gertrude Stein* (Philadelphia: University of Pennsylvania Press, 1965).

Hoshi, Kumiko, 'D. H. Lawrence and Hannah Höch: Representing Einstein and the Post-World War I World', *Études Lawrenciennes* 46 (October 2015), https://journals.openedition.org/lawrence/244.

Hoving, Kirsten A., 'The Surreal Science of Soap: Joseph Cornell's First Soap Bubble Set', *American Art* 20, no. 1 (Spring 2006), 14–35.

Israel, Nico, *Spirals: The Whirled Image in Twentieth-Century Literature and Art* (New York, NY: Columbia University Press, 2015).

Johnson, Ellwood, 'Wallace Stevens' Transforming Imagination', *The Wallace Stevens Journal* 8, no. 1 (Spring 1984), 28–38.

Johnson, Julie M., 'The Theory of Relativity in Modern Literature: An Overview and 'The Sound and the Fury', *Journal of Modern Literature* 10, no. 2 (June 1983), 217–30.

Jones, Amelia, *Irrational Modernism: A Neurasthenic History of New York Dada* (Cambridge, MA: MIT Press, 2004).

Kadri, Raihan, 'Dadaist Poker: The Body and the Reformation of Form', *Dada and Beyond: Vol. 1, Dada Discourses*, ed. Elza Adamowicz and Eric Robertson (New York: Rodopi, 2011), 145–56.

Kaempffert, Waldemar, 'How to Explain the Universe? Science in a Quandary', *The New York Times*, 11 January 1931, 120.

King, Elliott H., *Salvador Dali: Liquid Desire* (Melbourne: National Gallery of Victoria, 2009), 247.

Kelly, Jacinta, 'Purging the Birdcage: The Dissolution of Space in Mina Loy's Poetry', *Limina* 18 (2012), 1–12.

Kelvin, Lord (Sir William Thomson), *Popular Lectures and Addresses*, vol. 1 (London: Macmillan and Co., 1889).

Kennefick, Daniel, 'Testing Relativity from the 1919 Eclipse—A Question of Bias', *Physics Today* 62, no. 3 (March 2009), 37–42.

Kern, Stephen, *The Culture of Time and Space, 1880–1918* (Cambridge, MA: Harvard University Press, 1983).

Kinnahan, Linda A., *Poetics of the Feminine: Authority and Literary Tradition in William Carlos Williams, Mina Loy, Denise Levertov, and Kathleen Fraser* (Cambridge: Cambridge University Press, 1994).

Kostelanetz, Richard, 'Futurism (Italian)', *A Dictionary of the Avant-Gardes*, 2nd ed. (New York and London: Routledge, 2001), 231.

Kostelanetz, Richard, 'Futurist Music', *A Dictionary of the Avant-Gardes*, 2nd ed. (New York and London: Routledge, 2001), 233-4.

Kouidis, Virginia, *Mina Loy: American Modernist Poet* (Baton Rouge: Luisiana State University Press, 1980).

Kragh, Helge, 'Cyclic Models of the Relativistic Universe', arxiv:1308.0932 [physics.hist-ph] (2013), 1-9.

Kragh, Helge, *Quantum Generations* (Princeton, NJ: Princeton University Press, 1999).

Krikor, Mihran, *Röntgen Rays and Electro-Therapeutics: With Chapters on Radium and Phototherapy*, 2nd ed. (Philadelphia & London: J. B. Lippincott & co., 1910).

Krishna, Swathi and Srirupa Chatterjee, 'Mina Loy's Parturition and L'écriture Féminine', *The Explicator* 73, no. 4 (2015), 257-61.

Kruger, Jan-Louis, 'William Carlos Williams's Cubism: The Sensory Dimension', *Literator* 16, no. 2 (Fall 1995), 195-214.

Kuenzli, Rudolf and Francis Naumann (ed.), *Duchamp: Artist of the Century* (Cambridge, MA & London: MIT Press, 1996).

Lapin, Linda, 'Dada Queen in the Bad Boys Club: Baroness Elsa von Freytag-Loringhoven', *Southwest Review* 89, nos. 2-3 (2004), 307-19.

Laporte, Paul, 'Cubism and Science', *Journal of Aesthetics and Art Criticism* 7 (1949), 243-56.

Laporte, Paul, 'The Space-Time Concept in the Art of Picasso', *Magazine of Art* (1948), 26-32.

Le Bon, Gustave, *The Evolution of Matter*, trans. F. Legge (New York: Water Scott Publishing Co., 1907).

Leggett, B. J., 'Stevens' Psychology of Reading: "Man Carrying Thing and Its Sources"', *The Wallace Stevens Journal* 6, nos. 3-4 (Fall 1982), 51-9.

Leifer, Matthew S., 'Review of QBism: The Future of Quantum Physics', *Physics in Perspective* 19, no. 1 (2017), 76-83.

Lein, Julie Gonnering, 'Shades of Meaning: Mina Loy's Poetics of Luminous Opacity', *Modernism/modernity* 18, no. 3 (September 2011), 617-29.

Lejah, Michael, *Looking Askance: Skepticism and American Art from Eakins to Duchamp* (London: University of California Press, 2004).

Lewis, Lawrence Martine, 'Wallace Stevens and the Process Philosophy of Alfred North Whitehead' (University of Texas Dissertation, 1979).

Livingstone, Catriona, '"Embryo Lives": Virginia Woolf and Recapitulation Theory', BSLS 13th Annual Conference, Oxford Brookes University, 6th April 2018.

Lloyd, Margaret Glynn, *William Carlos Williams's Paterson: A Critical Reappraisal* (Plainsboro, NJ: Associated University Presses, 1980).

Lodge, Oliver, *The Ether of Space* (New York: Harper & Brothers, 1909).

Lodge, Oliver, '"Mind and Matter": A Criticism of Professor Haeckel (1904)', *The Hibbert Journal*, Vol. 3 (London: Williams & Norgate, 1905), 325–6.

Long, Rose-Carol Washton (ed.), *German Expressionism, Documents from the End of the Wilhelmine Empire to the Rise of National Socialism* (London: University of California Press, 1993).

Loy, Mina, 'Aphorisms on Futurism', *Camera Work*, vol. 45, ed. Alfred Stieglitz (1914), 13–15.

Loy, Mina, 'History of Religion & Eros' notes and drafts (1/2), The Beinecke Rare Books and Manuscripts Library.

Loy, Mina, 'Impossible Opus', Mina Loy Papers YCAL MSS6/5, The Beinecke Rare Books and Manuscripts Library, Folder 96.

Loy, Mina, *Insel* (Brooklyn, NY: Melville House Publishing, 2014).

Loy, Mina, 'Insel Draft 2', The Beinecke Rare Books and Manuscripts Library, MSS 6/3, Folder 41.

Loy, Mina, *Islands in the Air*, YCAL MSS 6/4, Folders 58–9.

Loy, Mina, *The Lost Lunar Baedeker*, ed. Roger L. Conover (Manchester: Carcanet, 1997).

Loy, Mina, 'Love Songs. I–IV', *Others* 1, no. 1 (1915), 6–8.

Loy, Mina, *Stories and Essays of Mina Loy*, ed. Sara Crangle (Illinois & London: Dalkey Archive Press, 2011).

Loy, Mina, 'Two Plays', *Rogue* (August 1915), 15.

MacGowan, Christopher J., *William Carlos Williams's Early Poetry: The Visual Arts Background* (Ann Arbor, MI: UMI Research Press, 1984).

Mancini, JoAnne M., '"One Term Is as Fatuous as Another": Responses to the Armory Show Reconsidered', *American Quarterly* 51, no. 4 (December 1999), 833–70.

Mansfield, Elizabeth C. and H. Harvard Arnason, *A History of Modern Art: Painting, Sculpture, Architecture, Photography* (Hoboken, NJ: Prentice Hall PTR, 1998).

Marinetti, F. T., 'Contempt for Woman' (1911), *Futurism: An Anthology*, ed. Lawrence Rainey, Christine Poggi, et al. (New Haven & London: Yale University Press, 2009), 86–7.

Marinetti, F. T., 'Electrical War', *Futurism: An Anthology*, ed. Lawrence Rainey, Christine Poggi, et al. (New Haven & London: Yale University Press, 2009), 98–104.

Marinetti, F. T., 'The Founding and Manifesto of Futurism', *Futurism: An Anthology*, ed. Lawrence Rainey, Christine Poggi, et al. (New Haven & London: Yale University Press, 2009), 49–53.

Marinetti, F. T., 'Geometrical and Mechanical Splendour and the Numerical Sensibility', *Futurism: An Anthology*, ed. Lawrence Rainey, Christine Poggi, et al. (New Haven & London: Yale University Press, 2009), 175–80.

Marinetti, F. T., 'Manifeste du futurisme', *LE FIGARO*, LV, 3. 51 (Saturday 20 February 1909), 1.

Marinetti, F. T., 'Technical Manifesto of Futurist Literature', *Futurism: An Anthology*, ed. Lawrence Rainey, Christine Poggi, et al. (New Haven & London: Yale University Press, 2009), 119–25.

Marinetti, F. T., 'Words-in-Freedom', *Futurism: An Anthology*, ed. Lawrence Rainey, Christine Poggi, et al. (New Haven & London: Yale University Press, 2009), 143–51.

Martz, Louis, 'Wallace Stevens: The World as Meditation', *Wallace Stevens: A Collection of Critical Essays*, ed. Marie Borroff (New Jersey: Englewood Cliffs, 1963), 133–50.

McAdie, Alexander, 'Relativity and the Absurdities of Alice', *The Atlantic Monthly* (June 1921), https://www.theatlantic.com/magazine/archive/1921/06/relativity-and-the-absurdities-of-alice/303933/ (Accessed 7 January 2020).

McCabe, Susan, 'Stevens, Bishop, and Ashbery: A Surrealist Lineage', *The Wallace Stevens Journal* 22, no. 2 (Fall 1998), 149–69.

McDaniel, Judith, 'Wallace Stevens and the Scientific Imagination', *Contemporary Literature* 15, no. 2 (Spring 1974), 221–37.

McLeod, Glen, 'Stevens and Surrealism: The Genesis of "The Man with the Blue Guitar"', *American Literature* 59, no. 3 (October 1987), 359–77.

McLeod, Glen, *Wallace Stevens and Modern Art* (New Haven & London: Yale University Press, 1993).

McWhorter, Ellen, 'Body Matters: Mina Loy and the Art of Intuition', *European Journal of American Studies* 10, no. 2 (Summer 2015), document 12.

Meade, Alexa, Christopher Fuchs and John Phillip Santos, 'Q3 Quantum Metaphysics', Peace and Security in a Quantum Age: Moment, Matter, Mind and Metaphysics Project Q Symposium, University of Sydney (2016), https://vimeo.com/167261302.

Mermin, N. David, 'Physics: QBism Puts the Scientist Back into Science', *Nature* 507 (2014), 421–3.

Middleton, Peter, *Physics Envy: American Poetry and Science in the Cold War and after* (Chicago & London: University of Chicago Press, 2015).

Miller, Arthur J., *Imagery in Scientific Thought* (Cambridge, MA: The MIT Press, 1986).

Mindell, David P., 'The Tree of Life: Metaphor, Model, and Heuristic Device', *Systematic Biology* 62, no. 3 (May 2013), 479–89.

Moholy-Nagy, László, *The New Vision* (New York: Wittenborn, 1946).

Moholy-Nagy, László, *Vision in Motion* (Chicago: Paul Theobold, 1947).

Morrisson, Mark, *Modern Alchemy: Occultism and the Emergence of Atomic Theory* (Oxford: Oxford Scholarship Online, 2007).

Morrisson, Mark, *Modernism, Science, and Technology* (London: Bloomsbury Academic, 2017).

Natale, Simone, 'A Cosmology of Invisible Fluids: Wireless, X-Rays, and Psychical Research around 1900', *Canadian Journal of Communication* 36, no. 2 (2011), 263–75.

Natarajan, Vasant, 'What Einstein Meant when He Said "God does not play dice ..."', *Resonance* 13, no. 7 (July 2008), 655–61.

Newcomb, John Timberman, *How Did Poetry Survive?* (Urbana: University of Illinois Press, 2012).

Nicolescu, Basarab, *From Modernity to Cosmodernity: Science, Culture, and Spirituality* (New York: State University of New York Press, 2014), 170–4.

Nijs, Pieter de, 'Marcel Duchamp and Alfred Jarry', *Relief* 10, no. 1 (2006), 77–98.

Noble, Mark, *American Poetic Materialism from Whitman to Stevens* (New York: Cambridge University Press, 2015).

Opperman, Serpil, 'Quantum Physics and Literature: How They Meet the Universe Halfway', *Anglia* 133, no. 1 (2015), 87–104.

Parkinson, Gavin, *Surrealism, Art and Modern Science: Relativity, Quantum Mechanics, Epistemology* (New Haven and London: Yale University Press, 2008).

Parkinson, Gavin, 'Surrealism and Quantum Mechanics: Dispersal and Fragmentation in Art, Life, and Physics', *Science in Context* 17, no. 4 (2004), 557–77.

Penrose, Roger, 'Introduction', in Albert Einstein, *Relativity: The Special and General Theory*, trans. Robert W. Lawson (New York: Pi Press, 2005), ix–xxvi.

Perloff, Marjorie, *The Futurist Moment: Avant-Garde, Avant Guerre, and the Language of Rupture* (Chicago: University of Chicago Press, 2003).

Pinkerton, Steve, *Blasphemous Modernism: The 20th-Century Word Made Flesh* (Oxford: Oxford Scholarship Online, 2017).

Planck, Max, *A Scientific Autobiography and Other Papers*, trans. Frank Gaynor (London: Williams & Norgate, 1950).

Podmore, Frank, *Mesmerism and Christian Science: A Short History of Mental Healing* (Cambridge: Cambridge University Press, 2011).

Poggioli, Renato, *Theory of the Avant Garde* (Oxford: Oxford University Press, 1968).

Price, Katy, *Loving Faster Than Light: Romance and Readers in Einstein's Universe* (Chicago & London: The University of Chicago Press, 2012).

Re, Lucia, 'Mina Loy and the Quest for a Futurist Feminist Woman', *The European Legacy* 14, no. 7 (2009), 799–819.

Reilly, Jane, 'Elsa von Freytag-Loringhoven', *Woman's Art Journal* 18, no. 1 (Spring–Summer 1997), 26–33.

Reiss, Robert, "My Baroness': Elsa von Freytag-Loringhoven', *New York Dada*, ed. Rudolf E. Kuenzli (New York: Willis Locker & Owens, 1986), 81–101.

Rexroth, Kenneth, *American Poetry in the Twentieth Century* (New York: Herder and Herder, 1971).

Ridge, Lola, 'Concerning Else von Freytag-Loringhoven', *The Little Review* 6, no. 6 (October 1919), 56.

Robbin, Tony, *Shadows of Reality: The Fourth Dimension in Relativity, Cubism, and Modern Thought* (New Haven & London: Yale University Press, 2006).

Robinson, Fred Miller, 'Poems That Took the Place of Mountains: Realization in Stevens and Cézanne', *The Centennial Review* 22, no. 3 (Summer 1978), 281–98.

Rodker, John, 'Dada and Else von Freytag von Loringhoven', *The Little Review* 7, no. 2 (Summer 1920), 34.

Rovelli, Carlo, *Helgoland* (London: Penguin Books, 2021).

Russell, Bertrand, *A B C of Relativity* (London: Routledge, 1997).

Rutherford, Ernest, 'The Scattering of α and β Particles by Matter and the Structure of the Atom', *Philosophical Magazine* 6, no. 21 (1911), 669–88.

Sauer, Tilman, David E. Rowe et al., *Beyond Einstein: Perspectives on Geometry, Gravitation, and Cosmology in the Twentieth Century* (Basel: Birkhäuser, 2018).

Schmid, Julie, 'Mina Loy's Futurist Theatre', *Performing Arts Journal* 18, no. 1 (January 1996), 1–7.

Schumacher, Claude, *Alfred Jarry and Guillaume Apollinaire* (London: Macmillan, 1984).

Schwarz, Daniel R., '"The Serenade of a Man Who Plays a Blue Guitar": The Presence of Modern Painting in Stevens' Poetry', *The Journal of Narrative Technique* 22, no. 2 (Spring 1992), 65–83.

Schweitzer, Cara, *Schrankenlose freiheit für Hannah Höch* (Copenhagen: Saga Egmont, 2014).

'Science Needs The Poet', *The New York Times*, 21 December 1930, 47.

Scroggins, Mark, *The Poem of a Life: A Biography of Louis Zukofsky* (New York: Shoemaker and Hoard, 2007).

Sharpe, Tony, *Wallace Stevens: A Literary Life* (London: Macmillan Press, 2000).

Shattuck, Roger, 'Love and Laughter: Surrealism Reappraised', *The History of Surrealism* (London: Penguin Books, 1978), 11–34.

'She Wore Mens Clothes', *The New York Times* (17 September 1910), https://home.cc.umanitoba.ca/~fgrove/bio/ill_pittsbNYTsep1910.html (Accessed 2 March 2020).

Shearer, Rhonda Roland and Stephen Jay Gould, 'Hidden in Plain Sight: Duchamp's *3 Standard Stoppages*, More Truly a "Stoppage" (An Invisible Mending) Than We Ever Realized', *Toutfait* (2019), https://www.toutfait.com/hidden-in-plain-sight-duchamps-3-standard-stoppagesmore-truly-a-stoppage-an-invisible-mending-than-we-ever-realized/.

Smart, John, *Modernism and after: English Literature 1910–1939* (Cambridge: Cambridge University Press, 2008).

Southall, Oliver, 'Desperate Measures: Williams's "new line" and the Poetical Economy of *Paterson*', *William Carlos Williams Review* 33, nos. 1–2 (2016), 207–36.

'Stars All Askew in the Heavens', *The New York Times* (10 November 1919), https://timesmachine.nytimes.com/timesmachine/1919/11/10/118180487.pdf (Accessed 9 January 2020).

Stein, Gertrude, 'Sacred Emily', *Geography and Plays* (1922), https://ebooks.adelaide.edu.au/s/stein/gertrude/geography_and_plays/Page_178.html (Accessed 8 August 2019).

Steiner, Wendy, *Venus in Exile: The Rejection of Beauty in Twentieth-century Art* (New York, NY: Simon & Schuster, 2001).

Steinman, Lisa, *Made in America* (New Haven & London: Yale University Press, 1987).

Steinmetz, C. P., *Four Lectures on Relativity* (New York: McGraw-Hill, 1923).

Stevens, Wallace, 'A Collect of Philosophy,' drafts, holograph and typescript, undated, YCAL MSS 545, Series 1, Wallace Stevens Collection. Yale Collection of American Literature, Beinecke Rare Books and Manuscript Library.

Stevens, Wallace, *The Collected Poems of Wallace Stevens* (London: Faber & Faber, 2006).

Stevens, Wallace, *The Letters of Wallace Stevens*, ed. Holly Stevens (New York: Alfred A. Knopff, 1966).

Stevens, Wallace, *The Necessary Angel* (New York: Vintage Books, 1951).

Stevens, Wallace, *Opus Posthumous* (London: Faber & Faber, 1957).

Stevens, Wallace, 'Peter Quince at the Clavier', *Others* 1, no. 2 (August 1915), 31–4.

Strehle, Susan, *Fiction in the Quantum Universe* (Chapel Hill, NC: The University of North Carolina Press, 1992).

Sutton, Walter, 'A Visit with William Carlos Williams', *Minnesota Review* 1, no. 3 (Spring 1961), 309–24.

Swabey, William Curtis, 'Science and the Modern World by A. N. Whitehead', *The Philosophical Review* 35, no. 3 (May 1926), 272–9.

Tashjian, Dickran, *Skyscraper Primitives: Dada and the American Avant-Garde, 1910–1925* (Middletown, CT: Wesleyan University Press, 1975).

Taylor, Linda Arbaugh, 'Lines of Contact: Mina Loy and William Carlos Williams', *William Carlos Williams Review* 16, no. 2 (Fall 1990), 26–47.

Tell, Darcy, 'The Armory Show at 100: Primary Documents', *Archives of American Art Journal* 51, nos. 3–4 (Fall 2012), 4–18.

Threlkeld, Isabella B., 'The Emergence of Futurism in Italy: 1900–1916—The Influence of Science on Art' (Unpublished MA Thesis, University of Nebraska, 1971).

Toll, Charles H., 'Review: [Untitled]', *The American Journal of Psychology* 38, no. 1 (1927), 138–4.

Tonini, Paulo, *I Manifesti del Futurismo Italiano 1909–1945* (Gussago: Edizioni dell'Arengario, 2011).

Trause, John J., 'William Carlos Williams and the Baroness', *The Rutherford Red Wheelbarrow*, ed. Jim Kline (Rutherford, NJ: White Chickens Press, 2011).

Tzara, Tristan, 'Seven Dada Manifestos', *The Dada Painters and Poets: An Anthology*, ed. Robert Motherwell (Belknap Press: Harvard University Press, 1989), 73–97.

'Uncertainty Principle', *Encyclopaedia Britannica* (Encyclopaedia Britannica inc., 1998)

'Unpopular Science', *Daily News*, 8 November 1919, 6.

Vetter, Lara, *Modernist Writings and Religio-Scientific Discourse* (London: Palgrave Macmillan, 2010).

Vetter, Lara, 'Theories of Spiritual Evolution, Christian Science, and the "Cosmopolitan Jew": Mina Loy and American Identity', *Journal of Modern Literature* 31, no. 1 (Fall 2007), 47–63.

Vendler, Helen, *On Extended Wings: Wallace Stevens' Longer Poems* (Cambridge: Harvard Press, 1969).

von Freytag-Loringhoven, Elsa, *Baroness Elsa*, ed. D.O. Spettigue and Paul I. Hjartarson (Ottawa: Oberon Press, 1992).

von Freytag-Loringhoven, Elsa, *Body Sweats: The Uncensored Writings of Elsa von Freytag-Loringhoven*, ed. Irene Gammel and Suzanne Zelazo (Cambridge, MA: MIT Press, 2011).

von Freytag-Loringhoven, Elsa, 'The Modest Woman', *The Little Review* (Summer 1920), 37–40.

von Freytag-Loringhoven, Elsa, Elsa von Freytag-Loringhoven Papers, Special Collections and University Archives, University of Maryland Libraries.

von Freytag-Loringhoven, Elsa, *Portrait of Marcel Duchamp*, photograph by Charles Sheeler, The Bluff Collection.

von Freytag-Loringhoven, Elsa, 'Selections from the Letters of Elsa Baroness von Freytag-Loringhoven', *transition* 11. (February 1928), 19–30.

Walter, Christina, 'Getting Impersonal: Mina Loy's Body Politics from "Feminist Manifesto" to *Insel*', *MFS Modern Fiction Studies* 55, no. 4 (Winter 2009), 663–92.

Wazeck, Milena, *Einstein's Opponents: The Public Controversy about the Theory of Relativity in the 1920s*, trans. Geoffrey S. Koby (Cambridge: Cambridge University Press, 2014).

White, John J., *Literary Futurism: Aspects of the First Avant Garde* (Oxford: Clarendon Press, 1990).

Whitehead, Alfred North, *Science and the Modern World* (Cambridge: Cambridge University Press, 1927).

Whitworth, Michael, 'The Clothbound Universe: Popular Physics Books, 1919–39', *Publishing History* 40 (1 January 1996), 53–82.

Whitworth, Michael, *Einstein's Wake* (Oxford: Oxford University Press, 2000).

Whitworth, Michael, 'Natural Science', *T. S. Eliot in Context*, ed. Jason Harding (Cambridge: Cambridge University Press, 2011), 340–2.

Wilde, Dana, 'Stevens, Modern Physics, and Wholeness', *The Wallace Stevens Journal* 20, no. 1 (Spring 1996), 3-4.

Williams, William Carlos, *The Autobiography of William Carlos Williams* (New York: New Directions, 1967).

Williams, William Carlos, *Collected Poems I 1909–1939* (Manchester: Carcanet Press, 2000).

Williams, William Carlos, *The Embodiment of Knowledge* (New York: New Directions, 1974).

Williams, William Carlos 'Embodiment of Knowledge [1/2]' (c. 1928–1930), YCAL MSS 116/40, The Beinecke Rare Books and Manuscripts Library, Folder 1018.

Williams, William Carlos, 'A Note on the Modern State of Poetry', The Beinecke Rare Books and Manuscripts Library, YCAL MSS 116/43, Folder 1092.

Williams, William Carlos, 'Introduction to *The Wedge*', *Poetry*, https://www.poetryfoundation.org/articles/69410/introduction-to-the-wedge (Accessed 16 March 2020).

Williams, William Carlos, 'Pastoral', 'Pastoral. II', 'The Ogre', 'Appeal', *Others* 1, no. 2 (August 1915), 23–5.

Williams, William Carlos, *Paterson* (New York: New Directions, 1963).

Williams, William Carlos, *Selected Essays of William Carlos Williams* (New York: Random House, 1954).

Williams, William Carlos, 'The Reader Critic', *The Little Review* 9, no. 1 (Stella Number, Autumn 1922), 59–60.

Williams, William Carlos, *Spring and All* (New York: New Directions, 2011).

Williams, William Carlos, 'St. Francis Einstein of the Daffodils', *Contact* 4 (Summer 1921), 2–4.

Wittman, Laura, 'Introduction to Part Three', *Futurism: An Anthology*, ed. Lawrence Rainey, Christine Poggi, et al. (New Haven & London: Yale University Press, 2009), 409–19.

Weaver, Mike, *William Carlos Williams: The American Background* (Cambridge: Cambridge University Press, 1971).

Wrighton, John, 'The Textual Ethics of Dada: A Case Study', *Textual Practice* 31, no. 1 (2017), 117–40.

Yew, Philip and Alex Murray (ed.), *The Modernism Handbook* (London & New York: Continuum Books, 2009).

Zayas, Marius de, 'What 291 Means to Me', *Camera Work* XLVII (January 1915), 73.

Zervos, Christian, 'Conversation avec Picasso', *Cahiers d'art* 10 (1935), 173.

Index

abstraction 5, 20, 23, 27–8, 33–4, 206, 210, 213, 219
Albright, D. 8, 194
Aleksa, V. 56–7, 60
Alexander, S. 180, 182
Analytical Cubism 25, 41, 44, 46
Anti-Matter Manifesto (Dalí) 202
Apollinaire, G. 43–7, 49, 200
atom 1, 15–17
atomic
    dissolution 33, 76, 119, 126–30
    spiritualism 107–18
    spirituality 110, 117
avant-garde art 23–30

Bachelard, G. 20
Balla, G. 95–7
Baroness 4, 6, 8, 26, 28, 31–5, 110, 131–3
    'Cosmic Sense Suicide' 175–6
    against Dada scientists 145–52
    'Life is science' 162–77
    'Narcissus – Icarus' 172–4
Bell, I. F. A. 6
Bergson, H. 100, 108, 125
Berlin. *See* Weimar Berlin
Besant, A. 114, 118
Big Bang Theory 168
blackbody radiation 14, 14 n.58
Boccioni, S. 95, 102–4
Boccioni, U. 94
Bohr, N. 16–19, 30, 77, 95, 105, 186, 186 n.30, 194, 202
Bohr-Rutherford model 77
Braque, G. 24, 41, 46–7
Breslin, J. E. 208
Breton, A. 27, 123, 199
The Bride Stripped Bare By Her Bachelors, Even (The Large Glass) (Duchamp) 146, 149, 176
Buffet-Picabia, G. 135
Burke, K. 219

Camera Work (Stieglitz) 81, 94, 135, 137
Carson, C. 155
Cavell, R. 151
Cézanne, P. 24, 28, 65, 191, 217
Christensen, P. 68
Christian Science 33, 80, 107–9, 114
Clairvoyance (Leadbeater) 115
classical physics 14–15, 18–19, 22, 185, 215
complex mathematics 54–63
'The Concept of Causality in Physics' (George) 214, 220–1
The Concept of Time (Heidegger) 56
Conover, R. 32, 79, 82 n.26, 88
Conquest of the Irrational (Dalí) 198, 202
Cornell, E. 13–14
Cortissoz, R. 24, 27
'Cosmic Arithmetic' (Clements) 165
'Cosmic Chemistry' (von Freytag-Loringhoven) 162–3, 165
Crease, R. P. 23
Critchley, S. 184 n.19
Crookes, W. 112, 114
Crossland, R. 7, 9, 34
Cubism 4, 24–5, 33, 40–4, 46–9, 53–6, 62, 73–4, 83 n.31, 141, 226–8
Cut with the Dada Kitchen Knife through the Last Weimar Beer-Belly Cultural Epoch in Germany (Höch) 155–6

Dada 4, 23–4, 26, 33
    Baroness against 145–52
    indeterminacy 133–45
Dalí, S. 196, 198, 201–3
'Destruction of Syntax – Radio Imagination – Words-in-Freedom' (Marinetti) 83, 91–2, 228
Dijkstra, B. 42, 62
Doetsch, G. 154
Donley, C. C. 57
Doreski, W. 205
Duchamp, M. 26, 28, 33, 42, 136, 139–53, 162, 164, 170, 176

DuPlessis, R. B. 78

Ebury, K. 7
Eddington, A. 2–3, 3 n.12, 12, 21, 40–1, 57, 73
Einstein, A. 2, 5, 7, 9–15, 17–18, 23, 27, 34
   in *Paterson* 70–4
   relativity (*See* relativity theory)
   Williams and 54–63
'Electrical War' (Marinetti) 88–91, 117, 121
electric light 92–3, 95–6
electromagnetism 7, 26, 33, 88, 108, 121, 124, 215, 230
Eliot, T. S. 2, 172, 200
Emerson, R. W. 188–9
Enduring Ornament 143
Enns, A. 98
The Ether of Space (Lodge) 112

Feynman, R. 60
'Fix' (von Freytag-Loringhoven) 159
Flowers (Gris) 50–2
Forcer, S. 134, 139
Forman, P. 145
'The Founding and Manifesto of Futurism' (Marinetti) 80, 82
Four Lectures on Relativity and Space (Steinmetz) 64
Freud, S. 197, 202
Friedman, A. J. 57
Friedmann, A. 171
Fuchs, C. 226
Futurism 25–6, 25 n.92, 76, 80–5, 87–90, 92, 94–5, 97, 103, 107, 116–18, 120, 123, 146–7, 150, 229

'Game Legend' (von Freytag-Loringhoven) 164
Gammel, I. 132, 140, 166
Gehrke, E. 157
General Relativity 13, 40, 57
George, A. 179–81, 214, 221–2
Ginanni, M. 104–5
God 141, 143–4
Goldhaber, A. S. 23
Gris, J. 46–7, 49–52, 61
Guitar and Clarinet (Gris) 49–50

Halliday, S. 30
Halter, P. 66
Hayden, S. 124
Heap, J. 26, 75, 131
Heidegger, M. 56, 64
Heisenberg, W. 18–20, 22, 27–30, 155, 183, 185–6, 186 n.30, 194, 196, 201–2, 204, 206, 210, 219
Henderson, L. D. 41, 46, 54, 110, 112
Higham, J. 5 n.15
Hjartarson, P. 132
Höch, H. 155–6
Huelsenbeck, R. 155–8
Hugnet, G. 152

impressionism 28, 42, 103, 217–18
Invisible Sleeping Woman, Lion, Horse (Dalí) 202–3, 208

Jeans, J. 2–3, 3 n.12
Jewell, E. A. 1–3
Johnson, J. M. 21
Jones, A. 132, 136
Joyce, J. 151

Kaempffert, W. 21
Kelly, J. 78
Khlebnikov, V. 90
'King Adam' (von Freytag-Loringhoven) 150
Kragh, H. 15–16, 171
Kreymborg, A. 5, 32

Laport, P. 73
Large Hadron Collider 15
Lawrence, D. H. 7
Leadbeater, C. 114–15, 118
Le Bon, G. 102
Leggett, B. J. 211
Lein, J. G. 97, 123
Leja, M. 141–2
Lemaître, G. 168
'Let's Murder the Moonlight' (Marinetti) 97, 103
Livingstone, C. 119
'Love-Chemical Relationship' (von Freytag-Loringhoven) 145–6, 164
Loy, M. 4, 7–8, 15, 26–9, 31–6, 79 n.18, 229–30

'Aphorisms on Futurism' 76, 81, 94–5, 111
atomic spiritualism 107–18
'electro-life' 110, 115, 117, 124
futurist satires 80–93, 98, 104, 121, 128
'History of Religion and Eros' 79, 79 n.19, 110–11, 117, 123
Insel 7, 79, 116, 118–27, 136
'Islands in the Air' 79, 99–100, 114, 117, 119
'man of electric vitality' 116, 118–26
nerve-vibrations 98, 100
'Parturition' 80–1, 93–108, 111, 115, 123–4, 127–8, 130
'The Sacred Prostitute' 89–90, 92
'Sketch of a Man on a Platform' 86–7
'Songs to Joannes' 85, 97, 122
'Three Moments in Paris' 84–5, 89
X-rays 100–1

McCabe, S. 196
MacColl, D. S. 27
McDaniel, J. 181–3
McLeod, G. 196, 210
McWhorter, E. 78
Made in America (Steinman) 7
'Manifesto of Mr Antipyrine' (Tzara) 165–6
'man of electric vitality.' *See* Loy, *Insel*
Marinetti, F. T. 7, 25, 80–92, 94, 97, 99, 101–3, 105, 107, 111, 116–17, 120–1, 129, 168
Martz, L. 210–11
Metzinger, J. 30
Meyer, A. 137
Michelson-Morley experiment 221
Middleton, P. 6, 8, 222
mimesis 44, 52, 54
modern physics 2, 7–9, 40–1, 74, 80, 91, 135, 137–8, 142, 185, 198, 208, 214, 222, 227
'The Modest Woman' (von Freytag-Loringhoven) 151
Moholy-Nagy, L. 54–8, 64, 73
Moore, M. 63–4
Morrisson, M. 109, 114

Natale, S. 109
Newcomb, J. T. 3

New Pathways in Science (Eddington) 21
new physics 2–3, 6–7, 9–10, 18, 22, 26–7, 39, 62, 64, 75–6, 94, 117, 129, 136, 142, 144, 151, 155, 182–4, 202, 223, 225, 228–9
Noble, M. 195
nutritious synthesis 198–9

Oelze, R. 33, 119

paradigm shift 9
The Paranoiac Face (Dalí) 202
Parkinson, G. 10, 20, 22, 27
'Parturition' (Loy) 80–1, 93–108, 111, 115, 123–4, 127–8, 130
Pascal 180–1, 207
Paulhan, J. 179–80, 184, 186–8, 190
Pauli, W. 161
perpetual motion 82, 99, 102, 105, 124, 166, 168, 170–3
physical vibration 93, 98
physics. *See also* classical physics; Einstein; modern physics; new physics; quantum physics
  poet and 30–7
  poetry and 5–9
  public interest in 3
Physics Envy (Middleton) 8
Picabia, F. 43, 148, 151
Picasso, P. 24, 29, 41, 45–7, 143, 196, 199–200, 210
Pierre, J. 135
Pinkerton, S. 78
Planck, M. 1, 14–15, 18, 31, 33, 179, 181–2, 214–16, 220–3
  discovery 185
  'The Meanings and Limits of Exact Science' 187, 191–2
planetary model 16–17, 77, 117
plum pudding model (Thomson) 15, 77
Podmore, F. 108–9
Poggi, C. 116
Portrait of Marcel Duchamp (von Freytag-Loringhoven) 141
Pound, E. 6
Prescott, T. 76, 97
Price, K. 57
psycho-physics 100

QBism 226, 226 n.2, 227
quanta 1, 14–16, 92, 184, 204
Quantum Mechanical Model (Schrödinger) 17
quantum mechanics 1, 7, 9, 17–20, 22–3, 27, 120, 133, 155, 176, 186, 189, 215, 226
quantum physics 14, 19, 29, 144, 155, 161, 180–1, 183, 187–8, 202, 223, 225, 227
quantum poetics 194
Quantum Poetics (Albright) 8
quantum revolution 17–22, 145, 163, 181
quantum theory 1, 10, 14–16, 21–2, 181–2, 185–6, 189, 227

Raynal, M. 29, 143
Reiss, R. 132
relativity theory 10–14, 19, 21–2, 31, 34, 40–1, 47, 54–6, 61–4, 66, 73–4, 81–2, 125, 136, 139, 142, 225–9
Rexroth, K. 147
Riordan, J. 64
Robbin, T. 46
Robinson, F. M. 217–18
Röntgen rays (X-rays) 77, 100–1
Rovelli, C. 225–6
Russell, B. 13
Rutherford, E. 15–16, 32, 77, 109

Schack, R. 226
Schamberg, M. 141
Schreiber, M. 108
Schrödinger, E. 17, 30, 144, 182–3, 186, 204
Schwarz, D. 205–6
Science and the Modern World (Whitehead) 41, 64, 183
'Second Manifesto of Surrealism' (Breton) 123
'Seven Dada Manifestos' (Tzara) 138–9
Shifting Gears (Tichi) 7
Southall, O. 72–3
space-time 9, 11–12, 33, 55–7, 62, 119
Spengler, O. 142
Steiglitz, A. 81, 94, 135, 137, 148
Stein, G. 193
Steinman, L. 7, 222
Steinmetz, C. P. 41, 64–6, 69, 73
Stevens, W. 4, 8, 27–8, 31–6, 179–82

'A Collect of Philosophy' 179–81, 184, 190, 213–14, 218, 222
Harmonium 188
'Imagination as Value' 207
'The Irrational Element in Poetry' 197–8, 211
'Man Carrying Thing' 211–12
'The Man on the Dump' 193–6
'The Man with the Blue Guitar' 199–200, 203, 210, 213
'The Noble Rider and the Sound of Words' 189
'Notes Toward a Supreme Fiction' 212, 215–16
'The Old Woman and the Statue' 209
'On Poetic Truth' 219
phantom problem 205–13
'Study of Two Pears' 191
and Surrealism 196–205
'St Francis Einstein' (Williams) 12, 33, 43, 54, 56–8, 61–70, 72
Strahlen (Insel) 122, 126
Street Light (Balla) 95–6
Sullivan, J. W. N. 21
superposition 183, 196–206, 213, 218, 220, 227, 229
Surrealism 5, 26–7, 120, 123, 196–201, 203, 229
Synthetic Cubism 25, 41, 44, 47

Tashjian, D. 135
'The Tendency to Abstraction in Modern Art and Science' (Heisenberg) 186
Thirlwall, J. C. 70
Thomson, J. J. 15, 77, 112
3 Standard Stoppages (Duchamp) 139, 144
Tichi, C. 7
Time and Free Will (Bergson) 100
timeline 232–4
Trower, S. 98
Tzara, T. 133–4, 138–40, 158, 165–6

uncertainty principle (Heisenberg) 18, 20, 215

'Variations' (Ginanni) 104
Vendler, H. 194
Vetter, L. 107–9
vision in relationships (Moholy-Nagy) 55
visualizability 186, 189, 194, 204

von Freytag-Loringhoven, E. 4, 33, 131, 143, 167, 169

Wahl, J. 179–80, 188
Weaver, M. 66
Weimar Berlin 33, 133, 152–62, 171, 176
Wein, W. 14, 14 n.58
Whitehead, A. N. 41, 64–5, 67–8, 73, 180, 182–3
White, J. J. 90, 108
Whitworth, M. 2–3, 7, 34–5, 62
Williams, W. C. 6, 8, 40 n.5, 177, 226–8
   and Einstein 54–63
   Kora In Hell 40
   Paterson 39–40, 70–4
   'The Poem as a Field of Action' 54, 69, 71, 73
   'Poetry as a Field of Action' 39, 41, 43
   The Red Wheelbarrow 45, 52, 61
   Spring and All 40, 43–54, 59, 61, 64, 67
   'St. Francis Einstein' 33, 56, 58, 61–3
   'To a Solitary Disciple' 48, 50
Wittman, L. 97, 120
Woolf, V. 7
The World as Space and Time (Friedmann) 171
Wrighton, J. 134

X-ray 3–4, 77, 89–90, 98, 100–1, 104, 106, 110, 121, 126, 148, 174–5, 189

Yeats, W. B. 7

Zang Tumb Tuum (Marinetti) 89
Zayas, M. de 135, 137–8, 164–5, 228
Zeitschrift für Physik (Friedmann) 171
Zukofsky, L. 2, 228

www.ingramcontent.com/pod-product-compliance
Lightning Source LLC
Chambersburg PA
CBHW062131300426
44115CB00012BA/1882